Enigma Books

Also published by Enigma Books

Dennis Wainstock

Election Year 1968

The Turning Point

Enigma Books

Published by Enigma Books, New York

Copyright © 2012 by Dennis Wainstock

First Paperback Edition

Printed in the United States of America

ISBN: 978-1-936274-41-3
e-ISBN: 978-1-936274-42-0

Publisher's Cataloging-In-Publication Data

Wainstock, Dennis, 1947–
    [Turning point]
    Election year 1968 : the turning point / Dennis Wainstock. -- 1st pbk. ed.

    p. : ill. ; cm.

    Originally published as: The turning point: the 1968 United States presidential campaign. Jefferson, N.C. : McFarland, c1988.
    Issued also as an ebook.
    Includes bibliographical references and index.
    ISBN: 978-1-936274-41-3

    1. Presidents--United States--Election--1968. 2. United States--Politics and government--1963-1969. I. Title. II. Title: Turning point

E851 .W35 2012
324.973/0923

To my students

Contents

Election Year 1968

Introduction

About This Book

The 1968 presidential election represented a turning away from eight years of Democratic liberal welfare reform and civil rights legislation and the beginning of a rightward drift which continued throughout the 1970s and into the 1980s. Unlike most elections, the economy was not the main issue. Unemployment was less than 4 percent. The dominant issues were law and order and the Vietnam War. While the former signaled a shift to the right, the latter's result was less decisive.

This study describes the process and analyzes the factors that moved the country to the right and led also to a lack of clear direction on Vietnam.

Scores of new source materials have become available since Theodore H. White and a team of English reporters wrote their election accounts in 1969. My research included 33 book-length memoirs and special studies, 35 personal interviews, 8 oral histories, and the papers of 10 leading participants, including Lyndon B. Johnson, Hubert H. Humphrey, and Eugene McCarthy. In addition I researched numerous newspapers, periodicals, convention proceedings, public papers, congressional hearings, and Department of Defense studies. I have tried to write as clear and balanced account as the sources permit.

Domestic Issues in the Johnson Presidency

By late 1967, law and order and the Vietnam War had overshadowed President Lyndon B. Johnson's quest for a Great Society. The public was frustrated with his war policy, tired of dissent and protest, and angered over riots and disorders. Moreover, policy debate over the war's direction divided the Democratic Party. But few expected Johnson to fold under the mounting pressures. At 59, he had been in politics for over thirty years, and his achievements were many and varied.

A descendant of frontierspeople, Johnson was born in Texas in 1908. He entered the United States House of Representatives in 1937, moved to the Senate in 1948, and when the Republicans lost control of Congress in 1954, became majority leader. He went to the 1960 Democratic convention in Los Angeles with 300 delegates but, unable to stop John F. Kennedy's bandwagon, settled for the vice presidency. On November 22, 1963, after Kennedy was assassinated in Dallas, Texas, Johnson became the thirty-sixth president of the United States.

As an able legislator, although not as urbane, rich, or handsome as Kennedy, Johnson entered the White House with a large measure of congressional respect and popular support. During his first year, he announced a "War on Poverty" and prodded Congress into adopting legislation to combat illiteracy and unemployment. He also attacked segregation. The Civil Rights Act of 1964 outlawed it in restaurants and motels, forbade discrimination in employment on the basis of sex as well as race, and ordered federal funds withheld from school districts that made inadequate progress toward desegregation.

After winning a landslide victory over Senator Barry Goldwater of Arizona in the 1964 election, Johnson, aided by large Democratic congressional majorities, achieved a program of welfare reform comparable in scope to President Franklin D. Roosevelt's New Deal. Johnson called his program "The Great Society."

It attacked a host of problems. In the Appalachian area, a poverty region extending from Pennsylvania to northern Alabama, it provided subsidies for the development of resources. It granted funds for urban renewal, and raised pensions and minimum wage benefits. In education, it aided schools in low income areas and provided scholarships to more than 140,000 needy college students. Medicare provided a basic health plan to provide up to 90 days of hospital care, 100 days of nursing-home care, and 100 home health-care visits to persons 65 and older. Conservation acts set aside land for parks and recreational use, protected numerous endangered species and safeguarded such threatened national areas as the Indiana dunes, Lake Michigan, California's giant redwoods, and several wild and scenic rivers.

During his second term, Johnson continued to break down the barriers of racial discrimination. Traditionally, white southerners had used literacy tests to deprive blacks of their franchise. If any county used literacy tests to disqualify more than half of its voting age population, the 1965 Voting

Rights Act provided federal supervision to allow anyone with a sixth-grade education to vote. Protected and encouraged by the 1964 and 1965 civil rights acts, black voter registration in the 11 southern states more than quadrupled between 1960 and 1969, to 3.2 million. In addition, the Civil Rights Act of 1968 forbade discrimination in renting or selling apartment buildings and provided penalties for interfering with the right of blacks to attend school or work.

While the various civil rights acts raised black expectations for a better life, many still found themselves without equal political rights, adequate education, social equality, and economic opportunity. Left unresolved, blacks considered these conditions intolerable.

Beginning in 1965, riots broke out in many of the nation's black ghettos. The first serious riot, triggered by a minor incident, occurred in August, 1965, in the Watts section of Los Angeles. Property damage totaled $140 million, 34 persons died, and over 1,000 persons were arrested. In subsequent summers, riots broke out in Los Angeles, San Francisco, Chicago, New York, Newark, and Detroit. The statistics were alarming: in Newark 26 dead, 1,000 injured, 1,400 arrested; in Detroit, 40 dead, 350 injured, and 3,800 arrested. Scores of homes and businesses were burned, sacked, and looted. Most of the violence and destruction took place within or on the fringes of the ghettos. In March, 1968, the National Advisory Commission on Civil Disorders, headed by former Illinois Governor Otto Kerner placed primary blame for the riots on appalling slum conditions and white racism and called for an all-out effort to provide slum dwellers with adequate housing, job-training, education, and welfare.[1]

After 1966, Johnson's antipoverty program, which failed to achieve its many goals, and public dissatisfaction with the Vietnam War brought a decline in popularity. Southern whites, who resented the federal government's civil rights efforts, joined northern whites, who blamed blacks for "crime in the streets," to produce an anti-Black backlash that seriously undermined Johnson's power. Moreover, the gradual escalation of American involvement in the Vietnam War diverted funds and attention from the Great Society. In the midterm elections, the Republicans made substantial gains, and the Gallup and Harris polls showed a dramatic decline in Johnson's poll ratings.

United States Involvement in Vietnam

The Vietnam War became Johnson's greatest foreign policy problem, and he never seemed to understand the complicated nature of the Vietnamese conflict.

Since the mid-nineteenth century, the Vietnamese had been under French colonial rule. In 1940, after the fall of France to Germany, the Japanese occupied northern French Indochina (Vietnam, Laos, and Cambodia) and the following year moved into the southern portion. By this time, the various Vietnamese resistance groups, including Vietnam's Communist party, had united to form the Vietminh, the League for Independence. After Japan's 1945 surrender, the Vietminh resisted French efforts to recover Indochina. Superior French firepower and conventional tactics were unsuited for Indochina's jungle and mountainous terrain, and they were unable to suppress the popular guerrilla movement. Even with $3 billion in American aid and over 200,000 French troops, they failed to break Vietminh dominance of the countryside or drive them from their strongholds in the areas north of Hanoi and Haiphong. In 1954, a major French military defeat at Dien Bien Phu, an outpost near the Laotian border, persuaded France to disengage.

Shortly thereafter, at Geneva, the French met with Ho Chi Minh's Hanoi-based government, France's puppet Bao Dai government, Britain, the Soviet Union, and China to find a solution to the conflict. Although Under Secretary of State Walter Bedell Smith attended some of the meetings, the United States signed no conference documents. In the 1954 Geneva Agreements, the countries involved agreed to give Indochina independence as three nations: Vietnam, Laos, and Cambodia. After France's defeat at Dien Bien Phu, its troops, including the Vietnamese who fought for France, withdrew into the half of Vietnam south of the 17th Parallel, and Vietminh forces withdrew to the north of that line. The agreements specified that the 17th Parallel was merely a temporary "military demarcation line" and scheduled an internationally supervised election for 1965 to elect a government for all of Vietnam.

But the election was never held. The United States installed Ngo Dinh Diem, an anti-Communist nationalist, at the head of France's abandoned colonial regime in Saigon and encouraged him to declare South Vietnam to be an independent nation. Ho Chi Minh denounced the cancellation of the election, but he was busy trying to rebuild North Vietnam and would not interfere for several years.

A member of the wealthy class, Diem followed unpopular policies which led to armed rebellion. He angered the peasants by cancelling their right to elect village chiefs, forced them to return lands to landlords, and used troops to collect rents. He alienated Buddhists by favoring Catholics, and nationalists by depending on the United States for economic and military aid. Most of Diem's government officials and army had come from

North Vietnam, and many South Vietnamese regarded them as carpet-baggers. In December, 1960, his opponents formed the National Liberation Front (NLF), whose leaders, mostly non-Communists, adopted a program calling for land reform, village self-rule, and armed resistance to Diem. They adopted guerrilla warfare. Their enemies called them the Vietcong, meaning South Vietnamese Communists, but only a few were Communists.

In 1963, disgusted with Diem's inability to win popular support, the United States withdrew its support from him, and his army officers killed him. After Diem's death, nine changes of government took place before General Nguyen Van Thieu and Air Marshal Nguyen Cao Ky took power. But they failed to win popular support and the Vietcong increased.

Between 1960 and 1963, President Kennedy increased the number of American military advisers from the 700 sent by President Dwight D. Eisenhower to 16,500. Technically, the advisers were giving aid and advice to the South Vietnamese Army, but their activities led them into combat. Kennedy justified American escalation by the so-called domino theory: if the Communists triumphed in South Vietnam, all countries in Southeast Asia would collapse to the Communists like a row of falling dominoes. "This view," recalled Jack Valenti, White House assistant under Johnson, "was staunchly held by every administration since 1950."[2]

When Johnson became president, he maintained that North Vietnam's arms and reinforcements to the Vietcong, not Saigon's unpopularity, was responsible for prolonging the war. But the Vietcong did not appear to be invaders. According to military doctrine, guerrillas cannot operate success-fully except where they have local support, which the Vietcong seemed to have throughout South Vietnam. Despite American military and economic aid throughout the 1950s and early 1960s, South Vietnam's political-military situation was unstable, and the political structure linking Saigon with the provinces was never secure. Desertion in the South Vietnamese army was high, and the Vietcong was gaining recruits.

No incident in the war is more clouded in controversy than that alleged to have taken place in the Tonkin Gulf in August of 1964. Americans awoke on August 2 to television and radio accounts of an attack upon a United States destroyer, the *Maddox,* in the Gulf of Tonkin off North Viet-nam. The news accounts said three North Vietnamese PT boats were driven off with the help of carrier-based fighter planes, with no reported damage to the destroyer, and added that the United States government called the alleged attack "unprovoked" and said the *Maddox* was on "routine patrol in international waters." Hanoi denied any attack and said that South Vietnamese vessels had raided North Vietnamese fishing boats and had, under the cover of the *Maddox,* bombarded North Vietnamese islands.

At first Secretary of Defense McNamara denied American complicity, but he later admitted before a congressional hearing that North Vietnamese islands had been bombarded and that the United States and South Vietnam had made joint raids against North Vietnam. The goal, he added, was to force North Vietnam to commit acts that would gain congressional authorization for whatever else "is necessary with respect to Vietnam."[3]

After the alleged attacks, which were later proven to be a fabrication by the United States, President Johnson warned the North Vietnamese that grave consequences would result from any further "unprovoked" offensive military action against United States Forces and ordered the *Maddox,* along with the destroyer *C. Turner Joy,* back into the danger zone. Two days later, on August 4, the United States reported another attack, which also caused no damage. Hanoi denied it. Johnson ordered American aircraft to hit North Vietnamese boats and naval installations along 100 miles of the coast. The air strikes damaged or destroyed 25 enemy boats and 90 percent of the oil storage tanks at Vinh, North Vietnam.

Buoyed by a Gallup poll showing 71 percent approved the air strikes, Johnson submitted to Congress the Southeast Asia (or "Gulf of Tonkin") Resolution, authorizing him to take all necessary measures to repel any armed force, to assist any member or protocol state of the Southeast Asia Collective Defense Treaty (Britain, France, Australia, New Zealand, Pakistan, and Thailand) requesting assistance in defense of its freedom. On August 7, 1964, the House passed it 416 to 0 and the Senate 88 to 2. (Wayne Morse, Oregon, and Ernest Gruening, Alaska, dissenting).

Rolling Thunder

On February 6, 1965, the Vietcong attacked the American installations at Pleiku and Camp Holloway, killing eight Americans and destroying five aircraft. In retaliation, Johnson ordered air strikes on military facilities in Dong Hoi and Chap Le barracks in North Vietnam.

The next day, February 7, McGeorge Bundy, presidential assistant, returned from a fact-finding tour of South Vietnam. He told Johnson that Saigon's defeat appeared inevitable unless the United States began sustained air reprisals against North Vietnam. Although Johnson had rejected similar proposals, he now agreed with this course of action. He did not want to be the first president "to lose a war."[4]

On February 13, Johnson cabled Ambassador Maxwell D. Taylor and General William C. Westmoreland, field commander in Vietnam, of his decision to implement "measured and limited air action" against selected targets in North Vietnam. "We of the American Mission," recalled Ambassador Taylor, "were elated over the approval of a policy which we had been urging for months.[5] But to Westmoreland, "I still saw no hope, in view of the restrictions imposed, that it would have any dramatic effect on the course of the war."[6]

In a memorandum to Johnson on February 17, Vice President Hubert Humphrey expressed serious reservations about American military escalation in Vietnam. He reminded Johnson of his recent campaign statements not to enlarge the war and of the public's fear of Goldwater's trigger-happy bombing image. Humphrey wrote:

> It is always hard to cut losses. But the Johnson Administration is in a stronger position to do so now than any Administration. Indeed it is the first year when we can face the Vietnam problem without being preoccupied with the political repercussions from the Republican right.... Our political problems are likely to come from new and different sources (Democratic liberals, independents, labor) if we pursue an enlarged military policy very long.
>
> The best possible outcome a year from now would be a Vietnam settlement which turns out to be better than was in the cards because LBJ's political talents for the first time came to grips with a fateful world crisis and did so successfully. It goes without saying that the subsequent domestic political benefits from such an outcome, and such a new dimension for the President, would be enormous.
>
> If, on the other hand, we find ourselves leading from frustration to escalation and end up short of a war with China but embroiled deeper in fighting in Vietnam over the next few months, political opposition will steadily mount. It will underwrite all the negativism and disillusionment which we already have about foreign involvement generally—with serious and direct effects for all the Democratic internationalist programs to which the Johnson Administration remains committed: AID (Agency for International Development), United Nations, arms control, and socially humane and constructive policies generally.[7]

Except for Ball, Humphrey found himself alone among his colleagues. "My ideas were well-intentioned," they said, "but not applicable." As a result, Johnson excluded him from Vietnam discussions for the rest of 1965. "No one ever said, 'You're out, and here are the reasons why,'" but "My views were not particularly welcome."[8]

On March 2, the first Rolling Thunder operation commenced with a joint attack by American and South Vietnamese planes on a North Vietnamese ammunition depot and naval base. In the early bombings, the administration carefully picked targets for their political and psychological considerations, but the Joint Chiefs of Staff sought a more sustained air campaign against long-range military targets. "Interference from Washington seriously hampered the campaign," complained General Westmoreland, "this or that target was not to be hit for this or that nebulous nonmilitary reason."[9] Ambassador Taylor agreed with the military view. He called "for a more dynamic schedule of strikes, a several week program, relentlessly marching north, to break the will of the North Vietnamese."[10] By mid-March, President Johnson accepted these recommendations, and air action against North Vietnam went from a sporadic, halting effort into a regular and continuous program.

Troop Escalation

On the morning of March 8, 1965, a United States Marine Corps Battalion Landing Team splashed ashore at Da Nang, South Vietnam, and a companion battalion landed by air later that day (a total of 3,500 Marines). Although over 20,000 American servicemen were in Vietnam, the Marine Corps battalions were the first combat units committed to action. Requested by General Westmoreland, their mission was to provide security for the Da Nang air base and release the South Vietnamese troops guarding it for offensive actions against the Vietcong.

By June, 1965, despite the air attacks and additional troop deployments, which now exceeded 50,000, the North Vietnamese and their Vietcong allies were winning the war. The American military command found that "the entire bastion was crumbling."[11] "It wasn't a matter of whether the North Vietnamese were going to win the war," recalled General Earle G. Wheeler, chairman of the Joint Chiefs of Staff. "It was just a question of when they were going to win it."[12]

On June 7, Westmoreland described the South Vietnamese army as near collapse and submitted a request for a large number of additional troops. "Without American reinforcements," he said in a message to Washington, "the ARVN (Army of the Republic of South Vietnam) would be unable to stand up to the pressure."[13] He asked for a quick deployment of the 1st Cavalry Division (eight battalions), an additional Marine battalion, and more tactical air units, helicopters and logistical troops, for a total request of 44 battalions (175,000 troops). These troops, added the Joint Chiefs of Staff, were only enough "to hold the fort" and more would be needed later.[14]

Westmoreland's request aroused considerable dissent. On June 25,

Ambassador Taylor's deputy, U. Alexis Johnson, urged Assistant Secretary of Defense John T. McNaughton not to bring in more troops. "The situation," said Johnson, "was in many ways no more serious than the previous year."[15] "Only the Vietnamese," argued Ambassador Taylor, "could save their own country and too aggressive use of foreign troops might even work against them in that regard."[16] "Before going big," said Assistant Secretary of State William P. Bundy, we need to find out how American troops would perform in Vietnam's environment.[17] "South Vietnam is a country with an army and no government," said Undersecretary of State George Ball. "Even if we were to commit five hundred thousand men to South Vietnam we would still lose."[18]

On July 20, after a five-day fact-finding visit to Saigon, Secretary of Defense Robert S. McNamara accepted the military's request for 175,000 more troops. He told Johnson that the Communists believe that South Vietnam is ready for "a complete takeover."[19] Along with the troop request, he advised calling up 235,000 men in the reserves and National Guard and adding 375,000 more men, through recruitment and draft calls, to the armed forces.

On July 21, in the Cabinet Room of the White House, President Johnson met with his advisers to discuss McNamara's report. All had read it. The president looked grave, even a little worn. After some discussion, he asked if everyone agreed with McNamara's report. All agreed except Ball. "I have grave doubts that any Western army can successfully fight Orientals in an Asian jungle." Johnson asked McNamara and General Wheeler to seriously ponder this question. He then asked the question most troubling him. "Wouldn't we lose all credibility by breaking the word of three presidents?" Ball replied, "We'll suffer the worst blow to our credibility when it is shown that the mightiest power on earth can't defeat a handful of miserable guerrillas."[20] But, "If the Communist world finds out we will not pursue our commitment to the end," argued Secretary of State Dean Rusk, "I don't know where they will stay their hand."[21] This also worried Johnson. He said later, "I was convinced that our retreat from this challenge would open the path to World War III."[22]

On July 28, 1965, at a televised news conference in the East Room of the White House, Johnson told the nation of his decision. He said:

> I have today ordered to Vietnam the Air Mobile Division and certain other forces which will raise our fighting strength from 75,000 to 125,000 men almost immediately. Additional force will be needed later, and they will be sent as requested. This will make it necessary to increase our active fighting forces

by raising the monthly draft call from 17,000 over a period of time, to 35,000 per month, and stepping up our campaign for voluntary enlistments....

These steps, like our actions in the past, are carefully measured to do what must be done to bring an end to aggression and a peaceful settlement. We do not want an expanding struggle with consequences that no one can foresee. Nor will we bluster or bully or flaunt our power.

But we will not surrender. And we will not retreat.[23]

Without a quick solution, the administration now found itself with an open-ended commitment to the Vietnam War. Westmoreland perceived a long war, with further troop deployments to follow: "I could make no estimate more precise than 'several years.'"[24] By the end of 1965, American troop levels had risen to 180,000, by the end of 1966 to 380,000, and by the end of 1967 to 500,000. By then, the war was costing $30 billion a year, and the casualty toll had risen to more than 25,000 American battle deaths and 100,000 wounded.

Controversy and Opposition

Johnson's Vietnam policy aroused intense opposition. Peace marches, pickets at the White House, campus protests, and draft-card burning became common. Thousands of young men left for Canada, went underground, or were sent to prison. In one rally, in October, 1967, 200,000 Americans marched against the war in Washington. The same month, October, the Harris poll recorded that public support for the war, 70 percent in February, had dropped to 51 percent, the lowest point up to that time.[25] The October Gallup poll showed Johnson's approval rating declining from 46 percent in February to 38 percent.[26] Among the war's opponents were retired generals James Gavin and Louris Norstad as well as many of the nation's leading Far Eastern experts. In late 1967, 30 members of the House appealed to Johnson to halt the air attacks on North Vietnam. Privately, Senator Fulbright exclaimed, "We go ahead treating this little pissant country as though we were up against Russia and China put together."[27]

In press editorials, church sermons, and political podiums, the war generated a major foreign policy debate. The hawks emphasized the country's moral responsibility to resist aggression, and its obligations under the Southeast Asia Treaty Organization (SEATO) pact. The doves said that SEATO was not a binding defense pact but only bound its members to consult in case of Communist aggression. If the Communists were allowed to take over one country, said the hawks, stressing the domino theory, they would soon take its neighbors continuing until they had conquered the whole world. The doves, rejecting the domino theory, noted the growing split between the Chinese and the Soviets and the traditional hostility of the Vietnamese to the Chinese. The hawks argued that the North Vietnamese provoked the conflict. But the doves said it was a popular revolt against a corrupt and repressive South Vietnamese regime and that the North Vietnamese had only increased their military activities in the South in proportion to United States involvement.

Positions varied on a solution to the war. The more extreme hawks favored the abolition of all bombing restrictions, sending ground troops into North Vietnam, and, if necessary, using atomic weapons. While some doves favored the immediate withdrawal of all United States troops, most urged Johnson to negotiate for the best terms to get out of the war, but all agreed that he should end the bombing as a means of drawing Hanoi into negotiations.

As the criticism mounted, the administration became more defensive and the language of its response on the war effort more shrill. Johnson and his advisers called critics of the war "nervous nellies" and "special pleaders." Westmoreland insisted that within two years the United States could phase down its military effort and withdraw some troops.[28] Ambassador to Vietnam Ellsworth Bunker said, "We could now see light at the end of the tunnel."[29] But the Joint Chiefs of Staff remained silent.

Despite official optimism, Johnson learned that his leading adviser, Secretary of Defense McNamara, was beginning to doubt the wisdom of escalation in Vietnam. His doubts surfaced in 1967 in off-the-record talks with journalists and in reports of "anguished" conversations with close friends, most notably Senator Robert F. Kennedy of New York.[30] "As McNamara's pessimism grew," recalled White House aide Doris Kearns, "his access to the President diminished. Johnson did not want to hear other people's doubts."[31] By the summer of 1967, recalled presidential assistant John P. Roche, McNamara was "a very disturbed guy."[32] "He lacked the innate toughness required in a 'War Minister,'" reported Joseph Alsop, and fellow columnist William S. White added that McNamara was "more bookish than martial in spirit and attitude."[33]

On November 28, 1967, against mounting press speculation of an open break, Johnson approved McNamara's resignation, taking effect in March, 1968, and appointed him president of the World Bank. "There never was any open break between them," insisted Press Secretary George Christian later.[34] "The job," recalled Roche, "was just too much for him."[35]

Meanwhile, the Republican Party was hoping to benefit from the mounting opposition to Johnson's war policy.

By early 1967, the field was still wide open. Governor George Romney of Michigan and former Vice President Richard M. Nixon were the two leading contenders. A member of the party's liberal wing, Romney was relatively unknown nationally, and Nixon had to overcome a loser image after his defeats to Kennedy in the 1960 presidential race and to Pat Brown in California's 1962 gubernatorial race. Despite New York Governor Nelson A. Rockefeller's expressed support for Romney, party leaders agreed that he would probably enter at a later date. Goldwater conservatives hoped Governor Ronald Reagan of California would enter, but he remained noncommittal. If Romney faltered and Rockefeller decided not to enter, Senator Charles H. Percy of Illinois and Mayor John V. Lindsay of New York appeared ready to run.

At the same time, the two parties faced a third party challenge from former segregationist Governor George C. Wallace of Alabama. By making law and order his main issue, he gained supporters from the white backlash to civil rights. At first, considered a minor figure by many, he would, by the fall of 1968, prove to be the most skillful southern politician to appear on the national scene since Governor Huey Long of Louisiana died in 1935, and the strongest third party challenger since Theodore Roosevelt ran on the Progressive Party's third party ticket in 1912.

Chapter I

The Challengers

Johnson's Reelection Strategy

In the fall of 1967, Johnson appeared determined to run again. He designated Postmaster General Lawrence F. O'Brien as the planner of overall
strategy, Washington lawyer James H. Rowe as chief adviser and liaison
officer with state delegations, and Vice President Humphrey as an alternative voice on the stump. O'Brien recommended that Johnson not make an
early announcement of candidacy or enter the primaries but to organize
behind the scenes and allow supporters in key primary states to work on his
behalf. Although Johnson agreed to avoid the primaries, his name, since he
was a prominent candidate, would automatically be placed on the Wisconsin, Nebraska, and Oregon ballots. In general, he followed O'Brien's
strategy.

The Dump Johnson Movement

Close friends since college days, antiwar activists Allard K. Lowenstein
and Curtis Gans were the two men most responsible for turning the
growing sentiment against Johnson's Vietnam policy into a real movement
to unseat him. Although Lowenstein, the older of the two, with thinning
hair and thick glasses, looked like an intellectual, he was a man of action,
not introspection. A staunch liberal, whose two great heroes and mentors
were Eleanor Roosevelt and socialist Norman Thomas, Lowenstein had

been president of the National Student Association (NSA), chairman of the students for Adlai Stevenson (Democratic candidate for president in 1952 and 1956), vice chairman of Americans for Democratic Action (ADA), and staff person for the Southern Christian Leadership Conference, Dr. Martin Luther King's civil rights organization. Slightly to the left of Lowenstein, Gans, a slim, dark New Yorker, was a former activist in the Students for a Democratic Society (SDS) and a long-time member of ADA.

Lowenstein and Gans disagreed on what strategy to adopt to unseat Johnson. Lowenstein advocated opposing Johnson through a third party bid with either Dr. King or Dr. Benjamin Spock, distinguished baby doctor and leftwing activist, at its head. Gans argued that a dump-Johnson move within the Democratic Party would have better results than a third party action.[1] Between November 1966 and early 1967, Lowenstein and Gans sounded out church groups and antiwar Democrats on their respective strategies. After discovering little sentiment for a third party challenge, Lowenstein adopted Gan's view.

In the spring of 1967, the two men recruited Washington lawyer Joseph L. Rauh and economist John Kenneth Galbraith, both important figures in ADA. "It's easier than you think," Galbraith told journalist David Halberstam, "because we believe it and we've thought it out and they haven't."[2] Galbraith and Rauh persuaded ADA to threaten Johnson with nonsupport unless he changed his war policy.[3] Meanwhile, they began looking for a candidate. They approached antiwar senators George McGovern of South Dakota and Frank Church of Idaho, but both were preoccupied with tough reelection campaigns. Senator Robert F. Kennedy of New York also declined. He explained that he did not want to hurt his nomination chances in 1972 by challenging Johnson in 1968.[4]

At midsummer, discouraged by their inability to get a candidate, Rauh and Galbraith, along with a number of other ADA liberals, decided on another approach. A better tactic, they agreed, was to concentrate on securing a peace plank in the platform. "This would be called the Peace Caucus," recalled Galbraith, "and it would seek to write into the platform such a strong expression of opposition that not even Johnson could be indifferent."[5] But after finding that delegates were pledged to candidates, not positions, they returned to Lowenstein's position that only political opposition would impress Johnson.

In mid-August, Lowenstein recruited a number of students at the NSA'S national convention in College Park, Maryland. "We had to start with the students," he explained later, "because we had no money and therefore no hope of getting anybody else to work for us."[6] The students formed a task force to begin mobilizing the campuses for the 1968 election. Sam Brown, a Harvard divinity student from Council Bluffs, Iowa, headed it. He used his father's credit card to visit scores of campuses throughout the country. Later, Brown recalled, he presented his father with a bill for $1500 and the words, "Thank you for your first campaign contribution."[7]

In search of funds, Lowenstein called on San Francisco lawyer Gerald Hill who headed the liberal 33,000-member California Democratic Council (CDC). With Hill's support, Lowenstein persuaded the CDC to give money to set up the Conference of Concerned Democrats (CCD).[8] Although it would later become the base for an informal national alliance of anti-Johnson political elements, it started out of Gans' Washington apartment and included a telephone answering service, a secretary, two credit cards, and very little money.[9]

Lowenstein and Gans worked as a team. Gans would enter a state first, compile a list of persons favorable to a dump-Johnson movement, then call Lowenstein who would confer with local politicians and activists and set up public meetings. If they went well, Gans stayed around to organize local chapters of the Conference of Concerned Democrats. "We compiled lists of sympathetic persons," recalled Gans, and "we had discussions with New York reform people like Bella Abzug."[10] In Eau Claire, Wisconsin, Don Peterson, a liberal ADA board member, told Lowenstein, "That sounds like what we should be doing."[11] In Minnesota, Alpha Smaby, a member of the state legislature with an impressive record in Minnesota politics, became the first elected official to join the dump-Johnson movement. In addition, Gans and Lowenstein obtained support from a number of liberal organizations: the Dissenting Democrats (a California based antiwar group organized by Robert Vaughn, the actor), the Hoosiers for a Democratic Alternative, the Coalition for a Democratic Alternative, and the Wisconsin Concerned Democrats.

To Lowenstein and others opposed to the war, Senator Kennedy of New York was the logical choice to challenge Johnson. Along with an abundance of charisma and high political standing, Kennedy, the brother of the late President John F. Kennedy, opposed the war and argued, like Lowenstein, that one man could make a difference and turn the country around.[12] In 1966, Dr. Spock and advisers Adam Walinsky and Pierre Salinger urged Kennedy to run.[13] By early 1967 Senators Eugene J. McCarthy of Minnesota and George McGovern agreed that Kennedy was the logical choice to challenge Johnson. He seemed intrigued by the idea, recalled McGovern, but "I became convinced that he was too 'practical' to challenge an incumbent Democrat President."[14]

Lowenstein first approached Kennedy on August 4, 1967. The two men spent several hours in uninterrupted talk on a flight to Los Angeles where Kennedy was to speak at a party fund-raising dinner. Lowenstein explained that the dump-Johnson movement was recruiting thousands of students and many party regulars. But he did not ask Kennedy to run. "I was a flea and he was an elephant," recalled Lowenstein, "and we had a lot more organizing to do before I could ask him that."[15] Kennedy appeared sympathetic to the cause but did not express an interest in running.

In late September, Lowenstein, accompanied by *Village Voice* reporter Jack Newfield and publisher James Loeb, visited Kennedy at Hickory Hill, his McLean, Virginia, home. Historian Arthur Schlesinger, Jr. (former speechwriter for John F. Kennedy), and Walinsky, Kennedy's speechwriter, were present. They assembled in the living room where Lowenstein, kicking off his shoes, sat down cross-legged on a thick chair, college-bull-session style. He stressed the "moral imperative" of stopping the war and denying Johnson renomination.[16] "Johnson," said Lowenstein, "might even pull out if defeated in the early primaries."[17] Kennedy agreed. Loeb asked, "Do you think his people will ask him not to run if he loses some early primaries?" "I'd like to see who the first person is," replied Kennedy, "who goes in there alone and says, please, Mister President, don't run."[18] "Johnson," insisted Lowenstein, "was more unpopular than the war."[19] Kennedy replied that he could not be the first to challenge Johnson. He feared that people would say that he was splitting the party out of ambition and envy. "No one would believe that I was doing it because of how I felt about Vietnam and poor people."[20]

Two weeks later, Lowenstein visited Kennedy at his New York office on East 45th Street. He pleaded with Kennedy to enter the race. "Everything is falling into place," said Lowenstein. "You have to get into it."[21] Kennedy declined. He said that potential supporters, like Mayor Richard J. Daley of Chicago, argued that entering now would hurt his chances in 1972. "The people who think that the honor and the future of this country are at stake," insisted Lowenstein, "don't give a shit what Mayor Daley and Chairman X and Governor Y think. We're going to do it and we're going to win, and it's a shame you're not with us because you could have been President."[22]

Lowenstein next approached Senator McGovern. Since Kennedy had declined, McGovern appeared interested, but he faced a tough reelection campaign in South Dakota.[23] "Would you mind," asked Lowenstein, "if I go to South Dakota and do a little looking around and see what the people think about this possibility?"[24] McGovern told him to "sample the waters."

After spending several days in the state, he reported that McGovern would have to run two very different campaigns and might lose reelection to the Senate.[25] McGovern then suggested seeking out a senator not up for reelection. Looking down the list of Democratic senators in the *Congressional Directory*, he checked the names of Lee Metcalf, the junior senator from Montana, and Eugene McCarthy. Shortly thereafter, McGovern checked back with his nominees. Metcalf had considered the idea "ridiculous," but to McGovern's surprise, McCarthy said that "he would consider it."[26]

Eugene J. McCarthy

A tall, trim figure with white hair, McCarthy, who in college excelled in economics, education, philosophy, and English, entered politics after teaching in public schools and private colleges for ten years. He served five terms in the House. First elected to the Senate in 1958, he won reelection by the largest popular majority ever received by a Democratic candidate in the history of Minnesota. His voting record did not always reflect his liberal philosophy. On civil rights, urban renewal, welfare, and labor issues, he consistently voted with the liberals; but unlike them, he voted in favor of maintaining the oil depletion allowance and, on one occasion, voted against the poll-tax amendment offered to the 1965 Voting Rights Act.[27] His opponents used these votes to discredit his liberal credentials.

Spurning Washington's social life, McCarthy preferred the company of intellectuals, poets, and books. His friends included journalists like Gilbert Harrison and Walter Lippmann or poets such as Reed Whittemore, James Dickey, and Robert Lowell. He was interested in theology, and his office bookshelves contained the *Summa Theologica* of St. Thomas Aquinas and St. Augustine's *City of God*. He often quoted from Thomas More's *Utopia*. He found few senators or senatorial duties that interested him. His Senate colleagues considered him intelligent but somewhat lazy and resented his habit of ridiculing other senators. He made comments such as "Birch Bayh (senator from Indiana) couldn't be found 'in a stubblefield'"; or "Charles Percy was a 'Hobbit —he never leaves a shadow, he never stands between the sun and a wall.'"[28]

An early supporter of the war, McCarthy was, by 1967, opposed to Johnson's Vietnam policy. On January 27, 1967, he joined with 14 other Democratic senators in signing a public letter urging Johnson not to resume bombing after the Christmas bombing halt (December 24, 1965, to January 31, 1966) and, the same day, made his first formal Senate statement against the war. "I felt," he recalled, "that the debate over our involvement in Vietnam, occasioned by the prospect of renewed bombing of the North was a proper point for the beginning of a much deeper and much more extensive discussion not only of Vietnam but also of the whole role of America in this second half of the twentieth century."[29] He urged the administration to concede some areas of South Vietnam to the Vietcong to stimulate peace talks. Up to that time, recalled Humphrey, McCarthy's criticism against the war "had been vague and periodic."[30]

In the spring and summer of 1967, McCarthy began to consider challenging Johnson in the 1968 primaries. Periodically, he would gather together friends and associates in New York and Washington to discuss the problems involved in running against an incumbent. On one occasion, he told Humphrey of his intentions. He spoke so casually about it, remarked Humphrey, that "I considered it sort of a lark on his part."[31] "I knew we had a candidate in mid-September," recalled Gans, "the only reason we delayed getting to McCarthy was Lowenstein's hope that Kennedy would change his mind or somebody more favorable, like McGovern, would be the candidate."[32]

On October 23, 1967, McCarthy met with Hill and Lowenstein over breakfast at the Ambassador Hotel in Los Angeles. At first, they discussed a slate of delegates, committed to an unnamed peace candidate, that the California Democratic Council could put forward for the June 4, 1968, California primary. Hill was optimistic that a peace candidate would not only win California but run well nationally. "Do you have any money? Can you get enough volunteers?" The questions and answers lasted an hour until McCarthy, seemingly satisfied, exclaimed, "You fellows have been talking about three or four names. I guess," he smiled, "you can cut it down to one."[33] McCarthy was in the race.

McCarthy began preparing for his campaign. Lowenstein, Gans, and Hill agreed that the CDC would provide the organizational structure for his national campaign. Although McCarthy had initially planned to announce his candidacy at the Conference of Concerned Democrats' convention scheduled in Chicago on December 2, 1967, he moved the date up to November 30 and decided to announce in the Senate Caucus Room. "The reason," he explained, "was that I did not wish to be represented as the candidate of any one special group," and "I had some reservations about the tone and the criticism of the Administration by some of the Concerned Democrats." Meanwhile, he concentrated his efforts to win over college students. "Meeting with these students," he said later, "re-enforced my belief that it was vitally important that the young people be given a chance to participate in the politics of 1968."[34]

In late November, McCarthy called on Kennedy. The meeting was brief, about seven minutes. "Whatever my personal feelings," said McCarthy, "you're the logical candidate. But since you won't run, I'm going to announce."[35] He added, "I'm not worried as to whether I'm a stalking horse for you. If you were to enter later on, I would not say I'd been tricked."[36] McCarthy neither disclosed his campaign plans nor asked Kennedy for advice. "He is a very strange fellow," remarked Kennedy later. "After all, I have had a little experience running primaries. But he didn't ask a single question."[37]

On November 30, 1967, McCarthy announced to reporters and well wishers, gathered in the Senate Caucus Room, that he would enter five or six Democratic primaries. His decision was made, he explained, after talking with numerous Democratic Party leaders and candidates in 26 states. He said:

> My decision to challenge the President's position has been strengthened by recent announcements from the Administration of plans for continued escalation and intensification of the war in Vietnam and, on the other hand, by the absence of any positive indications or suggestions for a compromise or negotiated political settlement. I am concerned that the Administration seems to have set no limits on the price that it will pay for military victory.

In his speech, McCarthy pointed to the human and financial costs of the war. He noted that American casualties, by November, 1967, included 15,058 dead and 94,469 wounded. The war cost the United States between $2 and $3 billion a month, caused a dangerous rise in inflation, and generated a deepening moral crisis in America. But he emphasized that he was not for peace at any price but for an "honorable, rational, and political solution" that would enhance our world position and "permit us to give the necessary attention to our other commitments abroad." He concluded:

> I am hopeful that a challenge may alleviate the sense of political helplessness and restore to many people the belief in the processes of American politics and of American government. On college campuses especially, but also among other thoughtful adult Americans, it may counter growing sense of alienation from politics which is currently reflected in a tendency to withdraw in participation and to make threats of support for a third party or fourth party or other irregular political movements.
>
> I do not see in my move any great threat to the unity and the strength of the Democratic Party.
>
> The issue of the war in Vietnam is not a separate issue but is one which

must be dealt with in the configuration of problems in which it occurs. It is within this context that I intend to take the case to the people of the United States.[38]

In the question-and-answer period, McCarthy joked with reporters. No, he told them, his entry was not political suicide although, he added, "it might be execution," but he assured them that the moment of decision "was nothing like St. Paul being knocked off his horse."[39] Asked if he had a chance to win, he replied in jest, "I think the President is the leading candidate for the Democratic nomination right now."[40] But when asked about Kennedy, McCarthy became serious. "If Kennedy had moved earlier," said McCarthy, "there'd have been no need for me to do anything," but he admitted that Kennedy "had made no commitment to stand aside all the way," and "there would surely be nothing illegal or contrary to American politics if he or someone else were to take advantage of what I'm doing."[41]

The press greeted McCarthy's candidacy with skepticism and sympathy. "Within the political fraternity," observed Kenneth Crawford of *Newsweek,* "McCarthy's own explanation of what he is up to is too lofty to be credited."[42] "Even if he won all primaries hands down," said Joseph Kraft, "Johnson could still have the nomination for the asking."[43] "His entry," said the *Washington Post,* "may channel into the political process dissent that often has been aimless and sometimes destructive."[44] "McCarthy is a thoughtful, responsible man," editorialized the *New York Times,* and "he can be expected to clarify the alternatives in Vietnam."[45]

To the foreign press, McCarthy appeared to be a dark horse without much credibility. "The ideal candidate could not be Senator McCarthy because he declared himself an enemy not of the man but of his Vietnam policy," reported Paris's *Le Figaro.* "McCarthy," stressed London's *Economist,* "will have to do phenomenally well in the primary elections."[46]

The Johnson camp considered McCarthy's candidacy linked to a future Kennedy challenge. They feared that McCarthy, after uniting the insurgent Democrats in the primaries, would throw his support to Kennedy sometime before the Democratic National Convention.[47] "If that is what he is doing he ought to say so," said Governor John B. Connally of Texas, Johnson's close friend.[48] McCarthy denied that Kennedy would step in as the convention neared and "pick up all the chips." But if that was his plan, warned McCarthy, "He will have a fight on his hands to see who has the most strength."[49]

McCarthy's entry did not greatly reduce Johnson's large Democratic following. In an early show of support, numerous Democratic governors and party organizations endorsed him for the nomination, and dovish senators Fulbright, Church, McGovern, Gaylord Nelson of Wisconsin, Wayne Morse of Oregon, and Joseph S. Clark of Pennsylvania did not endorse McCarthy.[50] The Gallup poll taken January 7, 1968, showed Democrats preferring Johnson to McCarthy 71 percent to 18 percent.[51] Nevertheless, McCarthy received pledges of support from over 800,000 persons and endorsements from several liberal publications: the *Nation, Progressive, New Republic,* and *New York Post.* The ADA's executive board voted 65 to 47 in his behalf. While many blacks and labor leaders regarded him as a one issue candidate, he obtained support from Dr. Martin Luther King (unofficially) and a few second-level labor leaders.[52]

McCarthy's Early Campaign

On December 2, 1967, McCarthy made his first official appearance before several thousand supporters at the Conference of Concerned Democrats' national convention held at Chicago's Conrad Hilton Hotel. In the introduction, Lowenstein gave a "rip-roaring speech" about what McCarthy was going to do to Johnson. "When a President is both wrong and unpopular," declared Lowenstein, "to refuse to oppose him is both a moral abdication and a political stupidity." He added, "If a man cheats you once, shame on him. But if he cheats you twice, shame on you!" While Lowenstein was speaking, some CCD participants observed McCarthy angrily kicking around a Dixie cup at the back of the hall. He considered Lowenstein's introduction incendiary and demagogic. "The tone," said McCarthy afterwards, "was not in the spirit of the campaign (on issues, not personality) which I intended to wage."[53] According to speechwriter Jeremy Larner, "He had deep misgivings about a group of young rebels using him as a battering-ram against his party."[54]

Taking the podium, McCarthy spoke against the Vietnam War. It was of questionable legality and constitutionality, he said, and it was the first war in this century in which the nation found itself without the support of decent world opinion. He said:

> A war which is not defensible even in military terms, which runs contrary to the advice of our greatest generals—Eisenhower, Ridgway, Bradley, and MacArthur—all of whom admonished us against becoming involved in a land war in Asia. Events have proved them right, as estimate after estimate as to the time of success and the military commitment necessary to success has had to be revised—always upward: more troops, more extensive bombing, a widening

and intensification of the war. Extension and intensification have been the rule, and projection after projection of success have proved wrong.

With the escalation of our military commitment has come a parallel of overleaping of objectives: from protecting South Vietnam, to nation building in South Vietnam, to protecting all of Southeast Asia, and ultimately to suggesting that the safety and security of the United States itself is at stake.

Finally, it is a war which is morally wrong. The most recent statement of objectives cannot be accepted as an honest judgment to justify the methods we are using as we have moved from limited targets and more destructive instruments of war, and also have extended the area of operations almost to the heart of North Vietnam.[55]

McCarthy's speech disappointed the audience. It was vague and wordy. "It was the speech of a college professor," remarked staffer Arthur Herzog, "not a candidate."[56] McCarthy spoke with no particular substance or feeling, recalled Larner.[57] "It was not a time for storming the walls," McCarthy said afterwards, "but for beginning a long march."[58] But from that day on, Lowenstein and McCarthy's relationship, never warm, cooled appreciably. "Lowenstein," observed Halberstam, "is in the McCarthy camp, but not of it; he is simply too much of a politician for McCarthy; who wants as few politicians near him as possible."[59]

McCarthy did not act like a professional politician. He started out with only $5000, announced before he even had a staff or a semblance of a campaign organization, refused to travel with a retinue, ate alone in restaurants, and considered the press an annoyance. "I think," said congressional reporter Grace Basett, "he thought he could campaign by just traveling around all alone like some medieval minstrel singing his song."[60] "Look here," said one supporter, "you've done a very unorthodox thing. You're ridden into the court. The penalty is death. You've got to have troops of your own."[61]

Slowly, McCarthy put together a national campaign organization. He picked 41-year-old Blair Clark, former vice president of CBS News, to head the campaign. After closing the CCD's national office, Gans became assistant campaign manager. Seymour M. Hersh, an Associated Press Pentagon reporter, became press secretary. He picked reporters Mary Lou Oates, of United Press International, and Peter Barnes, Associated Press, as his assistants. Jeremy Larner, a young writer, did the research and speechwriting, and Sam Brown became the national coordinator of students.

McCarthy's supporters considered his speeches soft, delivered with a lack of fervor, and even a little corny. Journalist I. F. Stone complained, "His speeches are 'dull, vague, and without either balls or poetry.'"[62]

"You're not in focus," said Arnold Hiatt, a Boston shoe company executive. "What do you expect me to do?" replied McCarthy. "Light bonfires on the hills?" "Some people can only see by that kind of light," contended Hiatt.[63] If he tried to satisfy the peace advocates by sharper attacks on the war, McCarthy feared losing the middle spread of voters. He did not want to "pound the pulpit," he explained, for "people don't want to be shouted at."[64] But California representative George Brown summarized the feeling of many McCarthy supporters. "He may not be the best man in the world," but "he's the best man we've got to give us a choice."[65]

Before the important March 12, 1968, New Hampshire primary, McCarthy won significant victories in Massachusetts, Minnesota, and California.

On March 5, 1968, McCarthy won Massachusetts' 72 delegates by default. At first, Johnson had considered a stand-in candidate for the April 30 primary. His choices included Speaker of the House John McCormack from Massachusetts, Senator Edward Kennedy of Massachusetts who, unlike Robert, Johnson personally liked, State Senate leader Maurice Donahue, and Larry O'Brien. Although Edward Kennedy did not want McCarthy to win the primary and control the Massachusetts delegation at the convention, he was a critic of the war and informed O'Brien that he did not wish to run against an antiwar candidate. McCormack urged O'Brien to run, but he, temporarily reversing his stand against Johnson entering primaries, now argued that the President himself should enter "since he could defeat McCarthy soundly and score a clear-cut victory over one of his main antiwar critics." Johnson listened but refused to make a decision. Consequently, on April 30, McCarthy, unchallenged except for write-in votes, won 50.7 percent of the vote. "Letting Gene McCarthy have the Massachusetts delegates was an annoyance to us," recalled O'Brien, "but the fact was that he could win the primaries and still not be nominated."[66]

On the same day McCarthy's Minnesota supporters showed their strength in the Twin Cities (Minneapolis-St. Paul) precinct elections. They unseated a large number of regular delegates. But they had failed to mount sufficient efforts in rural districts and were unable to control the Minnesota delegation to the national convention. Nevertheless, the events in the Twin Cities area were a preview of developments to come in New Hampshire. "It marked," observed *Newsweek* reporter Richard T. Stout, "the first determined steps of the Children's Crusade and the first major political expression of anti-administration sentiment."[67]

The McCarthyites also showed their organizing skills in California. State law determined a candidate's position on the ballot by whichever candidate first filed 13,467 signatures; by law, the gathering of signatures could not begin until the first minute of March 14 of the election year. Between midnight and nine o'clock on the morning of March 14, 1968, the California Democratic Council organized 500 petition-signing cocktail parties throughout the state. A typical petition party was at the home of Jack Morrison, county supervisor and unsuccessful candidate for mayor of San Francisco in 1967. In a few minutes, he obtained 117 signatures. At "The Factory," a large Hollywood discotheque, a thousand people signed the petition. A number of show business people, including Jan Sterling and Carl Reiner, threw parties, and Beverly Hills supporters organized a Paul Revere horseback petition campaign. By 9 a.m. the McCarthyites had collected 30,000 signatures and were the first to file. "This is a tremendous psychological victory for us," said campaign leader Edmund G. (Jerry) Brown, Jr. "We have a complete slate, our petitions are in, we have a campaign rolling, and Johnson has nothing."[68]

The New Hampshire Primary

McCarthy's staff split on the importance of entering the March 12 New Hampshire primary. Press attention, some staffers argued, was out of all proportion to its significance; the only statewide newspaper was the conservative *Manchester Union Leader* and it had no indigenous peace movement.[69] Brown advised McCarthy to wait for a more favorable primary: Wisconsin being the obvious one. But Clark, who had once owned a newspaper in New Hampshire, insisted that the voters would be receptive to McCarthy.[70] "Those of us who wanted him to enter," recalled Gans, "did so on the belief that he would make a respectable enough showing to better win subsequent primaries."[71] By the end of December, 1967, McCarthy realized that his campaign was stalling and began to view New Hampshire as a publicity-generator. "There had been increasing concern in the latter part of December about the credibility of the campaign," recalled Abigail McCarthy. Gene was not inclined to file, but "the pressures were great."[72] On January 3, he officially entered the contest.

McCarthy's staffers, mostly graduate students, set up the state headquarters in an old electrical appliance store in Concord. In charge was Sam Brown, Ben Stavis, a student of Chinese politics at Columbia University, Ben's wife Rosann, a New York University student, and Harold Ickes, Jr., son of Franklin D. Roosevelt's secretary of the interior. The star political recruit was Richard N. Goodwin, former presidential assistant to Kennedy and Johnson. Goodwin, swarthy, intense, was invariably found holding a cigar and wearing a dark suit. Towards the end of February Gans, understandably nervous since he had never run a campaign before, took over as campaign director.

Although Gans established a position of leadership and respect, he avoided the mundane, routine chores like addressing envelopes. One evening Stavis confronted him: "Curt do you know how the emperor opened the agricultural season in ancient China?" When Gans was unable to give the budding sinologist an answer, Stavis replied, "The emperor has a special silver spade, and when the court astronomers tell him the agricultural season should begin, he goes out and personally turns one spadeful of earth, symbolically participating in agricultural work. Then the millions of peasants go to work."[73] Gans got the point and was soon in the back room with the rest of the staff helping with the menial but necessary tasks.

The New Hampshire staff depended heavily on student volunteers. More than 2,000 students, from colleges as far away as Michigan and Virginia, campaigned full time, and high school students, to free more college students to canvass door-to-door, took over the routine chores of the local headquarters on weekends. "The young people," recalled McCarthy, "did everything from the most menial kind of campaign work to performing in the most demanding administrative offices."[74] Nonstudents played an important role too. New Hampshire's McCarthy Democrats shrewdly tailored ads and publicity to the local taste. One ad read, "Think of how you would feel if you woke up on Wednesday morning and realized Eugene McCarthy had won the New Hampshire primary and New Hampshire had changed the course of American politics."[75]

Hoping to tap the widespread anti-Johnson sentiment, the staff adopted a four-part strategy. First, McCarthy made several short swings throughout the state. He met workers at the factory gates, gave interviews to newspaper editors, and played hockey in Berlin. Second, an intensive media effort included full-page newspaper ads and radio and television commercials. Third, the staff used socially prominent people, like Paul Newman, to draw large crowds, and finally, they conducted door-to-door canvassing. "They had created," said Stavis later, "a super-machine, capable of being moved from state to state."[76]

Although Johnson refused to permit his name to be placed on the ballot, he did not stop the Democratic regulars from pursuing a vigorous write-in effort. His staunch supporters included state party leaders Governor John King and Senator Thomas McIntyre. Businessman Bernard L. Boutin organized 2,000 neighborhood coordinators for the Johnson write-in drive. He won support through promises of political jobs and favors. All that was needed, he said, was to get the voters to the polls.[77]

Early in the campaign, the regulars distributed serial-numbered pledge cards to all registered voters. They consisted of three sections. The first noted that "as expression of your support this card will be forwarded to the White House, Washington, D.C." The party kept the second section and the voter retained the third. The local newspapers reported that the pledge-card serial numbers meant retaliation for those who refused to sign. McCarthy's staff printed a poster "You don't have to sign anything for Gene McCarthy." McCarthy said that the pledge cards denied voters the basic American right of secret ballot.[78] "New Hampshire voters," reported the *New York Times,* "are reacting unfavorably to these pressure tactics."[79]

Pre-election indicators pointed to a low McCarthy vote. One survey reported that 60 percent of New Hampshire's voters had never heard of him, and opinion samplers gave him no more than 20 percent of the vote. Governor King described McCarthy's campaign as futile, and many regulars agreed that he would be lucky to obtain more than 11 percent of the vote.[80] But on March 12, when the Democratic votes were counted, McCarthy won 42.2 percent to Johnson's 49.4 percent. Johnson received 27,243 Democratic votes and 1,778 Republican votes, all write-ins, for a combined total of 29,021 votes. McCarthy won 23,280 Democratic votes and 5,511 Republican write-in votes for a total of 28,791 votes. Kennedy, who vetoed a write-in effort, acquired only 600 votes. Counting both the Democratic and Republican votes, McCarthy came within 230 votes of beating Johnson.

Although the regulars received a majority of the votes cast, McCarthy obtained 20 of the 24 convention delegates. The regulars, believing that the primary would be uncontested, had designated twice as many candidates as places on the delegation. They did this to give every regional and ethnic group some kind of recognition and to reward loyal Democrats with delegate seats. But, since the McCarthyites limited their number of candidates on a slate, the decision cost the regulars all but four delegate seats. "How do you tell the president," said McIntyre, "that even though he got most of the vote he got only four delegates?"[81]

On election night, McCarthy addressed his jubilant followers in the ballroom of the Sheraton Hotel in Manchester, New Hampshire. To shouts of "Chicago, Chicago," he told his supporters. "If we come to Chicago with this strength, there will be no violence and no demonstrations but a great victory celebration." He hugged two pretty young workers close to him. "Chi-ca-go, Chi-ca-go, Vic-to-ry, Vic-to-ry." The cheering was deafening now. "If I had failed," he said, "it would have been a great personal failure because I had the most intelligent campaign staff in the history of American politics, in the history of the world!"[82]

The press agreed that McCarthy's New Hampshire vote raised his political status. According to the *Progressive,* it made him a major contender.[83] "He proved," editorialized the *New Republic,* "that courage and intelligence aren't outmoded," and Rowland Evans and Robert Novak wrote that Wisconsin Democrats "now view McCarthy as the favorite."[84] "McCarthy's big vote," editorialized the *Washington Post,* "is a demonstration of significant opposition to the war."[85] But press secretary Christian emphasized, "We won the popular vote in New Hampshire with only a write-in vote."[86]

Although New Hampshire provided an important test for McCarthy's campaign, it was neither a clear-cut repudiation of the administration nor a total victory for the doves. Surveys by NBC and the Oliver Quayle Company concluded that the Democratic vote in New Hampshire was a vote of dissatisfaction with the Vietnam War, not a vote for a dovish stand.[87] "The hawks," recalled Gans, "voted for McCarthy for reasons other than the war."[88] Apparently, the common denominator was a deep dissatisfaction with the Johnson administration.

Robert F. Kennedy's Dilemma

Senator Kennedy had a very different background from Johnson and McCarthy. He was born to wealth as the seventh of nine children of Joseph P. Kennedy, a successful businessman and President Roosevelt's ambassador to Great Britain. Joseph instilled an almost obsessive compulsion for self-improvement in all his children, and he considered sports the best method to nurture the competitive instinct. Robert's sister Eunice recalled, "Daddy always entered us in public swimming races," and "the important thing was to win, don't come in second, or third, that doesn't count—but win, win, win, win."[89] Because Robert was the smallest, shyest, and least coordinated of his four brothers, he had to try harder to keep up. A Roman Catholic, and the most devout of the nine Kennedy children, he attended church regularly and served as an altar boy. At one time, he considered entering the priesthood. His wife Ethel Shakel was even more religious. They had 11 children.

From 1952 to 1963, Kennedy appeared to be conservative, and his various political roles earned him a reputation as ruthless. He worked for six months as junior counsel on Senator Joseph McCarthy's anticommunist investigative committee, taunted labor leaders during the McClellan Committee's investigation into labor racketeering, and testified in defense of legislation authorizing wiretapping. As President John F. Kennedy's attorney general, he participated in the decisions that enlarged America's Vietnam involvement from 800 advisers in 1961 to 16,000 in 1963.

After his brother's assassination on November 22, 1963, Kennedy underwent personal changes. "Out of that tragedy," recalled Humphrey, "he developed a compassion and understanding that he had seemed to lack previously."[90] He appeared more sympathetic to the problems of blacks, Mexican-Americans, and Indians. He began to feel a sense of community with other victims. Recalled Newfield, "Softer personal qualities long latent and repressed, came to the surface."[91]

Although not yet a dove, he became less hawkish on the war. On May 6, 1965, he spoke about the war for the first time in the Senate. He said that the administration should work harder for "honorable negotiations" between the Vietcong and the South Vietnamese government. In February, 1966, he told reporters that a reasonable solution to the war would include participation by the Vietcong in a coalition government. By 1967, he began calling for an unconditional cessation of the bombing of North Vietnam.

In 1967, despite favorable opinion polls, Kennedy did not consider a run for the nomination in his best interests. Except for Unruh and Iowa's Governor Harold E. Hughes, Kennedy knew that party leaders were against his entry and that antiwar senators up for reelection had to support Johnson or be hurt at the polls. Under these circumstances, Kennedy feared that his entry would split the party. The regulars would blame him for Johnson's defeat as well as the loss of other Democratic officeholders who would go down with the ticket.[92]

The "feud" issue was another concern. Kennedy did not want people to view his candidacy as a personality conflict with Johnson. Class differences and opposite temperaments separated the two men. Johnson resented Kennedy and his circle of urbane, educated, Eastern establishment people while Kennedy considered Johnson and his friends bad-mannered and crude. "Too much separates us," said Johnson later, "too much history, too many differences in temperament."[93]

Throughout the fall of 1967, Kennedy received conflicting advice from friends and associates on entering the race. Goodwin, Schlesinger, Walinsky, administrative assistant Joseph Dolan, and issue researchers Michael Schwartz and Lewis Kaden, argued that the war was too important an issue for Kennedy not to run. Opposed to this view were Kennedy's brother, Edward, and Stephen E. Smith, 1960 campaign strategist, Theodore C. Sorensen, former White House counsel, Pierre Salinger, former presidential appointments secretary, and Frederick G. Dutton, former White House adviser. They feared that the doves would lose influence if Kennedy challenged Johnson in the primaries and that Kennedy would tear the Democratic Party apart. He would, they said, have more power to determine the policies of the next four years if he stood heir to the 1972 nomination rather than become the cause of the party's defeat.[94]

McCarthy's entry increased the pressure on Kennedy to run. "The fact that Bob did not have a high opinion of McCarthy made his position all the more frustrating," recalled O'Brien.[95] Also, his failure to enter stimulated an anti-Kennedy backlash on the campuses. "For the first time in years," recalled Newfield, "Kennedy found himself being booed and heckled by college students."[96] "In his gut, he wanted to go," Kennedy told John Nolan, a former Department of Justice aide. "He felt it was the right thing to do, but his judgment told him his chances of success were so slim, it wasn't the right decision."[97]

Johnson's political advisers agreed that Kennedy was unlikely to enter the race. They concluded that Kennedy's political judgment was that he could not win the nomination and that his entry would split the party.[98] But Johnson was not persuaded. "That little runt will get in," he insisted. "I don't care what he says now."[99]

On January 30, 1968, to the disappointment of many friends and supporters, Kennedy appeared to have decided against entering the race. He told a group of Washington reporters that he would not become a candidate "under any foreseeable circumstances." Lowenstein insisted that he could have won. Walinsky threatened to quit and work independently against Johnson, and Fred Dutton warned that he was giving people the impression of backing off for "reasons of expediency."[100]

The Tet Offensive

On January 30, 1968, Tet, the Vietnamese Lunar New Year, the North Vietnamese and Vietcong launched a major offensive. They attacked 36 of South Vietnam's 44 provincial capitals, 5 of the 6 largest cities, and about one-fourth of the 242 district capitals. Some of the worst fighting occurred in Hue, the old imperial capital, leaving it almost destroyed and with more than 70 percent of its inhabitants homeless. The damage to Saigon was considerable. At the American embassy in Saigon, a squad of Vietcong blasted a hole in the wall surrounding the American embassy compound and entered the grounds, but United States military police and Marine guards prevented them from entering the embassy building itself and killed all the attackers. The fighting continued for many weeks before American and South Vietnamese troops regained the initiative. By then, American casualties totaled 2,000 dead, South Vietnamese twice as many, and enemy casualties close to 50,000.

Although aware of an enemy build-up, the extent and degree of the attack surprised the Johnson administration. "No one really expected the enemy to launch the attack during Tet," recalled General Wheeler.[101] "The major surprise," recalled National Security Adviser Walt W. Rostow, "was the number of provincial capitals attacked."[102] It was "a shock to all of us," added Johnson.[103]

But the administration claimed a decisive victory against the enemy. "They lost as many people at Tet as we have lost in the entire war," said Johnson.[104] "The ground lost was quickly recovered," recalled Christian, and "the best units of the Vietcong were decimated."[105] General Maxwell Taylor said later that the Tet offensive was "the greatest victory we ever scored in Viet Nam."[106] But "another victory or two like that," recalled Secretary of Defense Clark Clifford, "and we would be out of business. It was a disastrous defeat for us."[107]

In the wake of the Tet offensive, public support for the war fell, and most of the public media turned against it. Major publications like the *Wall Street Journal,* the *New York Post, Life, Look, Time,* and *Newsweek* and major television networks, CBS and NBC, came out against the war. Many newspapers moved to a more dovish position. "The whole Vietnam effort," editorialized the *Wall Street Journal,* "may be falling apart beneath our feet."[108] Even if Westmoreland is winning the war, remarked Lippmann, "there is still all Asia to be pacified before we have 'won'."[109] "It's increasingly clear," said newscaster Walter Cronkite in a television editorial, "that the only rational way out will be to negotiate."[110]

Opposition also came from Congress. A total of 139 House members—98 Republicans and 41 Democrats—joined in supporting a resolution calling for an immediate congressional review of the administration's policy in Southeast Asia.[111] "There is an awful lot of soul-searching going on up here," said one senior Democratic leader.[112] "We are destroying the country we profess to be saving," declared Senator Albert Gore of Tennessee, and "seriously damaging ourselves."[113]

Kennedy's Reassessment

With public opinion going against the war, Kennedy broke completely with the administration's Vietnam policy. Calling Johnson's claims of progress "illusory," he denied that there was "any prospect" of an American military victory. The United States, he told a Chicago audience on February 8, 1968, could not "resolve by military might a conflict whose issue depends upon the will and conviction of the South Vietnamese people." Kennedy received a thousand congratulatory telegrams, and a dozen major newspaper editorials praised his speech.[114]

Shortly thereafter, Kennedy again began to seriously consider entering. But unlike McCarthy, he would not enter solely to champion an issue, even the Vietnam War, but only if there existed a good chance of winning the nomination. He needed to know the result of the New Hampshire vote.

Consequently, on March 13, the day after McCarthy's large vote, Kennedy indicated that he might enter the race. He told reporters that he was "actively reconsidering the possibilities that are available to me." He explained that he no longer feared that his candidacy would divide the Democratic Party since McCarthy's showing indicated that it was already split.[115] But it was bad timing. To many, he looked like he was coming in after McCarthy had paved the way.

When McCarthy arrived at Washington, D.C.'s National Airport, reporters asked him to comment on Kennedy's reassessment. "Well," McCarthy's smile beginning to fade, "that's something you should ask him." When asked if he would withdraw if Kennedy entered, McCarthy replied coldly, "I don't intend to withdraw."[116]

On the evening of March 13, Edward Kennedy phoned Clark Clifford at his home and asked if he would meet with his brother and Sorensen. Clifford replied that he was available to meet Kennedy and Sorensen the next day at the pentagon.

At 11 o'clock the three men assembled at Clifford's Pentagon office. Kennedy said that Johnson's Vietnam policy was a failure. One way to correct the policy, said Kennedy, "would be for him [Kennedy] to become a candidate for the Democratic nomination for president, and if elected he could then change the policy. The other alternative was for him to find the means to persuade President Johnson to change the policy."[117] Clifford replied that he "would be making a grave mistake if he assumed that the situation in Vietnam would be the same in August (during the convention) as it is now." He urged Kennedy not to enter the race.[118]

Johnson rejected the commission proposal. "No matter how the arrangement was handled," he told Clifford, "it would still appear to be a political deal." He considered it "a form of blackmail, an ultimatum to the commander-in-chief."[119]

Some said Johnson's rejection of the commission plan played a role in Kennedy's decision to enter the race. But more likely McCarthy's large New Hampshire vote was the key factor. It showed that the party was seriously divided and that moderates would vote for an antiwar candidate. Kennedy then decided to enter the race.

Green Bay Meeting

On March 16, Edward Kennedy met with McCarthy at the Northland Hotel in Green Bay, Wisconsin. Gans and Goodwin, who had arranged the 2:00 a.m. meeting, hoped that Edward and McCarthy would agree to divide up the primaries. Edward said that Robert had instructed him to offer what help he could in Wisconsin. McCarthy replied that he needed no help. Edward then asked McCarthy to reserve Oregon for Robert. But McCarthy was adamantly opposed to dividing up the primaries he had already entered. He mentioned West Virginia, Louisiana, and Florida. But these were secondary primaries, and Edward remained silent. He made polite conversation for a little bit and then left. McCarthy turned to his wife Abigail, "That's the way they are. When it comes down to it, they never offer anything real."[120]

Long afterwards, those present at the Green Bay meeting differed as to who was at fault. Edward Kennedy blamed Abigail, but she denied being against an accommodation. "Edward wanted it," recalled Schlesinger, "but McCarthy was not in the mood or not prepared for that kind of discussion."[121] According to Gans, "McCarthy's sense was that he would bear both political profit and no loss by continuing to be the hero dealing with the opportunist who came in late."[122]

Kennedy's Announcement

On the morning of March 16, 1968, Kennedy, who had clipped his long hair for the occasion, strode into the old Senate Caucus Room and announced to reporters, cameramen, and well-wishers that he would enter the primaries in an all-out effort to win the nomination. More specifically, he stated his intention to enter the Nebraska, Oregon, and California primaries. (He would eventually add Indiana, District of Columbia, West Virginia, and New York.) He wished McCarthy well in the upcoming Wisconsin, Pennsylvania, and Massachusetts primaries. "In no state," he emphasized, "will my efforts be directed against Senator McCarthy." Kennedy explained his reasons for entering the race:

> In private talks and in public I have tried in vain to alter our course in Vietnam before it further saps our spirit and our manpower, further raises the risk of wider war and further destroys the country and the people it was meant to save....
>
> The remarkable New Hampshire campaign of Senator Eugene McCarthy

has proven how deep are the present divisions within our party and within our country. Until that was publicly clear my presence in the race would have been seen as a clash of personalities rather than issues.

But now that fight is won and over policies which I have long been challenging. I must enter that race. The fight is just beginning and I believe that I can win.

In the question and answer period, Kennedy discussed his Vietnam position. He said he intended to deescalate American involvement, turn more of the fighting over to the South Vietnamese, risk a bombing halt, and the Vietcong would have "a role in the future political process of South Vietnam."[123]

The press was critical of Kennedy's timing. The *Wall Street Journal* called it an opportunistic attempt "to seize the McCarthy victory for himself."[124] The *Evening Star* (Washington, D.C.) said it would "reinforce the charge of political opportunism" and the *Washington Post* reported that McCarthy deserved better treatment "at the hands of one who shares his cause but left him to test it first."[125]

To pollsters and Senate observers, Johnson appeared to be in some trouble. In late March, the Gallup poll reported that Democrats preferred Kennedy to Johnson by 44 to 41 percent and Johnson to McCarthy by 59 to 29 percent.[126] The judgment of some fifteen to twenty of my colleagues, said one Johnson senator, is that Kennedy has the capability of denying Johnson the nomination.[127] "Lyndon Johnson could not be elected dog-catcher in Missouri today," declared Senator Stuart Symington, and Senator Frank Church echoed, "I can't find a soul in Idaho who's really for him."[128]

While Johnson privately brooded over Kennedy's entry, his staff put on a positive front. "It wasn't a surprise," insisted Christian. "Johnson knew Kennedy was going to enter long before he did."[129] "If he wasn't in this before Bobby announced," said one campaign staffer, "he's in it up to his neck now. He will not turn this country over to Bobby—not a chance."[130] "He is trying," explained another staffer, "to hold sort of a Maginot Line against a blitzkrieg."[131] "Bobby Kennedy," said Johnson bitterly to a visitor, "has been a candidate since the first day I sat here."[132]

Despite the negative indicators, Johnson still outdistanced Kennedy in delegate support and held the support of the Democratic establishment. After the New Hampshire primary, a *New York Times* delegate survey indicated that Johnson controlled 1,725 convention votes, compared with a combined total of 790 for senators Kennedy and McCarthy and 61 for Wallace, the third party candidate.[133] The Johnson reelection campaign's state-by-state survey showed him winning renomination on the first ballot.[134] In addition, party chairmen, southern leaders, and power brokers in the big industrial states preferred the president to Kennedy. Although favorable to Kennedy, Mayor Richard J. Daley of Chicago, Governor Richard Hughes of New Jersey, and antiwar senators McGovern of South Dakota, Clark of Pennsylvania, and Morse of Oregon lined up behind Johnson. "The only thing to happen with an all-out fight," said Congressman Wayne L. Hays of Ohio, "would be to make it probable that Dick Nixon would be the next president of the United States."[135] "There is only one peace candidate this year," declared Democratic Chairman John Bailey, "and his name is Lyndon Johnson."[136]

McCarthy's supporters did not desert him. Although Lowenstein concentrated his efforts on his own race in Nassau County, Long Island, he remained with McCarthy. Goodwin stayed with McCarthy through Wisconsin and then parted on friendly terms. "Everybody's reaction," Rauh said later, "was one of bitter anger that after we tried to get Bobby to run he comes in after New Hampshire."[137] "He's a filthy, power-hungry politician like Lyndon Johnson," opined one Yale man. "He's shifty and obnoxious," said a McCarthy supporter at Claremont Men's College in California.[138] "Seeing the romance flower between them [the voters] and McCarthy," wrote *Washington Star* reporter Mary McGrory, "he moved with the ruthlessness of a Victorian father whose daughter has fallen in love with the dustman."[139]

The Nixon camp agreed that Kennedy's entry would irreparably split the Democratic Party and that Johnson could manipulate the war to his advantage and keep the nomination from Kennedy. But if he won the nomination, Nixon told his staff, "We can beat that little S.O.B."[140]

In the final analysis, the New Hampshire primary was pivotal in Kennedy's decision to enter the race. It indicated to him that the Democratic Party was already split and that the public would vote for an antiwar candidate. Thus Kennedy's entry after New Hampshire, though it angered some, made political sense.

Chapter II

The Republican Comeback

Background

The 1964 presidential election had been a political disaster for the Republican Party. Barry M. Goldwater of Arizona appeared too conservative for the voting public. His proposal to leave the protection of civil rights to the states angered blacks and Republican liberals. His criticism of social security, the Tennessee Valley Authority, and the Test-Ban Treaty, along with his apparent willingness to use nuclear weapons in Vietnam, scared moderates and independents. Many businessmen, who usually favored the Republicans, considered Johnson safer. Only a small number of major newspapers supported Goldwater. In a landslide, Johnson obtained 486 electoral and 43 million popular votes to Goldwater's 52 electoral and 27 million popular votes. Goldwater carried only his own state and 5 deep South states. And the Republicans lost 38 seats in the House, 2 in the Senate, and retained only 17 governorships and 7 state legislatures.

The Republicans made a comeback in the 1966 midterm elections. They gained 3 Senate seats, 47 House members, and 8 governorships. They controlled half of the country's statehouses, 17 state legislatures, and over 800 county offices. Republican Party leaders agreed that a strong anti-administration tide was running throughout the country, but they sought to avoid choosing another candidate like Goldwater who did not represent the political mainstream.

By 1968, the South had become an important new force in the Republican Party. In the post-Civil War years, Republicans in the South usually fell into one of three categories: eccentric, carpetbagger, or black. The 1928 presidential election, in which Herbert Hoover won 48 percent of the southern vote, marked the first time the Republicans broke the solid South. Since 1952, the region's share of the voting strength at the convention had risen from 19 to nearly 27 percent, and in 1968, the southerners had 356 of the convention votes.

George Romney

Shortly after the 1966 midterm elections, the polls showed Governor Romney of Michigan as the leading Republican candidate. The Harris poll indicated that American voters preferred Romney over Johnson by 54 to 46 percent, and the Gallup poll reported the preferences of Republicans as Romney 39 percent, Nixon 31 percent, Reagan 8 percent, Rockefeller and Percy 5 percent each, and Lindsay 2 percent.[1]

Governor Romney had been in politics for almost three decades. He was a Washington lobbyist and served as manpower specialist during World War II. After serving as president of the American Motors Corporation in the 1950s, he was elected governor of Michigan in 1962, by a margin of 80,573 votes. Deeply religious, a member of the Mormon Church, he neither smoked nor drank and would not talk politics on Sunday.

On issues, he was not always clear or consistent. He argued that large unions were the main cause of rising costs and prices. But as governor, he had sponsored a minimum wage law and promoted boosts in unemployment compensation benefits. He seemed favorable to civil rights. He once marched with Dr. Martin Luther King, Jr., fought for a state (and supported a federal) open occupancy housing law. A strong proponent of law and order, he told blacks that change would come about through the political process. At one point, he opposed a bombing halt in North Vietnam but later said he would consider it. He called McCarthy's proposals as amounting to "surrender to the enemy."[2]

Romney exhibited a number of weaknesses. His speeches, said party leaders, were often boring and unexciting. Newsman David Broder wrote of his "fuzziness on national and international issues," and political observers described him as "a finger-jabber, a lapel-grabber, and a fistpounder" who, when frustrated, would sometimes stomp his feet or turn his back.[3]

On September 4, 1967, when asked by Detroit television interviewer Lou Gordon to explain his Vietnam position, Romney replied that the generals and diplomatic corps had brainwashed him on a visit to Vietnam in 1965. "And they do a very thorough job," he insisted. But since returning, he had concluded that intervention in Vietnam was not in the nation's self-interest.[4]

Romney's remarks went unnoticed for several days until Gordon, who had decided that Romney's "brainwashing" statement would be a real attention-getter, alerted the *New York Times*. Five days later, the *New York Times'* headline read, ROMNEY ASSERTS HE UNDERWENT "BRAINWASHING" ON VIETNAM TRIP, and the national networks played the 30-second "brainwashing" clip, "shorn of background and circumstances."[5]

Romney's "brainwashing" remark generated a storm of protest, and his political standing plummeted overnight. After leading the Republican pack against President Johnson for over a year, Romney suddenly plunged to fourth place in the mid-September Harris poll. The *New York Times* called it an example of his "crippling lack of agility and verbal precision."[6] He never recovered from it.

When Romney officially entered in mid-November, 1967, his standing fell so low that observers considered him Nelson Rockefeller's stand-in. Rockefeller did give Romney financial assistance, political organizers, mailing lists, and research papers. While Rockefeller denied there was anything devious about his support for Romney, he added that he would not "go out and shoot people who wanted him [Rockefeller] to run."[7]

Once the frontrunner, Romney fell far behind Nixon. A January 1968 Gallup poll showed that Republicans favored Nixon three-to-one over Romney and three-to-two over Rockefeller, and a *Newsweek* delegate count gave Nixon 561 convention votes, only 106 shy of the number needed to win the nomination. According to Romney's own poll, taken by Market Opinion Research of Detroit, Nixon would obtain 70 percent of the New Hampshire vote to Romney's 10 percent.[8]

Richard M. Nixon

Born in 1913, Nixon grew up in Whittier, California, where his father operated a citrus farm and combination grocery store and gasoline station. In high school and later at Whittier College, a small Quaker institution, he won honors as a student leader and master debater. He graduated from Duke University Law School and, in 1940, married Thelma Patricia Ryan, a school teacher. During World War II, he served as an attorney in the Office of Price Administration and later entered the navy.

After the war, Nixon returned to California and entered politics. In

1946, he won a congressional seat by defeating nationally-known New Deal Democrat Jerry Voorhis, and in 1950 defeated Helen Gahagan Douglas to win a Senate seat. Nixon's early electoral victories were gained by intimating that his opponents were "soft on Communism."[9] During this period, he served as prosecutor for the House Committee on Un-American Activities. He won national prominence by helping to convict (on a perjury charge) Alger Hiss, a former State Department official accused of once belonging to the Communist Party.

After General Dwight D. Eisenhower picked Nixon as his running mate in 1952, the Democrats charged Nixon with having a secret campaign fund. Over a two-year period, his supporters had set-up a fund which collected and disbursed just over $18,000 to meet various political expenses.

Fearful that Eisenhower would drop him from the ticket, Nixon went on national television in Los Angeles, to give his famous "Checkers" speech. He said that Checkers, a little black-and-white spaniel that a Texas admirer had given his children, was a gift and "regardless of what they say about it, we are going to keep it."[10]

The speech generated favorable response. Over a million telegrams and letters of support arrived at Republican offices in Washington and state capitals, and contributions covered the $75,000 cost of the telecast. Most important, Eisenhower decided to keep him on the ticket. He told a cheering crowd in Cleveland, "I have seen brave men in tough situations, but I have never seen anyone come through in better fashion than Senator Nixon."[11]

Two incidents stand out in Nixon's vice presidency. In the spring of 1958, on a goodwill trip to Latin America, Nixon was stoned and spat upon by leftist students. This gave him notoriety and popular approval. On a trip to the Soviet Union in 1959, Nixon again won much applause by engaging Soviet premier Nikita Khrushchev in a spontaneous debate at the site of a model kitchen during a visit to a Moscow trade fair. Both episodes helped Nixon in his successful bid for the 1960 Republican presidential nomination.

After the 1960 election, some observers attributed Nixon's loss to John F. Kennedy, by 113,000 votes, to vote fraud in Illinois and Texas. In one Texas county, where only 4,895 voters were registered, 6,138 votes were counted. In Chicago, a voting machine recorded 121 votes after only 43 people had voted. Many Republican leaders, including Eisenhower, urged Nixon to contest the results. But after thoughtful review, Nixon refused. "If I demanded a recount and it turned out that despite the vote fraud Kennedy had still won," explained Nixon later, "charges of 'sore losers' would follow me through history and remove any possibility of a further political career."[12]

On September 27, 1962, at a press conference at Los Angeles' Statler Hilton Hotel, Nixon announced his decision to enter the race for governor of California.

During the campaign against the incumbent Pat Brown, Nixon encountered a number of difficulties. By denouncing the John Birch Society, he alienated the political right. Governor Brown accused him of using his position as vice president to help his brother get a secret loan from a major defense contractor. Although the charge was unsubstantiated, the media raised the issue throughout the campaign. Also, many Californians argued that Nixon sought the governorship only as a stepping-stone to a 1964 presidential candidacy. Out of nearly six million votes cast, Nixon lost to Brown by a margin of 297,000 votes. In his concession statement, Nixon angrily attacked the press. He said:

> I leave you gentlemen now and you will write it. You will interpret it. That's your right. But as I leave you I want you to know—just think how much you're going to be missing.
>
> You won't have Nixon to kick around anymore, because, gentlemen, this is my last press conference, and it will be one in which I have welcomed the opportunity to test wits with you. I have always respected you. I have sometimes disagreed with you. But unlike some people, I've never cancelled a subscription to a paper, and also, I never will.[13]

After his defeat and his emotional outburst to the press, Nixon's political career appeared to be over. ABC television aired a half-hour show entitled "The Political Obituary of Richard Nixon." "Let's look at the facts," Nixon told newspaperman Roscoe Drummond in 1963; "I have no staff.... I have no political base. Anybody who thinks I could be a candidate for anything in any year is off his rocker."[14] Shortly after, he accepted a $200,000 a year offer to join the New York law firm of Mudge, Stern, Baldwin, and Todd. This move seemed to seal Nixon's political retirement. Despite his defeat, he could have continued to play an important leadership role in California's Republican Party, but in New York, Rockefeller was the Republican leader.

But Nixon was unable to stay away from politics for long and was soon back in the national limelight. At the 1964 Republican National Convention in San Francisco, he skillfully established himself in the role of party unifier. But Goldwater's acceptance speech, to Nixon's dismay, was a "strident and divisive speech" which alienated the liberals and allowed the Democrats to depict the nominee as "a dangerous right-winger." Despite Goldwater's devastating loss, Nixon's efforts, which included 150 appearances in 36 states, increased his standing among party leaders, gained him national attention, and made a favorable impression on conservatives.[15]

From 1964 to 1966, Nixon continued his efforts for Republican candidates. Traveling 127,000 miles, he visited 40 states, and spoke before more than 400 groups in support of congressional and gubernatorial candidates. He helped raise more than $4 million in party contributions and formed "Congress 66" to help elect Republican congressmen. His enthusiastic campaign efforts identified him as a central participant in the midterm Republican victories.

After the election, hoping to let Romney take the heat from the press and public, Nixon remained unofficially undecided on running in 1968. "Not only would this allow me more independence," he told his advisers, "but the speculation about my intentions guaranteed far more media attention than I would have if I announced."[16]

In early 1967, Nixon began assembling a topnotch campaign staff. He made his law partner, John Mitchell, campaign manager, and picked Peter Flanigin, an investment banker, for deputy manager. He put Maurice Stans, another investment banker, in charge of gathering money; in March, 1967, he organized the "Nixon for President Committee." Nixon's personal staff included Robert H. Finch, Richard G. Kleindienst, John W. Sears, Robert Haldeman and Dwight Chapin, former advertising men; Robert Ellsworth, a former congressman from Kansas; and Rose Mary Woods. In charge of media and press campaign were Herbert Klein, a public affairs officer, and his longtime associate, Ronald Ziegler. The research team included two former editorial writers, Raymond E. Price and Patrick Buchanan, and William Safire, a public relations man.

Nixon's biggest handicap was a loser image. He had not won an election on his own since 1950, and even his strongest supporters wondered if he could win. Nixon's problem, wrote columnist Drew Pearson, "is the sickening fear among rank-and-file Republicans that Nixon can't win." "If I can't establish in these miserable primaries that I am a winner," Nixon told friends, "I'm out of it."[17]

Nixon portrayed himself as a centrist candidate, the party unifier. He cultivated the image of the experienced professional acceptable to all factions. The press talked of a "New Nixon" who would not say "a sharp word about any opponent."[18] But said the *Economist* (London), "It remains to be seen whether the 'old' Nixon has been suppressed permanently."[19]

Until early 1968, Nixon advocated holding out for a military victory in

Vietnam. He charged Johnson with "frittering away" America's military and economic advantages. "The only effective way to convince Hanoi that peace is in their interests," argued Nixon, "is to prosecute the war more effectively." He maintained that the choice was not, as the doves argued, "between this war and no war," but between this war and an even bigger war later against a stronger Communist presence: "If South Vietnam is lost and the Pacific becomes a Red Sea, we could be confronted with a world war where the odds against us would be far greater."[20]

As the New Hampshire primary approached, Nixon began to sound less hawkish. He was persuaded by party leaders that a "Republican hawk" could not win the presidency."[21] He said that the war "cannot be won by military means alone" and pledged that "new leadership will end the war and win the peace in the Pacific." But he refused to give details and denied rumors that he had a secret plan to end the war. "A pledge to end the war," editoralized the *Washington Post*, "cannot help but stir hopes, but Mr. Nixon must not be offended if he is asked how he proposes to do it."[22]

Nixon took a hardline on the law and order issue and seemed to equivocate on civil rights. He said that doubling the rate of criminal convictions would do more to eliminate crime than Johnson's "war on poverty."[23] He rejected forcible integration and said that each state and city should make its own decision on open housing. The *New York Times* reported,

"He is now suggesting that the nation and congress have done about as much as they can to guarantee equal rights."[24]

Rejecting government welfare programs, Nixon advocated black capitalism to raise black's economic status. He would use the tax and credit powers of the Department of Treasury to create black capitalism in the slums. This would require technical assistance, loan guarantees, new capital sources, and tax incentives to industry to provide job training and education so blacks could establish their own businesses. "Black ownership," he explained, "would mean black pride, black jobs, black opportunity and, yes, black power."[25] The Congress of Racial Equality (CORE) endorsed his proposal.

On February 2, 1968, at a news conference at the Holiday Inn in Manchester, New Hampshire, Nixon announced his candidacy. "Ladies and gentlemen," he deadpanned, "as we start this campaign there's one thing we should say at the outset—this is not my last press conference."[26] He said that he would enter the Wisconsin, Indiana, South Dakota, and Oregon primaries and would avoid primaries, like Pennsylvania, Massachusetts, Ohio, and California, where favorite sons were running. "Victory for the Republican Party," he declared, "is more important than the ambition of one man." His background and experience, he said, made him the candidate "who can win and can do the job."[27]

Romney Withdraws

By late February, 1968, George Romney considered the race hopeless. The national polls indicated a decisive Nixon victory in New Hampshire, and Romney's private polls showed him trailing Nixon by more than five-to-one.[28] In addition, contributions had fallen off considerably. Romney had already spent $1 million and his campaign would require another $2 million to carry him to the August convention. His advisers argued that political observers would interpret an early pullout as proof that he had been Rockefeller's stalking horse, but Romney feared that a landslide defeat would destroy his chances to influence the nomination.[29]

On February 28, while in Washington to attend the midwinter Republican governors' conference, Romney announced to reporters that he was withdrawing from the race. He expressed gratitude to Rockefeller and Governor John H. Chafee of Rhode Island, the only governors to endorse him. He pledged his "wholehearted support" to any new candidate his fellow Republican governors endorsed, but he did not name his choice. He gave three reasons for his decisions: his candidacy had not won the wide acceptance with rank and file Republicans; it was desirable that he be enabled to make plans to support another candidate; and he had concluded that he could best serve his country otherwise than as a candidate.[30]

Romney's withdrawal came as a political surprise. While party leaders agreed that his race appeared hopeless, they were surprised that he withdrew before the test of the New Hampshire primary. Reporters covering his campaign described him as a man with a mission and considered withdrawal "quite literally the last thing in the world he would do."[31]

Nixon's staff welcomed Romney's withdrawal, but Nixon was concerned that running unopposed in New Hampshire would not help erase his loser image. "I was disappointed," recalled Nixon. "Now I would win without having actually defeated an opponent in the election" and that was "the reason I had decided to enter the primaries in the first place."[32]

While Governor Reagan continued to stress his noncandidate status, Rockefeller reaffirmed his draft position. "I'm not a candidate," he declared but he was available for a draft and would welcome write-in campaigns in the primaries. Significantly, Romney gave no endorsement—an indication of resentment at his patron's emerging availability.

Nelson A. Rockefeller

Born into one of America's wealthiest families, Rockefeller early entered public service. From 1940 to 1945, he worked in Washington as co-ordinator for Latin American affairs and assistant Secretary of State. In the Eisenhower Administration, he served as Secretary of Health, Education, and Welfare, and became the president's special assistant in the White House. In 1958, he was elected governor of New York. As governor, he acquired thousands of acres of new parklands and spent $1.7 billion to attack water pollution. In education, he increased guaranteed student loans and expanded the state university of New York. He established the most comprehensive state program of medical aid in the nation and helped pass New York's biggest bond issue ($2.5 billion) to improve the transportation system. He also built housing and hospitals, raised minimum wages, and added consumer protection and narcotic control laws.

Rockefeller had many enemies in the Republican Party. In 1960, he had generated a storm of censure by divorcing his wife to marry a woman who had given up custody of her children to win her divorce. Despite the controversy, he entered the 1964 primaries, lost to Goldwater, and refused to support him in the general campaign. This, many western Republicans argued, "sabotaged" his candidacy. "His major liability," remarked Eisenhower in 1968, "is that his becoming a candidate would resurrect all the hard feelings of 1964, at a time when it is imperative to get the party together."[33]

After Rockefeller's reelection for governor in 1966, he adopted a non-candidacy stance. His closest supporters argued that any overt move for the nomination would resurrect the hatreds of the 1964 race and quickly unite the conservatives against him. But in June, 1967, he said he might accept favorite son status for New York and in December, at a Republican governors' meeting in Palm Beach, he said that he would accept a presidential draft but did not consider such a move likely. He joked to friends, "Washington's a great place to visit, but who'd want to live there?" He added coyly, "I'm not burning my draft card."[34]

By remaining a noncandidate. Rockefeller avoided taking an early stand on the Vietnam issue. He told friends that he was "really agonizing" over the political effect of making an early commitment on Vietnam because he believed that Johnson would begin peace negotiations before the November elections. Top aides advised him to describe the war as "a grave crisis" which demonstrates "the need for new leadership." "The apparent belief in both the Nixon and Rockefeller camps," editorialized the *New York Times,* "is that the Republicans can win the Presidency by censoring Administration policies in Vietnam but keeping vague, their own proposals for change."[35]

By early 1968, Rockefeller had emerged as the rallying point for young, urban, liberal Republicans who considered Romney unable to stop Nixon. Among them was Maryland Governor Spiro Agnew. In early January, 1968, he set up a draft Rockefeller movement in Maryland and in mid-March became the head of a national Rockefeller draft committee. If Rockefeller won the nomination, he hoped to play a large role in the campaign. "Agnew," remarked a Maryland newspaperman, "acted as if he had reached the big time at last."[36]

The polls favored Rockefeller, but most party regulars preferred Nixon. A Harris poll, taken in March, 1968, indicated that voters preferred Rockefeller 41 percent to Johnson's 34 percent, whereas Nixon and Johnson tied at 39 percent. But among rank and file Republicans (who made up about a quarter of the electorate), Nixon led 56 percent to Rockefeller's 32. Republican county chairmen favored Nixon over Rockefeller five-to-one. "What he is looking for," declared the *Washington Post,* "is a strong groundswell of popular support."[37]

On March 10, two days before the New Hampshire primary, Rockefeller's advisers arranged a carefully publicized three-hour meeting of 32 Republican Party leaders in Rockefeller's New York Fifth Avenue apartment. They included staunch supporters Mayor Lindsay of New York, and Governors Agnew of Maryland, Tom R. McCall of Oregon, John H. Chafee of Rhode Island, Winthrop Rockefeller of Arkansas, Raymond P. Shafer of Pennsylvania, Harold LeVander of Minnesota, and John A. Love of Colorado.

Also in the group was William E. Miller, Goldwater's 1964 running mate. He was now a Rockefeller supporter. Miller said, "The Governor has proven to be a greater vote-getter among a greater cross-section of Americans than Mr. Nixon."[38] Publicly, they issued a statement: "There was very strong sentiment that Governor Rockefeller should get into the race," but privately, they reported that sentiment for entering the race "was not nearly so one-sided as expected."[39] The lack of representation from the big Midwestern States, the South, and the party leadership in Congress added to the inclusiveness of the result.

Ronald Reagan

Although the polls favored Nixon and Rockefeller, Ronald Reagan, despite his noncandidacy posture, was a formidable contender. Throughout

1967 and 1968, the Harris poll showed him running ahead of all other Republican candidates in the South, the conservative rural areas, and with those who had voted for Goldwater. As a popular fund-raising speaker, who had raised a total of $1.5 million for the party, he had broadened his appeal and placed numerous party officials politically in his debt.

Born in 1911, Reagan grew up in the small town of Tampico, Illinois, the son of an Irish shoe salesman. Athletic as a youth, he spent his summers as a lifeguard and claimed to have saved 77 bathers from drowning. At Illinois' Eureka College, he majored in economics and sociology and lettered in football, basketball, and track. After landing a job in Des Moines, Iowa, as a sportscaster, he acquired a reputation as one of the best baseball commentators in the Midwest. In 1937, he went to Hollywood, became a movie star, and made, all told, 80 films including training and morale-boosting efforts for the air force during World War II.

Reagan gradually changed from a New Deal Democrat to a conservative Republican. As president of the Screen Actors Guild, he lined up its members behind the efforts of the House Committee on Un-American activities to ferret out communists in Hollywood. He resigned from the board of the Hollywood Independent Citizens Committee of Arts, Science, and Professions when it was exposed as a "Communist front organization." "Light was dawning in some obscure region of my head," he said afterwards; "I was beginning to see the seamy side of liberalism." In the 1950s, he spoke on the topics, "Losing Freedom by Installments" and "Communist Subversion in Hollywood" to some 250,000 General Electric workers across the country. "A great deal of his conversion," explained one commentator, "can be traced to his speaking tours."[40]

During Goldwater's 1964 presidential campaign, Reagan delivered his basic General Electric speech on national television. It was a blend of free enterprise "heroics" and criticism of government spending. Although some Goldwater staffers were upset because it attacked the Social Security system, it netted the party over $50,000 in contributions and helped launch Reagan on a successful bid for the governorship of California in 1966.

As governor, Reagan proposed a conservative program but was unable to implement it all. He hoped to generate $38 million in new funds by charging tuition at the University of California and its state colleges, but the liberals and the Board of Regents blocked his efforts. Opponents also defeated his attempt to trim the state's mental health budget. He was forced to change his proposed 10 percent across-the-board cuts in all spending programs to 6 percent. While campaigning on the promise to reduce taxes, he wound up raising them by $943 million to cover the highest budget in history, nearly \$5.1 billion. California Democrats admitted that Reagan could grasp the "financial realities," and out-of-state journalists admitted that he was not "half as alarming" as he appeared.

On national issues, Reagan took a hard-line stand on law and order, called the nation's welfare program a failure, and advocated reducing the government's role in the economy. He called civil rights rioters "mad dogs" and student demonstrators "rabble-rousers and hate-mongers."[41] While admitting that "something should be done" to help minorities, he considered the 1964 and 1965 federal civil rights acts unconstitutional.[42] He called welfare a "colossal failure" and was proud to have vetoed more anti-poverty projects than any other governor. In fiscal matters, he called for a reduction in federal spending and implementation of a federal revenue-sharing program with the states. To London's *The Listener,* "His anti-government, anti-politician, anti-intellectual, anti-internationalist, and anti-Negro posture shows him to be in tune with the national mood."[43]

Reagan adopted a noncandidacy posture for 1968. "If Reagan campaigned in the primaries in the face of earlier declarations of no interest," explained Clifton White, "he would appear opportunistic, and Californians consider their governor the highest position in the world."[44] More likely he feared losing to Nixon in the primaries. "His only hope," said columnist Warren Weaver, Jr., "was if Nixon faltered."

Charles H. Percy

Elected in 1966, 47-year-old Senator Charles Percy of Illinois, bright, eager, and handsome, was standing in the wings. Once president of Bell and Howell, his political star rose after he became chairman of the Republican Platform Committee in 1960. He had few enemies, and party leaders agreed that he had the qualities, "glamour and youth and unscarred success," to unify the party. However, Theodore White wrote that Percy, although attractive to young voters, "lacked the political machinery, the allies or the knowledge to translate his popular appeal to real power within his party."[45] Percy was dovish on Vietnam and moderately liberal on domestic issues. "Many believe," he said, "that escalation of U.S. combat efforts would end the war more quickly. However, each American escalation has been matched by the other side." He would shift more responsibility for fighting the war to the South Vietnamese, and he would raise taxes to finance the war. "I think it is unconscionable to pass the cost of the war on to future generations,"[46] he said. On domestic issues, he argued that the pendulum had gone too far in protecting the criminal against society, proposed a federal-state tax sharing plan, called for a cut in federal spending, and looked to the private sector to become more involved in solving public problems.

John V. Lindsay

John Lindsay, the first Republican mayor of New York in this century was also standing in the wings. But as a New Yorker and a liberal Republican, he could not make a move without Rockefeller's support. He was dovish. "The war in Vietnam," he warned, "has estranged the majority of the American people from their own government, endangered our precarious economy, paralyzed our national will and crippled our ability to deal with our critical domestic problems." He described the nation's cities as "seething with the gravest domestic crisis since the Civil War" and said that poverty was the cause of the crime. "If we are to eliminate crime and violence in this country," he said, "we must eliminate the hopelessness, futility, and alienation from which they spring."[47]

But Romney had preempted the liberal challenge, and Rockefeller seemed ready to jump into the fray, leaving Lindsay and Percy no opening to enter the race.

Harold E. Stassen

A progressive Republican, Harold E. Stassen, who also ran in 1948 and 1952, was a candidate. As governor of Minnesota in the early 1940s, he pushed through a Labor Peace Act, installed an effective civil service system, and became the first governor to desegregate the National Guard. Under Eisenhower, he served in a number of important positions; including the National Security Council of the United Nations and the Cabinet. Eisenhower referred to Stassen as his "secretary for peace" and assigned him the project of planning for world arms control. As the 1968 primaries neared, Stassen called for a reversal of Johnson's war policies and a stronger commitment to overcome the problems in the cities. He pledged to "correct completely, thoroughly and immediately the tragic error of the Johnson-Humphrey Administration in turning the Vietnamese struggle into an American war," and he asked for a "major commitment of resources to overcome the neglect of our big cities."[48]

But since he had virtually no support, Stassen viewed his candidacy more as a forum for expressing his liberal views and influencing opinion against the war than as a serious attempt for the nomination.

The New Hampshire Primary

In New Hampshire's March 12 primary, Nixon won a landslide victory. Out of the 106,000 Republican votes cast, he obtained 84,005, Rockefeller 11,691, Romney 1,743, Stassen 429, and Reagan 326. Nixon won more votes than any candidate in any presidential primary in New Hampshire's history; and his total was larger than the combined votes of all other Democratic, Republican, and write-in candidates. Rockefeller got only about half of the 19,504 votes he got in 1964. He claimed that the vote was "not politically significant," but party leaders concluded that it was a severe blow to him. New Hampshire had "ruptured the loser image," wrote Theodore White; and the *Wall Street Journal* declared that the Republicans have a chance such as they haven't had since the Eisenhower victories."[49]

Rockefeller's Noncandidacy

In mid-March, Rockefeller became convinced that entering the race was not in his best interest. Along with his poor New Hampshire showing, the polls indicated future losses in upcoming primaries, particularly Wisconsin and Oregon. On March 19, only 17 Republican senators showed up for a meeting arranged by Senator Scott, and they were not enthusiastic over a Rockefeller candidacy. Among governors, Rockefeller could count only on Agnew and Shafer. Kennedy's entrance took away potential liberal democratic supporters. But the main consideration, insisted Emmett John Hughes, Rockefeller's top political adviser, was lack of party support: "He couldn't get nominated in any case."[50]

On March 21, at New York's Hilton Hotel, Rockefeller announced to cameramen and reporters that he would not enter the race. In an even, serious voice, the 59-year-old governor read a prepared statement. His first words were blunt: "I have decided today to reiterate unequivocally that I am not a candidate campaigning directly or indirectly for the presidency of the United States." He stated his readiness to answer a draft call, but "would do nothing in the future by word or deed to encourage such a call," and asked his supporters to withdraw his name from the Oregon primary. He listed the reasons for his decision:

> Ideally, the Presidential candidate of each of our two major parties should reflect as broadly as possible the will and the spirit of each party and its leadership across the country.
>
> By this criteria I could not truthfully claim such a Republican following

today. Quite frankly, I find it clear at this time that a considerable majority of the party's leaders wants the candidacy of former Vice President Richard Nixon, and it appears equally clear that they are keenly concerned and anxious to avoid any such divisive challenge within the party as marked the 1964 campaign.[51]

The press agreed that Rockefeller's refusal to run meant Nixon's nomination by "default." "Nixon has the nomination 'all but in the bag,'" editorialized the *Wall Street Journal*.[52] "The professionals have triumphed over the people," said the *New Republic*.[53] "Only an improbable series of Nixon blunders," said newsman Roscoe Drummond, "would keep him from the nomination."[54]

Some observers considered Rockefeller's announcement a tactical move to limit the relevance of the primaries. But according to Hughes, it was not a maneuver, but "a genuine statement of his feelings."[55]

Other politicians responded variously to Rockefeller's announcement. Mayor Lindsay admitted he was "disappointed," and Senator Morton said that Rockefeller had made "a tragic mistake and failed to comprehend the 'depth and breadth' of his party strength." Nixon told reporters that he took "nothing for granted," and Reagan said, "Rockefeller's decision would make subsequent primary victories for Mr. Nixon inconclusive."[56] "It leaves Wisconsin's Liberal Republicans with only one alternative," said McCarthy, "to cross over and vote for him on April 2."[57]

Rockefeller had failed to give Spiro Agnew, head of the national draft Rockefeller headquarters in Annapolis, advance notice. "Rockefeller had a list of people he was to call before making his announcement," recalled Hughes. But Rockefeller's public relations adviser, Ted Braun, insisted that "it would just upset you to have these conversations before you go into your press conference."[58] Agnew had invited the press to his office to watch what he expected to be Rockefeller's announcement of candidacy. After hearing Rockefeller's withdrawal, observers noted, Agnew "just sat there frozen...saw his jaw open slightly for a second," and "a kind of barely perceptible sick grin came over his face for an instant."[60] "It made Agnew look like a total fool," recalled Hughes. "He never forgave 'Rocky' for it."[61] Agnew's move towards Nixon began at that moment.

As the April 2 Wisconsin primary approached, Nixon was running unopposed. Romney had dropped out, and Reagan and Rockefeller said they were not candidates. To many observers, it looked like Nixon would be the nominee. But he still had his loser image to contend with and the convention was only months away.

Chapter III

The Turning Point

Despite McCarthy's large New Hampshire showing, political observers agreed that Johnson was going to seek reelection. The convention date (August 26) was scheduled around his birthday (August 27). So late a time could benefit only an incumbent. The White House had financed and organized the campaign for a pro-Johnson slate in New Hampshire, and cabinet members were campaigning for him in Wisconsin. "I had always expected Johnson to be the candidate," said Lawrence F. O'Brien, "probably of a divided party, but nonetheless, our candidate."[1]

Johnson Ponders Reelection

Since 1964, Johnson had been thinking of not running for reelection. His wife, Lady Bird, urged him not to run again. He had suffered a serious heart attack in 1955, and she was worried about his health.[2] He told Humphrey in 1964 that he would not run again. Humphrey did not believe him and acted on that assumption.[3] "Johnson had often threatened not to run," recalled Edgar Borman, Humphrey's political confident and physician, "but no one ever took these protestations seriously, least of all Humphrey."[4]

In September, 1967, Johnson asked George Christian and Governor John Connally of Texas, to draw up a withdrawal statement. Christian and Connally agreed that withdrawal was in Johnson's best interest. "We talked a long time about it," recalled Christian. "I got a lot of thoughts from the Governor on how Johnson might phrase the statement, then I wrote it."[5] But Johnson decided to wait until some dramatic moment before giving it.

Throughout the fall, Johnson told a few close associates that he might not run again. On October 3 he told his cabinet that he might not enter the race.[6] He told Mary Rather, his secretary, that he was "99 percent certain that he would not run again." He also told Arthur Krim, adviser on party affairs, that "the Democratic committee should make no organizational or fund-raising plans for 1968 on the assumption that I would head the ticket."[7]

On November 20, he met with General William C. Westmoreland, back from Vietnam on a public relations visit. He explained that his health was not good and that his two daughters wanted him to retire. He asked, "Would the troops think their commander-in-chief had let them down if he withdrew from the race?" "If the troops knew why he made such a decision," replied Westmoreland, "they would understand." "Westmoreland was a man I could trust," said Johnson afterwards, "and he never as far as I know, even told his wife."[8]

In mid-January, 1968, Johnson asked Busby to draft a withdrawal statement and give it to Christian to combine with the one written earlier. Johnson said that he would announce his withdrawal at the end of his State of the Union Address, on January 19th. The final draft read: "With the priorities thus divided, and with due concern for the future of my country, I have prayerfully concluded that I will not be a candidate for reelection."[9]

But Johnson failed to read the withdrawal statement on January 19th. "When I went to the Capitol that night," he explained, "I thought I had the statement with me, but when I reached into my pocket at the end of my speech, it wasn't there."[10] "He had resolved beforehand," said Christian later, "that he wasn't ready to give it."[11]

Post-Tet Troop Requests

On February 12, 1968, General Westmoreland asked for an additional 10,000 American troops. He feared another round of attacks. According to General Maxwell Taylor,

> Westy was particularly uneasy about a renewal of the campaign in the northern provinces abutting on the DMZ in the area where the Khe Sanh outpost of the Marines had been under heavy pressure for several months.[12]

"With additional reinforcements," recalled Westmoreland, "I could strengthen the north without risking further weakening of forces in the south, around Saigon."[13] Johnson agreed to send additional troops.

On February 28, Wheeler met with Johnson and his advisers. Wheeler

asked for an immediate reserve force of about two divisions and recommended that the administration seriously consider a three-phase preliminary
proposal worked out by Westmoreland and him. The total came to slightly
more than 205,000 additional troops. "What are the alternatives?" asked
Johnson. "In his [Westmoreland's] judgment," replied

Wheeler, "if we did not send troops in the numbers suggested, we
might have to give up territory, probably the two northernmost provinces
of South Vietnam." "The addition of 205,000 more troops would not make
a major difference," said Secretary of Defense McNamara. The North Vietnamese would only add troops to meet our increase.[14] Walt W. Rostow,
National Security adviser, supported the military's recommendations and
added, "We should not rule out the invasion of Laos, Cambodia, and North
Vietnam."[15] Clifford recommended opening up new peace efforts. Johnson
said that he needed more information and asked Clifford to head a task
force to "consider their demanding problems."[16]

Clifford's Task Force

Shortly after the February 28 meeting, Johnson instructed Rostow to
draft a directive to Clifford's task force to guide its work. "I made sure that
every facet of the troop decision was canvassed," recalled Rostow.[17]
According to Johnson, the directive called for a broad analysis of alternatives.[18] But Clifford, who denied receiving a directive, considered his task,
not to examine other alternatives, but only procedures to fulfill Westmoreland's request. "We were not instructed to assess the need for substantial
increase in men and material," recalled Clifford, "we were to devise the
means by which they could be provided."[19] Johnson later called Clifford's
version "totally inaccurate." He cited his directive as well as Rusk's instruc-
tions to the situation presented to us by General Wheeler and his preliminary proposal."[20] Hoopes, explaining these contractions, said that Johnson never signed the directive, and its contents were unknown to most of
the Task Force members.

Between February 28 and March 4, Clifford's Task Force met daily to
prepare their report for Johnson. The group included Rusk, McNamara,
William Bundy, Generals Wheeler and Taylor, CIA Director Richard
Helms, Deputy Secretary of Defense Paul H. Nitze, Assistant Secretary of
Defense for International Security Affairs Paul C. Warnke, Under Secretary
of State Nicholas Katzenbach, Secretary of the Treasury Henry H. Fowler,
and Assistant Secretary of Defense for Public Affairs Phil G. Goulding.
Clifford broke the group into teams. He assigned papers on short and mid-
term troop deployments, air and naval campaigns against North Vietnam,

need for reserve call-ups, and cost.

The participants expressed "little or no enthusiasm" for sending 205,000 more troops, recalled General Taylor, and "centered on whether we should readjust our strategy and, if so, the new direction to give it."[21]

In the day-long Task Force sessions, Clifford examined every aspect of the Vietnam War. Until then, he had never analyzed the war in detail. The air war, he learned, had not limited the North Vietnamese's ability to supply troops and material to the South. By early 1968, despite the aerial interdiction, North Vietnamese infiltration had risen three to four times above the rate of a year earlier. The Joint Chiefs of Staff explained that the military did not have a plan for victory. The president, they said, had forbidden them to invade North Vietnam, mine Haiphong harbor, or pursue the enemy into Laos and Cambodia. Clifford agreed that the restrictions were wisely designed to prevent the United States from being drawn into a longer war, and he would not recommend their cancellation. But given these circumstances, he asked the military how could the United States win? None had an answer.[22]

The Clifford Task Force report recommended rejection of the military's recommendation for 205,000 additional troops. To fulfill that request, it noted, the administration would have to increase the strength of the armed forces by some 511,000 men by June 30, 1969. This would mean calling up 262,000 reservists, increasing draft calls, and extending terms of service. But the additional troops would not assure a more favorable military position. The enemy would compensate by increasing its troops. Instead, it recommended immediate deployment of 22,000 troops and periodic reviews to determine whether additional troops were necessary.[23]

In early March, Johnson and his advisers met on several occasions to discuss the Clifford report. Johnson was troubled by its "negative approach to any possible negotiations."[24] Rostow favored "a negotiating initiative" in 1968, near the end of the Communist winter-spring offensive "when the Communists had tried their hardest and failed."[25] Rusk argued for an unconditional partial bombing halt, and Johnson said that he would give it careful thought.[26] Rusk said that the very nature of the military was to request more troops. "Give the Generals one-half of the troops they ask for," he said, "then double their mission, and that will be about right."[27]

Whether Johnson was ready to send additional troops remained unclear. "I had almost been ready to call up a large number of reserves," he said later, but "my opinion had changed as a result of what I had heard from my advisers and what I saw happening on the ground in Vietnam."[28] He complained to Christian: "The military talk too big about success, body count, and all that."[29] Wheeler informed Westmoreland that Johnson would not approve 205,000 additional troops "or anything approaching it."[30] However, the question of sending large numbers of additional troops remained open.[31]

Clifford's Reassessment

By mid-March, Clifford had become convinced that a change in policy was necessary to avoid disaster. "After Tet," he said later, "there was no suggestion that we could see any light at the end of the tunnel."[32] He was now persuaded that a substantial troop increase would only "increase the devastation and the Americanization of the war" and that "disengagement was in the United States' best interest."[33]

Clifford's changed views on the war pitted him against Johnson, Rusk, and Rostow. "The president," recalled Clifford, "was deeply concerned and angered."[34] "The impact on the President," explained Westmoreland, was "considerably stronger than if some admitted dove had come up with a similar conclusion."[35] But Clifford lost little of his influence and, according to Christian, "continued to present his views forcefully to the end."[36] The differences with Rusk, Clifford later stressed, were not personal and "neither of us made any effort when apart from the other to undermine the other's position with the President."[37] Clifford appeared "very vague," said Rostow. "He lectured us on the impossibility of military victory, but he did not advocate anything operational."[38] "Rostow's attitude towards me," recalled Clifford, "was that I'd come in rather late in the whole picture," and that "I didn't understand a great many facets of it that he and others understood."[39]

Johnson Searches for a Policy

After the Tet offensive, with the help of Harry McPherson, a trusted assistant, Johnson had begun preparing a speech to explain the military situation and future decisions on Vietnam. But the confusing military situation caused Johnson to postpone it. By mid-March, he had given the speech a lot of thought. He planned to describe the military situation in Vietnam and make a serious peace proposal. "I would announce my decision on politics, but I decided to hold that very close until the last minute."[40]

The bombing halt issue resurfaced at Cabinet meetings on March 20 and 22. Clifford proposed a bombing halt north of the 20th parallel if Hanoi agreed to withdraw its forces from the DMZ, and Rusk repeated his proposal of an unconditional partial bombing halt.[41] It was the clearest recollection of several participants, said Townsend Hoopes, that it was

Clifford, not Rusk, who "argued for a partial bombing halt without condi-tions."[42] Rusk "really didn't have in mind a bombing cutback," insisted Clifford, but "thought we could use the period of bad weather in North Vietnam to make a lot over a bombing pause." It wouldn't cost much, and if the other continued to attack, would justify committing more force.[43] Johnson asked for further study on bombing halt initiatives. "I was weighing one aspect that others around me were not," he recalled. "I was judging the possible impact of a peace move linked with an announcement of my decision to withdraw from politics at the end of my turn."[44]

Discouraged by the results of the March 20 and 22 Cabinet meetings, Clifford suggested that Johnson consider another meeting with the "wise men," a special group of presidential advisers. Clifford knew that their support for Johnson's war policy had eroded since the November 2, 1967, meeting, and Clifford hoped that they would persuade him to change it. "I knew," recalled Clifford, "that Dean Acheson and McGeorge Bundy were in the process of re-evaluation; that Tet had had a substantial impact upon the thinking of both these men."[45] Johnson asked Rostow to set up a meeting.

The "wise men" assembled at the State Department on March 25. They included Bundy, Ball, General Taylor, Arthur Goldberg, Dean Acheson (secretary of state under President Truman), Douglas Dillon (secretary of the treasury under President Kennedy), Cyrus Vance (deputy secretary of defense under McNamara), Arthur Dean (chief Korean War negotiator), John J. McCloy (High Commissioner to West Germany under President Truman), General Omar Bradley (World War II commander), General Matthew Ridgway (Korean War commander), Robert Murphy (a senior career ambassador of the Truman-Eisenhower administrations), Henry Cabot Lodge (former senator and twice ambassador to Saigon), and Abe Fortas (a sitting associate justice of the Supreme Court).

At 7:30 in the evening, the "wise men" assembled in Rusk's office to listen to three government officials describe the Vietnam situation. Deputy Assistant Secretary of State Philip C. Habib reviewed the political situation; Major General William DePuy spoke on the American military position; and CIA analyst George Carver, discussed pacification and the condition of the enemy. To expel the North Vietnamese from the South and pacify the country, they said, would take "at least five to ten more years."[46] "That assessment," recalled Johnson, "did not square with the situation as I understood it."[47] But Maxwell Taylor "found nothing unusual in what they said on this occasion." Though Habib "seemed slightly more pessimistic about the political situation than I had expected."[48]

At lunch in the White House on the following day, March 26, the "wise men" met with Johnson and Generals Wheeler and Creighton W. Abrams. Johnson asked the generals to give a description of the military situation. "We don't want an inspirational talk or a gloom talk," he explained. "Just give them the factual, cold, honest picture as you see it."[49] Abrams, deputy to Westmoreland in Vietnam, said he was training the South Vietnamese army with the object of "Vietnamizing" the war.[50] The South Vietnamese and allied forces, said Wheeler, were on the offensive, and he blamed the press for all "the doom and gloom" in the United States.[51] When asked whether the enemy would carry out another series of attacks like Tet, he flatly replied "No." Once Saigon completed its military build-up, he insisted the South Vietnamese Army would take on a larger share of the fighting. "I would have to quit if I didn't believe that."[52]

After lunch, the "wise men" retired to the Cabinet Room with Johnson. Bundy told him that the group's position had changed since November. The dominant sentiment, said Bundy, was that the burden of proof rested on those urging a troop increase and that extension of the conflict was not in America's national interest. "All of us got the impression," recalled Dean Acheson, "that there was no military conclusion in sight. We felt time was running out."[53]

Johnson had placed great faith in the opinions of this group of men and was now visibly impressed by their arguments. "This dramatic and unexpected reversal of position on the part of so many respected friends," recalled Taylor, "made a deep impression on the President."[54] "There is no doubt," recalled Ball, "that the unexpected negative conclusions of the 'elder statesmen' profoundly shook the President."[55] "The meeting with the Wise Men served the purpose that I hoped it would." Clifford said later, "It really shook the President."[56] "I had always regarded the majority of them as very steady and balanced," recalled Johnson. "If they had been so deeply influenced by the reports of the Tet offensive, what must the average citizen in the country be thinking?"[57]

The Speech

The exact moment when Johnson decided to offer a bombing halt north of the 20th parallel and couple it with his withdrawal from the race remained unclear.

But right up to the day of his speech, Johnson was unsure of his decision. On the morning of his speech, March 31, he showed Humphrey two endings: one with and the other without his withdrawal statement. Humphrey said that Johnson had not yet decided which one to use.[58] The withdrawal decision shifted back and forth throughout the day, recalled Busby. At one point, Johnson said, "I'm not going to know probably until I get in there whether I'm going to use that speech." When Busby asked, "What do you think the chances are that this will happen?" Johnson replied, "Forty to 60 percent against running."[59]

At 9 p.m., on Sunday, March 31, Johnson addressed the nation from the Oval Office. He announced a partial suspension of the bombing of North Vietnam as a new initiative to reduce the level of violence and lead to peace talks.

> Tonight, I renew the offer made last August—to stop the bombardment of North Vietnam. We ask that talks begin promptly, that they be serious talks on the substance of peace. We assume that during those talks Hanoi will not take advantage of our restraint.
>
> We are prepared to move immediately toward peace through negotiations.
>
> So, tonight, in the hope that this action will lead to early talks, I am taking the first step to de-escalate the conflict. We are reducing—substantially reducing—the present level of hostilities.
>
> And we are doing so unilaterally, and at once.
>
> Tonight, I have ordered our aircraft and our naval vessels to make no attacks on North Vietnam, except in the area north of the Demilitarized Zone where the continuing enemy build-up directly threatens allied forward positions and where the movements of their troops and supplies are clearly related to that threat.
>
> The area in which we are stopping our attacks includes almost 90 percent of North Vietnam's population, and most of its territory. Thus, there will be no attacks around the principal populated areas, or in the food-producing areas of North Vietnam.
>
> Even this very limited bombing of the North could come to an early end —if our restraint is matched by restraint in Hanoi. But I cannot in good conscience stop all bombing so long as to do so would immediately and directly endanger the lives of our men and our allies. Whether a complete bombing halt becomes possible in the future will be determined by events....
>
> Now, as in the past, the United States is ready to send its representatives to any forum, at any time, to discuss the means of bringing this ugly war to an end.
>
> I am designating one of our most distinguished Americans, Ambassador Averell Harriman, as my personal representative for such talks. In addition, I have asked Ambassador Llewellyn Thompson, who returned from Moscow for consultation, to be available to join Ambassador Harriman at Geneva, or any other suitable place—just as soon as Hanoi agrees to a conference.
>
> I call upon President Ho Chi Minh to respond positively, and favorably, to this new step toward peace.

Johnson did not place any conditions on the bombing halt nor mention any conditions under which he would resume bombing. He did not indicate what would happen if the negotiations failed and stressed only that the United States would equip the South Vietnamese Army to defend its territory.

After announcing a slight 13,500 increase of men in Vietnam, Johnson ended with his dramatic withdrawal statement:

> With America's sons in the fields far away, with America's future under challenge right here at home, with our hopes and the world's hopes for peace in the balance every day, I do not believe that I should devote an hour or a day of my time to any personal partisan causes or to any duties other than the awesome duties of this office—the Presidency of your country.
>
> Accordingly, I shall not seek, and I will not accept, the nomination of my Party for another term as your President.[60]

Epilogue

At a press conference on the afternoon of April 3, 1968, Johnson reported that the North Vietnamese were ready to meet with American representatives to discuss "unconditional cessation of the United States bombing raids and all other acts of war against the Democratic Republic of Vietnam so that talks may start." He said that we would establish contact with the representatives of North Vietnam and that consultations with the South Vietnamese and our other allies were now taking place.[61]

The following day, April 4, the administration placed a ceiling of 549,000 on United States forces in South Vietnam. This meant that none of the requested 205,000 reinforcements would be sent to Vietnam.

Reaction and Analysis

Johnson's withdrawal took the Democrats by surprise; Eugene McCarthy declared, "We must all pay honor and tribute to a man who has been in politics for his entire lifetime."[62] Robert Kennedy was speechless: "I don't know quite what to say." Vice President Humphrey told reporters, "This is a very sad moment for me."[63] O'Brien said, "I had never imagined that he would withdraw."[64]

Republicans were equally surprised. "This is a year of surprises," said Nixon, "but I must say I didn't expect President Johnson to withdraw from the race."[65] "I almost fell off the couch," recalled Kleindienst.[66] Rockefeller and Reagan were stunned.[67] Sears recalled, "In the years I've spent in politics, I'd have to say this was the single most surprising thing that has ever happened."[68]

Former Governor George Wallace of Alabama, third-party candidate, said Johnson's withdrawal enhanced his candidacy among southerners and conservatives. They would reject the Democratic nominee, said Wallace, because all the candidates, McCarthy, Kennedy, and Humphrey, were too liberal for them. "Despite Wallace's presence on the ballot," said the *New York Times,* "Nixon will do much better in Texas and the rest of the South now that Johnson is out of the race."[69]

The press supported Johnson's withdrawal. "His decision," said newsman William S. White, "may return domestic tranquility and unity to a nation torn by war."[70] "He put himself in position to act on the question of Vietnam," said Wicker, "without incurring the charge that he was merely seeking re-election."[71] "He made a personal sacrifice," editorialized the *Washington Post,* "in the name of national unity that entitles him to a very special place in the annals of American history."[72]

Johnson's challengers were now without a target. "At once," said Newfield, "Kennedy had lost his chief issue."[73] McCarthy was deprived of the "Johnson issue," said the *Nation,* "the issue on which he might have won."[74] "Johnson's decision," said the *Wall Street Journal,* "instantly cooled the controversy."[75]

Although Johnson told reporters that his decision not to seek reelection was "irrevocable," political observers agreed that changed circumstances might compel him to accept a convention draft. "Intuitively," said Senator Frank J. Lausche of Ohio, "I am of the belief that a clamor will arise at the Democratic National Convention for him to change his decision." "If he should succeed in the renewed peace effort announced in his speech last night," editorialized the *New York Times,* "he could yet emerge as the President who brought peace to Vietnam and whose reelection was mandatory to nail down the terms of that peace."[76]

The reasons behind Johnson's decision not to seek reelection remain unclear.

Johnson said that many factors influenced his decision. He feared that he would not survive another four years and that race riots might occur during the fall campaign and hinder a proper response. Also, his influence with Congress had lessened since 1964, and he would not be able to get much more social legislation. He hoped withdrawal from the race would help "heal wounds and restore unity." Above all, he insisted that his withdrawal was "a serious and sincere effort to find a road to peace."[77]

Johnson's closest advisers attributed his withdrawal to the Vietnam War. The country was so deeply divided, recalled Clifford, that Johnson thought "it was in the public interest that he not conduct the race in

1968."[78] Johnson wanted to go down in history as a "peace president," said General Wheeler later.[79] By not running for reelection, explained Jack Valenti, his trusted aide, he could better persuade Hanoi that his plans for peace were "not politically motivated."[80] "Plainly," said the *Nation,* "the President's move was a monumental gamble for nine months' time to redeem his policies in Vietnam."[81]

But Johnson did not have to withdraw from the race as a peace gesture. The presidency gave him the means to greatly influence events and polls. If he desired, he could undercut his opponents with further peace initiatives. He did not have to expand "the extra effort."

To some observers, Johnson's decision was motivated by the New Hampshire primary and the fear of losing Wisconsin and other primaries. "McCarthy's New Hampshire vote did it," argued Goodwin.[82] "The McCarthy problem," said Christian later, "had to be there."[83] "Reports were coming in," observed Theodore White, "that he was going to lose Wisconsin and be repudiated."[84] Rauh was more emphatic: "He was going to get the shit kicked out of him in Wisconsin."[85] "Then he would have been an emperor without clothes," added Gans.[86] Later Johnson told Walter Cronkite, "What did they expect, Walter? That bastard McCarthy came within an inch of kicking me in New Hampshire, and he was about to tear my ass off in Wisconsin. What else could I do?"[87]

There was some question whether Robert Kennedy's entry played a factor. "Johnson was desperately afraid of being defeated by Kennedy," argued Frank F. Mankiewicz, Kennedy's press secretary.[88] "There was not a shadow of a doubt," added Berman, "that Johnson thought Kennedy and McCarthy were the principal cause of his downfall, and he had no notion of having his grand gesture of pulling out accrue to their benefit." But others disagreed. "Kennedy's entry did not have anything to do with Johnson's withdrawal," insisted Rauh.[89] "Kennedy's entry," recalled Christian, "may have entered Johnson's mind but not in his decision."[90] "What scared me when Kennedy got in," recalled Busby, "was that it killed off any chance that Johnson would withdraw because he didn't want to appear like he was running from Kennedy."[91]

Although the reasons behind Johnson's withdrawal remain unclear, it surprised everyone. Most important, by linking it with a bombing cutback and rejection of further massive troop increases, he changed the direction of the war: from military escalation to negotiation. His actions signaled to the North Vietnamese a genuine desire to begin peace negotiations.

Chapter IV

Aftermath of Johnson's Withdrawal

Robert Kennedy Takes the Lead

Johnson's withdrawal made Kennedy the leading Democratic candidate, but Democratic regulars considered him a divisive force. The business community and labor leaders, including AFL-CIO president George Meany, associated him with the commotion frightening the country. He had developed a reputation for "radicalism." The South, reported the *Wall Street Journal,* regarded Kennedy "as only slightly less dangerous than Mao Tse-tung."[1]

Kennedy and his strategists, including Lawrence F. O'Brien who resigned his position as postmaster general, focused their strategy on winning key primaries.

Kennedy could not win enough delegates in the primaries to win the nomination, but by scoring impressive victories, he hoped to boost his poll standings and thus persuade the delegates that he had the best chance to win in November. If Kennedy beat McCarthy in Nebraska (May 14) and Oregon (May 28), Kennedy's strategists agreed that McCarthy might withdraw from the California (June 5), and New York (June 18) primaries. They considered Humphrey to have little popular support in the key primary states. And they hoped to forge a coalition of blacks, blue-collar whites, and college students.

On April 3, 1968, Kennedy and Sorensen met with Johnson in the Cabinet Room with Walt Rostow and Charles Murphy, Johnson's friend and adviser, also present. Kennedy had requested the meeting to discover if Johnson intended to marshal forces against him. Murphy's notes reflected the tenor of the discussion:

> Senator Kennedy: Are you opposed to my effort?...
>
> The President: I'm not that pure, but I am that scared. The situation of the country is critical. I will try to run this office so as to have as much support and as few problems as possible.
>
> I will tell the Vice President about the same things I'm telling you. I don't know whether he will run or not. If he asks my advice, I won't give it.
>
> If I had thought I could get into the campaign and hold the country together, I would have run myself. If I campaign for someone else, it will defeat what I am trying to do.
>
> My objective is to stay out of pre-convention politics. I have no plans to get into it. That might change at any time. I might have to disagree with you tomorrow. I might say who I'm going to vote for, but I do not plan to do so.
>
> I do not want to mislead you or deceive you, and I must preserve my freedom of action, but I want to follow the course stated in my speech (keeping the Presidency out of the campaign) if I can. But I must be free to react to future developments.
>
> I am no king maker and don't want to be. I did not talk to Daley about this in Chicago....
>
> Senator Kennedy: If you decide later on to take a position, can we talk to you prior to that?
>
> The President: Yes, unless I lose my head and pop off. I will try to honor your request.
>
> Senator Kennedy: I wanted to know, because if I should hear reports that you are doing so and so, I wanted to know whether to believe them.
>
> The President: If I move, you'll know.[2]

Hubert H. Humphrey

On April 1, 1968, Humphrey and friends assembled in his Washington apartment. They included staffers William Connell, Bill Walsh, and Norman Sherman and close friends Gus Tyler, Richard Maguire, Max Kampelman and Edgar Berman. Humphrey told them to go slow, "not make it appear that he was dancing on a dead man's coffin," and to say nothing, "not even to speculate on what he would do." He wanted to get a reading from around the country. "I had been through abortive efforts at the nomination before," recalled Humphrey, "and I was simply not about to make the effort again unless the odds were at least a little in my favor."[3]

Humphrey grew up in Doland, South Dakota, where he learned politics from his father, a pharmacist and one of the town's political leaders. The Great Depression forced him to move the family drugstore to Huron, South Dakota. Humphrey was unhappy working in the drugstore and enrolled as a political science major at the University of Minnesota in Minneapolis. He was elected to Phi Beta Kappa and received his B.A. degree magna cum laude in 1939. The following year he received a master's degree from Louisiana State University and went on to teach political science at the University of Minnesota and Macalester College in St. Paul. During the early 1940s, he pulled together a farmer-labor coalition in Minneapolis to win two terms as clean-up mayor of the corruption-ridden city.

In 1948, Humphrey rose to national prominence after he led the fight for a strong civil rights plank at the Democratic National Convention. First elected to the Senate in 1948, he described his early years there as the most miserable period of his life: "I was looked on there as a political accident, a flaming liberal, a very dangerous fellow."[4] In 1960, he lost the crucial West Virginia primary to John Kennedy. But at the 1964 Democratic National Convention, Johnson, a friend since the 1950s, picked Humphrey as his running mate.

Humphrey was a staunch supporter of liberal causes. He played a key role in passage of the Medicare bill, the Peace Corps, the Food-for-Peace Program, the 1963 nuclear test ban treaty, and the 1964 civil rights law. In 1960, Humphrey voted 213 out of 214 times as favored by the AFL-CIO's Committee on Political Education; and while majority whip, between 1961 and 1964, his labor record was also a near-perfect 97 percent.[5] "I was one of the leaders," recalled Humphrey, "who fought the conservative coalition of Republicans and southerners year-in and year-out until they were slowly beaten down."[6]

Although Humphrey had opposed the initial 1965 Vietnam air and troop build-up, by 1966 he had become a staunch supporter of the administration's Vietnam policy. On a fact-finding trip to Vietnam in 1966, he explained, "It was ... the experience of meeting our enlisted men and field officers. Their spirits were high, their dedication impressive, though some were just hours away from jungle missions where they had been wounded, where men alongside had been killed."[7] He admitted to becoming the administration's spokesman for the war. In a "Meet the Press" interview in 1966, he said, "These are great commitments. I think there is a tremendous opening here for realizing the dream of the Great Society in the great area of Asia, not just here at home, and I regret that we have not been able to dramatize it more."[8]

After a second visit to Vietnam in the fall of 1967, Humphrey again began to question Johnson's Vietnam policy. Official reports on the war were inaccurate, American reporters on the war told him. They said that the United States controlled the South Vietnamese economy and American troops did most of the fighting. "I did not want to believe them," recalled Humphrey, "but they were so unemotionally firm in their descriptions, that I began to hear what they were saying." He privately hoped for a negotiated settlement.[9]

On April 3, 1968, shortly after Kennedy's meeting, Humphrey met with Johnson, Rostow, and Charles Murphy. If Humphrey chose to run, Johnson said that he would offer help in ways consistent with his withdrawal statement. According to Murphy's notes:

> Humphrey's problem was money and organization. This the President cannot assure the Vice President because he could not assure it for himself. The President said that he should recall what happened in the West Virginia primary in 1960, because that is the kind of thing he would be up against. He thought the Vice President had always been more charitable about those events than himself. He suggested the Vice President make his decision soon and bear in mind that the heart of the matter lay not with the southerners who, in the end, might support him, but with the following states: New Jersey, Pennsylvania, Illinois, Michigan, Ohio, and Indiana. He did not know where Daley and Hughes [Governor Richard J. Hughes of New Jersey] and the others would come out....
>
> The Vice President stated he had been in preliminary contact with Daley and Hughes and they appear not yet to have made up their minds. He had the impression that they were not willing to be 'blitzed' and had not yet committed themselves....
>
> The President said he thought it possible that, in the end, Daley and Hughes would go with Kennedy.[10]

While Humphrey assumed that Johnson would support him, his friends and associates were not so certain. They wondered if Johnson would withhold support in hopes of a convention draft.[11] Berman said that Johnson could not be sure Humphrey would continue to carry out the administration's Vietnam policies. Humphrey's only real assurance, recalled Berman, was the president's "vindictive hatred of Gene McCarthy and especially Bobby Kennedy."[12] Some of Humphrey's associates preferred that Johnson continue his nonendorsement position. They hoped that Johnson would pursue peace in Vietnam and leave Humphrey free to reestablish himself nationally as a viable candidate.[13]

Humphrey's supporters included party regulars, labor leaders, farm groups, businessmen, and southern Democrats. Party support included most of the National Democratic Committee, about 70 percent of the Democratic county chairmen, and some 20 of the 24 Democratic governors.

Mayors Joseph Barr of Pittsburgh, A. J. Cervantes of St. Louis, and Ivan Allen of Atlanta, former governors Terry Sanford of North Carolina and Grant Sawyer of Nevada, as well as Governors Connally of Texas and Hughes of New Jersey rallied to Humphrey's banner. Meany publically urged Humphrey to run, and private support came from I. W. Abel, president of the United Steelworkers' Union, and Joe Beirne, head of the Communications Workers of America. Support came from such diverse southern figures as Edgar Brown of Barnwell County, South Carolina, one of the region's staunchest conservatives, and Barney Weeks of Birmingham, president of the Alabama Labor Council and a leader in liberal causes.

The National Federation of Grain Cooperatives endorsed Humphrey. At a meeting he was introduced with the prayer "that this man will eventually be chosen President of the United States." He told the farmers, "If nothing ever happens from here on out, I'm satisfied," but smiling, he quickly added, "Of course, if something else does happen that will be all right too."[14]

Shortly after Johnson's withdrawal, Humphrey conferred on separate occasions with Kenneth O'Donnell, representing Kennedy and McCarthy. O'Donnell arranged through Berman to meet Humphrey. O'Donnell said that Kennedy was going to win and that Humphrey could choose any position in the new administration. If Bobby won, replied Humphrey, he'd be with him all the way. In the McCarthy-Humphrey meeting, McCarthy complained about Kennedy's tactics and said that he now understood how Humphrey had felt under the "Kennedy steamroller in West Virginia."[15] The two men agreed to assess their positions after the California primary.

By mid-April, Humphrey had firmly decided to enter the race and began recruiting a campaign staff. Senators Fred Harris of Oklahoma and Walter Mondale of Minnesota became national co-chairmen of United Democrats for Humphrey. Key lieutenants included Secretary of Agriculture Orville Freeman, former United States ambassador to Poland John Gronouski, economist Robert Nathan, and Richard Maguire, veteran of the 1964 presidential campaign. Humphrey's vice presidential staff, Connally, executive assistant John Reilly, foreign affairs adviser and speechwriter John Stewart, and William T. Sherman, press secretary, all became part of the team. Washington lawyers David Ginsburg, James Rowe, and Kampelman, and Minneapolis hotel owner Robert Short led the Citizens for Humphrey.

Advisers included Berman, Secretary of Labor Willard Wirtz, ambassador to the United Nations Ball, former chairman of the Council of Economic Advisers Walter W. Heller, and Professors Zbigniew R. Brzezinski and Marshall D. Shulman of Columbia University, both experts on Soviet policy.

Since the primaries chose only a small number of delegates, Humphrey's strategy focused on winning support in the district caucuses and state conventions where party bosses controlled large delegate blocs. He would work quietly to win their support. "I won't do much between now and August," said Humphrey. "You don't improve your case or argument by overexposure prematurely."[16]

Humphrey's Announcement

On April 27, the 56-year-old Humphrey announced his candidacy to friends and reporters jammed into Washington's Shoreham Hotel. The audience, warmed by a preluncheon reception, was all Humphrey's. It cheered him at the beginning, interrupted his speech two dozen times with applause, and drowned out the band's rendition of "The Minnesota Rouser" with loud clapping and cheering. Blinking back tears, Muriel stood beside her husband to share in the ovations. She described the day as "thrilling and exciting." The guests included George Meany, Clarence Mitchell (Washington representative of the National Association for the Advancement of Colored People), Governor Hulett C. Smith of West Virginia, Senators Carl Hayden of Arizona and Harrison A. Williams of New Jersey, and congressmen James G. O'Hara of Michigan, Fred B. Rooney and William S. Moorhead of Pennsylvania, Al Ullman of Oregon, Spark M. Matsunaga of Hawaii, and W. R. Poage, Richard C. White, James C. Wright, and Abraham Kazen, all of Texas. Skirting the Vietnam issue, Humphrey stated his goals in broad terms:

> I believe this nation can finally break across the threshold of what no previous society has ever dared dream or achieve, the building of a social order of both freedom and compassion, of both enterprise and peace.
>
> I believe we can finally create a nation where human equality and human opportunity not only exist side by side but nourish and reinforce each other....
>
> I believe we can make law and order not only compatible with justice and human progress but their unflinching guardians.
>
> I believe that we can build cities and neighborhoods where all our citizens may walk together in safety and in pride and in the spirit of true community....
>
> For 1968, this year is not the year for frenzied or inflammatory rhetoric nor is it the year for searching out and seeking and finding scapegoats for our problems.

I submit that 1968 is the year for common sense to the American people.[17]

The press split on Humphrey's candidacy. The *St. Louis Post Dispatch* called him "more acceptable to all wings of the Democratic Party," but the *Washington Post* editorialized, "If the vice president wishes to wear the familiar mantle of the Democratic New Deal, he will have to wear the hair shirt that goes with it.[18] The *New York Times* added, "Humphrey will have to establish that his years as a Johnson cheerleader has not stripped him of capacity for critical analysis and independent creativity."[19]

Humphrey's announcement did not surprise the other candidates. Kennedy "warmly welcomed" Humphrey's announcement but criticized his unwillingness to enter the primaries. McCarthy told reporters that Humphrey's entry would not affect his campaign plans "very much" and added there "wasn't much in the way of policy in his speech."[20] On the Republican side, Nixon welcomed Humphrey's entry and emphasized that he was "an eloquent spokesman for the Johnson Administration." Governor Reagan dismissed Humphrey's entry as "inconsequential," and Wallace said that Humphrey's bid was "of little or no importance to his own independent campaign."[21]

George C. Wallace

On April 1, 1968, running on the American Independent Party's third-party ticket, Wallace announced his candidacy. "When both national political parties say we've got to remove the causes of rioting, looting, and burning," declared Wallace, "they're saying that these anarchists have a cause. They've got to stop saying there's a cause for the breaking down of law and order. Poverty is not a cause for anarchy."[22]

A county judge, state legislator, and protégé of Governor Jim Folsom, Wallace was elected governor of Alabama in 1963. At his inauguration, on the steps of the state capital in Montgomery, where Jefferson Davis took the oath of office as president of the Confederacy, Wallace declared "in the name of the greatest people that have ever trod this earth, I draw the line in the dust and toss the gauntlet before the feet of tyranny. And I say segregation now, segregation tomorrow, segregation forever!"[23]

In 1963, he threatened to "stand in the schoolhouse door" and bar the way, rather than follow a federal court order to admit black students to the University of Alabama. Though he backed down at the last minute and followed the court order, the incident made him a national figure. In 1966, he overcame Alabama's rule that a governor could not succeed himself by running his wife, Lurleen. After she won, he became her chief adviser. His 1964 primary showings in Wisconsin (34 percent), Indiana (38 percent), and Maryland (43 percent), persuaded him to try for a presidential bid in 1968.

Apart from his segregationist views, Wallace was more liberal than his national reputation indicated. He advocated extensive health and hospital programs and pushed hard for technical education. He piled up an impressive record in attracting industry to Alabama and built a vast highway system.[24]

Wallace obtained ballot status in all 50 states and had little trouble raising money. It was untrue, he insisted, that he was being financed by mysterious sources. Most of his money, he said, came through the mail from common people in average contributions of $5 to $15. His staff, all Alabamians, set up a "dollar-a-month" plan with the use of a computerized system of numbered pledge cards. Wallace collected $4.7 million in campaign contributions of less than $100 dollars. Wealthy contributors included Colonel Sanders, the Kentucky Fried Chicken King, Edward Ball, a Florida lawyer related to the DuPonts, Paul Pewitt, the potato and oil magnate, H. L. Hunt, a multimillionaire archconservative, and actor John Wayne, who sent three checks for $10,000 each and on the back inscribed "Sock it to 'em, George."[25]

Wallace's goal was to deadlock the election. The constitution stipulated that if no presidential candidate received a majority of the electoral votes, 270, in the Electoral College, the House of Representatives, with each of the states having one vote, would decide the election. But if a deadlock resulted, Wallace had no intention of allowing Congressmen to decide the results. He would offer to trade his electoral votes to the candidate who agreed to implement more of his program. He hoped to carry the 16 southern and border states, plus Delaware, representing a total of 177 electoral votes. If he got 177 electoral votes, there would be no majority either for Nixon or Humphrey and the election would go to the House of Representatives.

Chapter V

The Democratic Primaries

The Wisconsin Primary

In Wisconsin, McCarthy found a large base of liberal support. The liberal University of Wisconsin, located near the state capital in Madison, provided McCarthy with foot soldiers and ready forums. McCarthy's supporters also included numerous businessmen and suburban Republicans who liked his moderate tone. The state's liberal newspapers, including the *Madison Capital Times,* endorsed him. While most of the state's labor unions continued to support Johnson (the United Auto Workers remained neutral), McCarthy won endorsements from the Meat Cutters Union and the Amalgamated Clothing Workers Union in Milwaukee.

The national staff moved state headquarters from Madison to Milwaukee to permit closer coordination of the state-wide campaign. New staffers included Ted Warshafsky and Frank Campenni of the Milwaukee McCarthy committee and some young lawyers and students who had helped in New Hampshire. In tour, they recruited friends and relatives, and Curtis Gans and Sam Brown drew extensively on their National Student Association (NSA) contacts.

McCarthy's staff split on the importance of Wisconsin's black votes. Gans, Richard N. Goodwin, and Warshafsky agreed that a play for the black vote would hurt McCarthy with the blue-collar workers. Gans was more concerned with the immediate problem of Milwaukee than with appealing to Kennedy's black supporters in other primary states, and Stavis agreed that civil rights had been so strongly stressed in New Hampshire that the campaign had defined the issue adequately. Seymour Hersh, McCarthy's press secretary, and his aide Mary Lou Gates resigned in protest, and the newspapers reported it. This angered McCarthy's black supporters, and some liberals threatened to cut off contributions. Goodwin said that the story had been blown out of proportion, and McCarthy added, "I couldn't say anything that would do the damage that the story had done."[1]

The incident compelled McCarthy to increase his efforts to win Wisconsin's black voters. He began talking about "white racism," took a five-mile publicity walk through Milwaukee's black ghetto, and expanded his campaign staff to include a number of black advisers. But he realized that he was unable to compete with Kennedy on the race issue, and he did not campaign heavily in the black ghettos. "He sort of had the feeling," said Brown later, "that he had voted right for many years on the Civil Rights issue and that blacks would understand that."[2]

The controversy had little effect on the April 2 primary. McCarthy won 56.2 percent of the 733,000 votes cast to Johnson's 34.6 percent. On write-ins, Kennedy received 6.4 percent to Humphrey's 0.5. But after Johnson's withdrawal, McCarthy's victory appeared anticlimactic.

Martin Luther King's Assassination

At the beginning of April 1968, Dr. Martin Luther King, Jr., preaching the doctrine of nonviolence, went to Memphis, Tennessee, to lead a march for striking black garbagemen. Black militants and their followers turned the peaceful march into a rock-throwing melee resulting in one dead, many injuries and arrests, and the call-up of the National Guard. Dr. King was disappointed but urged his supporters not to be disheartened. On April 4, he was shot by an assassin while standing on the balcony of the Lorraine Motel.

The nation's blacks responded to King's murder with grief and outrage, and violence and rioting broke out in over 125 cities. The riots began in the South, in Greensboro and Nashville, and spread to the slums of Chicago, Kansas City, Baltimore, Detroit, and Washington. Over 70,000 troops and guardsmen were called out. The riots left 46 persons dead and $50 million in property destroyed. Washington alone, said one observer, "took on the appearance of the besieged capital of a banana republic."[3] The riots, remarked Theodore White, "literally terrified white America."[4]

The Connecticut Primary

Middle-aged liberals headed Connecticut's McCarthy organization. They included Anne Wexler, vice chairman of the Westport Democratic County Committee, the Rev. Joseph Duffy, director of the Center for Urban Studies at Hartford Seminary, and Chester Kerr, director of the Yale University Press. In addition, a list of celebrities, writers William Shirer, William Styron, Barbara Tuchman and Arthur Miller, and actor Paul Newman all volunteered their efforts to the state organization. The Connecticut people printed their own literature and devised their own campaign buttons.

Since 1955, local party committee meetings had chosen the 960 delegates to the Connecticut state convention, and the party chairman selected the entire 44 member state delegation and directed them how to vote at the National Convention. But Geoff Cowan, a Yale Law School student, found a provision in a 1955 election law which allowed for a local party primary if 5 percent of the registered party members signed a petition. McCarthy's supporters obtained the necessary petition signatures, chose a slate of delegates in opposition to the regulars, and gained the right to hold primaries in 30 cities, including the major population centers in Hartford and New Haven. On April 10, McCarthy, the only candidate on the ballot, won 44 percent of the 67,781 votes cast. The remaining 56 percent went to the local slates of the regular party organization: most of which were officially uncommitted. In total, the McCarthy forces won 145 delegates to the June 22 state convention.

The Pennsylvania Primary

In Pennsylvania, the party regulars held the advantage. Before the April 23 primary, they had chosen the delegates-at-large (one-fourth of the delegation). Because the primary was nonbinding, McCarthy could obtain 100 percent of the preferential vote and still not get a single delegate to the convention. In addition, the ballot did not identify the delegate's presidential preference: voters would have to know this beforehand. But he decided to enter after the mid-February straw polls indicated that his support was substantial.

McCarthy's supporters adopted a strategy to fit the circumstances. They decided to run many candidates and depend on percentages. Between 12 and 16 McCarthy delegate candidates filed for the four delegate seats in each district. Because the regulars were better organized in the major cities, the McCarthyites concentrated their efforts in the suburbs and small towns.

They ran slates of delegates directly opposed to the organization slates.

On April 23, McCarthy won a landslide victory. He won 71.6 percent of the vote (428,259 votes) to Johnson, Humphrey, and Kennedy's combined 23.4 percent (137,693 votes) in write-ins. This was the first time in recent Pennsylvania history that voters elected nonorganization delegates; but despite McCarthy's large showing, fewer than 20 percent of the Pennsylvania delegation would support him at the national convention.

The Polls

As the May 7 Indiana primary approached, the public opinion polls were inconclusive. A nationwide Gallup poll reported McCarthy with 33 percent, Kennedy 28, and Humphrey 25. The Harris poll reported Humphrey with 38 percent, Kennedy 27, and McCarthy 25. A California poll found McCarthy running twice as strong among Republicans as Humphrey or Kennedy. But by two to one, a poll taken by the American Society of Newspaper Editors predicted that Humphrey would run against Nixon.[5]

Smear Tactics

Before the Indiana primary, the Citizens for Kennedy, under the chairmanship of Dr. Martin Shepherd, began distributing copies of McCarthy's voting record to universities and local Democratic organizations throughout the country. According to the fact sheet, he had voted against a 1960 minimum wage law, against a cut in the oil depletion allowance, and against repeal of the poll tax in the 1965 Voting Rights Act. In defense, McCarthy said that he had always advocated the expansion of minimum wage coverage and, except for one occasion, supported the oil-depletion allowance. He admitted that he had voted against the Poll-Tax Amendment offered to the 1964 Civil Rights Bill. He did it, he said, to avoid hindering the Justice Department's case before the Supreme Court to outlaw poll taxes under the Constitution.[6]

Kennedy and staff denied responsibility for distributing the fact sheet. They claimed that Dr. Shepherd was acting on his own. "Had it been our attack," insisted Steve Smith, "we would have done a better job."[7] (A Kennedy staffer later said that Salinger was responsible for the fact sheet operation).[8] Despite the denials, the fact sheets would continue to surface throughout the Indiana, Nebraska, Oregon and California primaries.

In response, McCarthy's supporters escalated their attacks on Kennedy. They pointed to his past association with Wisconsin's infamous "Communists-in-the-State-Department" Senator Joseph F. McCarthy and charged Kennedy, as attorney general, with interfering with the civil liberties of labor leader James R. Hoffa, supporting wiretap legislation, and refusing to support southern civil rights' workers. In addition the McCarthy people set up a very efficient intelligence network within the Kennedy circles.[9]

The Indiana Primary

Indiana was a conservative state. With the exception of 1964, its people had voted Republican since 1936. In 1960, Nixon carried the state by over 225,000 votes; and in the 1964 primary, Wallace obtained one-third of the votes against a Johnson stand-in. "Indiana," wrote David Halberstam, "harbored old and powerful prejudices against Catholics." Also, its people were suspicious of outsiders. McCarthy remarked, "It was as though they have to think Indiana for fear that if they do not, it will be absorbed by the outside world."[10]

At first, Kennedy hesitated to enter the contest. His candidacy automatically placed him in Nebraska, Oregon, and South Dakota—states which required that all active candidates appear on the ballot. He added California, New York, and the District of Columbia to his list but left out Indiana. His staff noted that Indiana's Democratic organization, with 50,000 state jobholders and 91 to 92 county chairmen beholden to it, was solidly behind Governor Roger D. Branigin, Humphrey's stand-in. But as the deadline for entry neared, Kennedy decided to enter. Fearful of losing Nebraska, or some later primary, he considered an early win necessary to knock out McCarthy.[11]

Kennedy used his staff and financial resources to the fullest. O'Brien, Goodwin, who defected from McCarthy's campaign, Edward Kennedy, Steve Smith, Joseph Dolan, longtime friend and advance man Jerry Bruno, and former Democratic chairman of Massachusetts, Gerry Doherty, planned and coordinated the effort. They agreed that Kennedy needed time to confer with people, and a train, the tried and true method of the past, was the perfect device.[12] They decided on the route around Indianapolis on the Wabash and picked out about eight or nine cities and towns. Kennedy's staff spent at least $750,000 on radio and television commercials. They bought up so much television and radio time that the other candidates had to rely almost solely on smaller radio stations to carry their ads. They also saturated Indiana's suburbs with billboards, launched a mail campaign to all registered Democratic voters, and arranged with all the state's newspapers to carry advertising inserts in the form of tabloid newspapers (2.5 million copies were printed).

Because Indianians were on edge following the riots after King's assassination, Kennedy stressed his commitment to law and order. He emphasized that violence was unacceptable as an expression of dissent. The *Indianapolis News* reported that his conservative approach indicated that Kennedy "hopes to make a favorable impression on Hoosiers," and the *New York Times* reported that the angry young spokesman for the poor had become the sole defender of law and order."[13] But Indiana's blacks did not desert him. "He had such a grip on them," said newsman Wicker, that "he could afford to openly appeal to unsympathetic whites."[14]

Kennedy's presence provoked scenes of wild and frenzied jubilation. At a Mexican-American high school rally in Hammond, teenagers rushing to the platform overturned the rostrum; and in the small town of Mishawaka, the overenthusiastic crowd hurled him against the side of his car, chipped his left front tooth and split his lip. In Indianapolis's black section kids and adults rushed to him. "The Kennedy mystique," wrote Jules Witcover, "constituted a tremendous pulling force."[15] "The style is neither elegant nor polished," reported Joseph Alsop, "yet what comes through most strong is a sense of deep and true concern."[16]

Others feared and hated Kennedy. Reporters accused him of instances of "blatant demagoguery," and some viewers insisted that his speeches stirred his young followers to frenzy. "It was amazing," recalled Lamer, "how many would tell you they hated him."[17] Kennedy's manner, nervous, hands trembling, betrayed an anticipation of hostility from the crowd. "Frankly," Kennedy told Newfield, "I don't understand it. I see people out there call me names, and say they want to actually hit me, and I just don't know what to say about it."[18]

On March 16, the day Kennedy announced his candidacy, McCarthy entered the Indiana primary. He had originally by-passed Indiana because of its conservative sentiment and well-organized Democratic machine, but Kennedy's entry persuaded him to enter. "He would not," explained Herzog, "give Kennedy any presents."[19]

McCarthy's low-key campaign style appealed to Indiana's white middle-class suburban voters. Canvassers portrayed him as a multi-issue candidate and avoided the Vietnam issue. He focused his efforts in the state's smaller cities, like Kokomo, Wabash, Peru, and Muncie, because he had done so well in such areas in New Hampshire and Wisconsin and because these were the centers of power of Governor Branigin whose votes McCarthy hoped to capture.

Severe internal problems weakened McCarthy's Indiana campaign. Tension developed between his local Indiana organization and his national staff. The Hoosiers filled the top campaign positions with college kids, but the national staff was reluctant to share power with them. Loss of sleep and pressure of work contributed to colds and viruses which knocked out a large portion of the headquarters staff. McCarthy's unwillingness to stick to his schedule contributed to low staff morale and generated concern about his leadership qualities. "To have appointments swept away," recalled Abigail McCarthy, "was damaging to morale and left resentment."[20]

Governor Roger D. Branigin, the third candidate, represented the Democratic machine and was assumed to be Humphrey's stand-in. He called out-of-state campaigners "interlopers" and argued that "it would be advantageous to Indiana not to commit itself to anyone at this stage." The *Indianapolis Star,* the state's most popular paper, supported Branigin, ignored McCarthy, and assailed Kennedy "brutality" in daily cartoon and editorial. After the Humphrey forces hinted that Branigin was being considered for the vice presidential slot, Indiana's newspapers played it up in almost daily headlines.[21]

By May 7, Kennedy had successfully forged a coalition of blacks and lower-income whites to win the Indiana primary. In a record turnout of 764,000 Democrats he obtained 320,485 votes (42 percent) against McCarthy's 209,165 (27 percent), and Branigin's 234,312 (30.7 percent). Kennedy won 10 of the 11 congressional districts and 57 of the state's 92 counties. He polled 86 percent of the black vote, carried white backlash bastions like Hammond, Gary, South Bend, and East Chicago, and found support among blue-collar workers in the cities as well as rural whites. Nonetheless, party regulars were not persuaded to ditch their favorite Humphrey.

Jammed together in the Indianapolis Sheraton-Lincoln Hotel's Cole Porter Room, Kennedy's supporters gave him the hero's treatment. They shouted, "Sock it to 'em Bobby." Kennedy replied, "This was a vote for a change in the United States." Across the street, in the Claypool Hotel, McCarthy's supporters welcomed him "with squeals of delight." "How long can your father go on losing primaries?" a newsman asked Mary McCarthy. "I don't understand the question," she replied. "This is the first primary he has lost out of six. Five out of six is a pretty good record."[22]

The District of Columbia

On March 25, McCarthy withdrew from a previously agreed upon joint effort with the Kennedy forces for the May 7 District of Columbia primary. This surprised McCarthy's supporters. "We had an absolute firm agreement of joint headquarters," recalled Rauh. "I don't know why he withdrew."[23] "The Kennedy campaign," explained McCarthy later, "was using the joint effort to suggest that I had accepted his offer of help in primaries he had not entered," but "there were no indications that the Kennedy supporters were preparing to help me, except as it might serve their own campaign."[24] "His analysis was not unreasonable," recalled Schlesinger. "Each, I would guess, preferred Hubert Humphrey to the other."[25]

After McCarthy withdrew, his followers supported Kennedy's slate, represented by Channing E. Phillips, a black minister. Two-thirds of the District's 810,000 residents were black, and Kennedy's staff successfully geared its efforts to win their support. Consequently, on May 7, his vote was substantial. He obtained 62 percent of the vote to Humphrey's 37. "But here a light turnout and Mr. Humphrey's inaction," reported the *Washington Post,* "makes this only mildly interesting as a test for popularity."[26]

The Nebraska Primary

Kennedy attracted large crowds as he stumped the wheat-filled Nebraska prairies by car and train. Dissatisfaction in this farm state was widespread because grain and livestock prices had not kept up with the rising cost of farming. About 14,000 turned out to hear him at the University of Nebraska Coliseum, the largest crowd in the state's political history; 5,000 came to see him at Hartington, a northeast town of 1,600; and 6,000 turned out at Wayne, a town of 4,200. The NBC Oliver Quaryle pre-election poll showed Kennedy with 47 percent of the vote, McCarthy 22, and Johnson and Humphrey 16 percent together in write-ins.[27]

At one point, O'Brien accidentally encountered Humphrey at an Omaha hotel. "Humphrey," recalled Kampelman, "had an understanding with Kennedy and was convinced he [Kennedy] would withdraw after California and throw his support behind him."[28] "Hubert greeted me warmly," recalled O'Brien:

> I commented on the progress he had been making in terms of delegate support. He agreed that he was doing well but he said he didn't know if it were lasting strength, as he felt much of it was less pro-Humphrey than anti-Kennedy....
>
> I reminded him of his commitment to meet with Bob and me at some mid-point in the campaign, and he said that was still his intention, and that he would await word from me on what I thought was the appropriate time. After an hour's visit, that was how we left it.[29]

McCarthy's Nebraska campaign was almost totally unorganized. A state McCarthy organization did not exist nor did any major state political figure support him. This made fundraising difficult. Moreover, McCarthy spent only four days in the state. "We had to concentrate our money, time, and effort there, giving Nebraska little more than a quick once-over and hoping for the best."[30] According to observers, he appeared "unimpressive," and his rebuttals to the Kennedy camp's continuing distribution of the facts sheets "took on a petulant tone."[31]

On May 14, Kennedy chalked up another win. He polled 32 percent of the vote to McCarthy's 31. Johnson and Humphrey obtained a total of 14 percent in write-ins. Kennedy carried 88 of the state's 93 counties and obtained 85 percent of the black, 60 percent of the ethnic white, and 60 percent of the farm vote. Nebraska, said Kennedy, showed that the Democratic voters wanted "a different course of action than that followed by the Johnson-Humphrey Administration," and he invited McCarthy to join forces with him.[32]

McCarthy appeared undaunted by his defeat. He rejected Kennedy's invitation to join forces and insisted that the loss would not harm his efforts in Oregon and California. "There was weariness," reported newsmen, "but no sign of gloom at the McCarthy headquarters."[33] "In the history of the westward movement," said McCarthy at a post-election rally at Lincoln, "it had been a relatively easy task to get the wagons to the Missouri, but after the crossing of the Missouri the real test took place on the Oregon Trail." And, he declared, "We are going on to Oregon."[34]

The Oregon Primary

In Oregon, Kennedy faced an uphill battle. The state lacked the great social problems found in the urban areas of the Northeast and Midwest. Only 1 percent of the population was black and 10 percent was Catholic, and it had almost no Mexican or East European blue-collar workers. Its makeup was mostly Protestant, suburban, well educated and middle-class. Kennedy's role in the Senate Rackets Committee investigation of Teamster corruption in Portland had turned the influential labor unions against him. Also, Oregon's people were issue-oriented, less dazzled by Kennedy's charisma and glamour, and considered him "too tricky." "It's that pushiness," explained a Portland hotel clerk, "what we call that Eastern edge that Oregonians don't like."[35] Kennedy's impulsive swim in the cold, dangerous Pacific surf reinforced those impressions. "The Oregonians," said Andreas Tueber, a McCarthyite, "reacted to that like, 'That's silly!'"[36]

Kennedy had assigned a low priority and budget to Oregon and lacked a well organized campaign apparatus. A month before the vote, on April 28, his main headquarters in Portland consisted of two desks and three people, and a telephone strike hindered installation of campaign communications equipment. State Congresswoman Edith Green headed the campaign, but her personal organization did not follow her into the Kennedy camp.

Continuing his whistle-stop tours, Kennedy focused his attack on Humphrey. He told crowds at Oregon City, Salem, Albany, and Eugene, "If I do poorly in Oregon, it's the Vice President who will benefit. He's my major opponent at this time." "If I get beaten in a primary," he told reporters, "I'm not a very viable candidate.... I have to win in Oregon."[37]

Kennedy called on McCarthy to join him and present a solid front against Humphrey. "The forces of the status quo," he told McCarthy's supporters, "can win in Chicago relying only on political pressures instead of the popular will if the verdict of the primaries is clouded. That is why I hope all those who seek a new direction for this country will join with me in this effort." "Kennedy's offer," replied McCarthy angrily, "was in bad taste." He intended to "go all the way to Chicago and beyond—and no concessions and no compromises."[38]

On May 24, the Friday before the election, a nationally syndicated column by Drew Pearson and Jack Anderson charged that Kennedy, while attorney general, had ordered a wiretap on Dr. King's phone. The column appeared in four Oregon newspapers. According to the columnists, Kennedy feared that Communists were behind King's movement. In October, 1963, Kennedy ordered the FBI to tap King's phone, and he received regular reports on King's activities—right up until the time of his death."[39]

Kennedy and his staff declined to discuss the matter. Press Secretary Salinger told reporters, "Senator Kennedy has never discussed individual cases and isn't going to now." "It should be pointed out," said one Kennedy staffer, "that there were two other attorney generals and one other president in the time between the alleged tap and the conversations reported by Pearson."[40] But in the wake of King's assassination, the column was damaging.

When McCarthy challenged Kennedy to a television debate, he adopted the frontrunner's standard no-debate position. He said that any major confrontation would jeopardize what looked like a narrow victory. Almost six weeks of nonstop campaigning, insisted Green and Dutton, had left Kennedy groggy with fatigue. He needed, they argued, a chance to refresh himself for the questions, which was impossible in the last frantic days before the election. But Walinsky contended that the failure to debate "fed the idea that McCarthy was intellectually superior and that Bobby was a tough little prosecutor cashing in on the family name and wealth."[41]

Oregon's basically middle-class, relatively well educated people responded favorably to McCarthy. He was a Midwesterner in a state resentful of Easterners and a college professor in a state where education was the major industry. Also, when McCarthy announced his candidacy on the last day of November, liberal Oregonians already were in the vanguard of the dump-Johnson movement. His quiet style, editorialized the *Oregon-Journal,* is a relaxing change from Johnson's "revival-meeting oratory" and Kennedy's "frantic outreach for teen-age adulation."[42]

As was not so in Indiana and Nebraska, McCarthy's campaign organization was in top form. Every cent was poured into Oregon, which had to be won if McCarthy was to stay in serious contention. Staffers mounted an effective radio and newspaper campaign, and advance planning and staff work provided him with excellent crowds. His Oregon organization, McCarthy told reporters, "is far better than in other primary states. So, if I fail, I won't have anyone to blame but myself."[43]

The attacks on McCarthy's voting record, the "smear sheets," as the McCarthyites called them, continued to bob up in Oregon. Despite the denials, McCarthy angrily accused Kennedy's staff of an organized effort to smear and distort his record. Escalating his attacks against Kennedy, McCarthy taunted him for not having entered the New Hampshire primary and for supporting Johnson's war policy for so long. In contrast, Kennedy's criticisms did not take on McCarthy's sharp edge. He was fearful of antagonizing McCarthy's student followers, whose support he later hoped to acquire.[44]

On May 21, at an airborne news conference on a flight from Klamath Falls to Coos Bay, Oregon, McCarthy insinuated that he preferred Humphrey to Kennedy. If McCarthy lost Oregon and California, asked the reporters, "would he support Humphrey or Kennedy?" "I could support Vice President Humphrey if he changed his position on Vietnam," replied McCarthy, "and possibly Senator Kennedy if there were a change in his campaign methods."[45]

After McCarthy's remarks went over the news wire, some of his supporters accused him of "selling out," and a number of staff members threatened to resign. "McCarthy," said Stout later, "seemed to be giving truth to the Kennedy claim he was but a stalking horse for Humphrey."[46] "It was now clear," recalled Larner, "that McCarthy hated Bobby Kennedy, that on a personal level he preferred Humphrey."[47]

At San Francisco's Cow Palace the next evening, May 22, McCarthy tried to reassure his followers by attacking Humphrey and Kennedy equally. McCarthy blamed his two Democratic opponents for the nation's "disastrous adventures" overseas:

> During the early 1960s, Senator Kennedy played a prominent role in formulating policies which resulted in disastrous adventures. These policies grew from a systematic misconception of America and its role in the world.
>
> I am not convinced that Senator Kennedy has entirely renounced that misconception. I have not heard him criticize the military in this nation, or the Department of State, or the CIA.
>
> Kennedy continues to call upon America to assume the moral leadership of the planet—the very presumption that Senator J. William Fulbright called the arrogance of power....
>
> The Vice President is the "new champion" of these policies. Not merely did he defend the war, he defended every assumption which produced the war—America's moral mission in the world, the great threat from China, the theory of monolithic Communist conspiracy and the duty to impose American idealism upon foreign cultures. These myths have the enthusiastic support of the Vice President.[48]

But apparently unwilling to criticize Humphrey with the same fervor as he did Kennedy, McCarthy slurred the remarks on Humphrey in a subdued, rapid tone, "suggesting that he found them distasteful."[49]

On May 25, Kennedy and McCarthy almost collided at the Portland zoo. Learning of Kennedy's schedule, McCarthy's staff purposely sent their candidate to the zoo. They sought a face-to-face encounter to force Kennedy to an exchange of views. Shortly after arriving at the zoo's main entrance, Kennedy learned that McCarthy was campaigning nearby and heading in his direction. He hurriedly left for his car, but three McCarthy students prevented his exit by standing in front of his car with outstretched hands. The television crews showed McCarthy coming and Kennedy leaving. That night, recalled Larner, all Oregon saw McCarthyites shaking hands with Kennedy's abandoned press.[50]

Later that day, McCarthy spoke to over 5,000 persons at Portland's Memorial Coliseum. It was, reported the *New York Times,* "his hardest-hitting exhibition in six months of campaigning."[51] He directed most of his remarks against Kennedy. He and his supporters, said McCarthy, had not "reassessed" their position nor changed their minds, and he feigned surprise that Kennedy found "no difference between his approach and my approach to the politics of 1968."

One difference ... is that I was prepared to run in the New Hampshire primary and I was prepared to challenge the re-nomination of the President and of the Vice President while he was saying that he was for the re-election of both of them.

But now he says there are no differences and suggests we ought to get together with you-know-who surrendering.... We have in mind no such surrender and no such accommodation.... Mr. Kennedy had not brought any new politics to the scene. What Mr. Kennedy had brought ... was an effort to add up a consensus, somehow out of appeals to minorities.

The problem confronting both Mr. Kennedy and Vice President Humphrey ... is that each of them in a particular way has obligations to the past and is under some pressure to defend old mistakes.[52]

The Humphrey camp considered Kennedy their main opponent and agreed that a McCarthy victory would benefit Humphrey. According to Larner, McCarthy "was getting some financial support from friends of Hubert Humphrey."[53] "The more McCarthy cuts down Kennedy," said newsman James Reston, "the more he helps Humphrey."[54]

Fearful of defeat, Kennedy stepped up his campaign efforts. In the last critical week, he averaged 16-hour days, canvassed 50,000 homes, sent out 320,000 letters, and published six regional tabloids. He began his day before 7 a.m., often skipped lunch, and campaigned until 3 a.m. The crowds were small, and he began "to show some panic."[55] He sensed defeat, recalled Newfield. "There was no playback to his emotions."[56] "All that week he had been tired," observed Theodore White. "The deep tan, burned in by weeks of campaigning in the sun, lay over the exhaustion."[57]

Despite Kennedy's last-ditch efforts, he lost Oregon, McCarthy obtained 45 percent, Kennedy 39 percent, Johnson 12 percent, and Humphrey 4 percent in write-ins. This was the first political loss ever suffered by a member of his family in 27 years since John F. Kennedy's first congressional race in 1946. The state "is all one great white middle-class suburb," said a Kennedy staffer, and "we frightened them."[58]

When McCarthy arrived at headquarters, his staff and supporters went wild. They chanted, "Gene in '68, Bobby'll have to wait." "Here we had the right issues and the right candidate," declared McCarthy. "We're on our way solid to Chicago and beyond." Tears welling in their eyes, his supporters sang "The Battle Hymn of the Republic," and "California Here I Come." "In victory or defeat," recalled Stout, "the McCarthy election night celebrations were much the same. But this night in Oregon outdid them all."[59]

Kennedy took his loss stoically. "It would appear," he told reporters, "that McCarthy has won the primary. I congratulate him." When reporters asked him to comment on his previous statement that a defeat in any primary would no longer make him a viable candidate, he replied, with a small laugh, "I've slept on it. I'm just going to try to ask that I be tested before the voters of California." Would he now consider California the ultimate test of his candidacy? "That," he answered, "would come close to describing how I feel."[60] He also agreed to debate McCarthy.

The press agreed that Kennedy's loss seriously hurt his chances for the nomination. Party leaders, wrote columnists Evans and Novak, "expressed a new sense of personal emancipation."[61] With his loss, said the *Omaha World Herald,* "went a good part of his chance for the Democratic nomination."[62] "Senator McCarthy is once again established as a powerful contender," editorialized the *New York Times.* "Nevertheless," said the *Los Angeles Times,* "there remains the important California primary, where the Kennedy image of invincibility might yet be restored by a solid win over McCarthy."[63]

Humphrey's Delegate Lead

While Kennedy and McCarthy were battling in the primaries, Humphrey was winning nonprimary party caucuses and state conventions. In April and May, he won the majority of delegates in Delaware, Alaska, Hawaii, Wyoming, Arizona, Maryland, Nevada, New Jersey, Pennsylvania, Missouri, Maine, and Vermont. Louisiana's 36-vote delegation gave favorite-son status to Governor John McKeithen, a strong Humphrey supporter. "It is rather clear," said Mayor Alioto, "that the non-primary states are moving very heavily in the direction of the Vice President."[64] *Newsweek* delegate survey showed 1, 280 delegates (1, 312 needed to win) solid or leaning to Humphrey, 714 leaning to Kennedy, and 280 favoring McCarthy; and a CBS survey reported Humphrey with 1,483 delegates, enough to win the nomination. Kennedy's staff placed Humphrey's number at 1,000 delegates.

The California Primary

California would send 174 delegates to the August Democratic convention. Over four million of its seven million registered voters were Democrats. According to the state's polls, they favored Kennedy. The Oliver Quayle poll gave him 38 percent to McCarthy's 24 percent, and the Don Muchmore poll predicted that Kennedy would take about 40 percent of the vote, McCarthy 25 percent, and California's Attorney General Thomas Lynch, assumed to be Vice President Humphrey's stand-in, 25 percent.

Kennedy considered a victory in California crucial to staying in the race.

His Oregon defeat spoiled his chance to confront party leaders with a clear mandate from grass-roots Democrats. He needed a big victory to offset the Oregon loss and provide a springboard toward the New York primary and the convention.

Kennedy's California organization was in top form. It included 100 headquarters scattered throughout the state, thousands of volunteer workers, an extensive canvassing and polling operation, a fund-raising unit, and a media blitz. Because of California's size, he could not blanket the state in a short time. To a large extent, he had to rely on radio, newspaper, and television advertising. At an immense cost he had pre-empted much of the available time on both television and radio. "We're not playing pushball anymore," declared a Kennedy staffer. "We're going out and run a real Kennedy campaign."[65]

Kennedy's staunchest California backers were the minorities and the poor. His close friendship with migrant workers organizer Cesar Chavez gave him a powerful in with California's Mexican-Americans and black voters. In a motorcade through the Mexican-American suburbs south of Los Angeles and in the black area of Oakland, he experienced the wildest crowds: "Children leap and shriek and grown men risk the wheels of Kennedy's car just to pound his arm or grasp his hand."[66]

McCarthy's California organization also was in top form. His staff had divided the state in half. Gerald Hill headed the northern part and Gans the southern half. Over 200 McCarthy headquarters and neighborhood centers were scattered throughout the state. Because McCarthy's Oregon victory had generated new contributions, huge sums of money were available to purchase television and radio time. Hoping for another Kennedy loss, Humphrey's contributors, with his staff's permission, donated $50,000.[67]

But McCarthy could still not compete with Kennedy in money, staff, personnel or campaign expertise.

McCarthy focused his efforts on California's students, suburban liberals, and Jews. Appearing on college campuses, he directed his remarks to issues that interested Californians: population growth, education needs, race, urbanization, conservation, water, air pollution, and agriculture. He got some support in black and Mexican-American areas. He worked the black areas of Watts, Compton, West Oakland, and the Fillmore District of San Francisco and spoke at Mexican rallies in both Los Angeles and San Francisco.

In California, Kennedy's staff accused McCarthy of distorting Kennedy's record. They pointed to full page ads placed in the *San Francisco Chronicle* and the *Los Angeles Times* in late May charging Kennedy with responsibility for the decision that led the United States to land marines in the Dominican Republic in 1965, and claiming that McCarthy was the first man to say "Let the killing stop" in Vietnam and the first with the guts to add "Why are we there?"[68] Actually, Kennedy was not in the Johnson administration during the 1965 Dominican Republic crisis nor was McCarthy the first senator to speak out against the war. Later, Larner insisted that Thomas Finney approved the ad, but Stout claimed that it inadvertently slipped by Finney's scrutiny.[69]

After the Oregon loss, Kennedy could no longer refuse McCarthy's challenge to debate, and arrangements were made for the candidates to appear on a special program of ABC's "Issues and Answers" set for Saturday, June 1, in San Francisco.

Kennedy and his advisers spent Saturday on the top floor of the Fairmont Hotel on Nob Hill preparing for the debate. He hoped to accomplish three things: establish his experience against McCarthy's ten-year age advantage, demonstrate his grasp of the issues, and dispel his ruthless image. Advisers urged Kennedy to remind the audience of his past experience in government. But Kennedy seemed distracted by the beautiful day and would often stare out the window. Around noon he went off to Fisherman's Wharf to campaign a little but was back for another session and a nap before the debate.

On Saturday, Finney flew to San Francisco to meet with McCarthy. Finney persuaded him to secretly check out of the Fairmont Hotel, where Kennedy was staying, and get a room in the Hilton Hotel. Finney sought to keep McCarthy away from close friends, particularly poet Robert Lowell, and prepare for the debate. But Lowell, along with Shana Alexander, Mary McGrory, and Blair Clark, discovered the ruse and by late afternoon had found McCarthy. Consequently, instead of preparing for the debate, McCarthy spent the afternoon singing Irish songs, reading poetry, and listening to Lowell who "scoffed at the elaborate preparations and belittled the idea McCarthy had to match Kennedy little fact for little fact, for McCarthy was above such things."[70]

At 6:30 in the evening, McCarthy and Kennedy met at Station KGO-TV, an ABC affiliate. The format was more like a joint press conference than a formal debate. Three cameras focused on five seats around a small table. Three ABC reporters, Robert Clark, William H. Lawrence, and Frank Reynolds, the moderator, would take turns asking questions, and each candidate had the right to reply to the other's first answer. Only a small group of reporters were admitted into the studio, but a larger number watched on monitors.

The first question concerned Vietnam. "If in fact you were President, what would you do at this time that President Johnson is not doing in order to bring peace in Vietnam?" McCarthy answered first:

> I think these are the important positions that have to be taken: one, de-escalation of the war, and secondly, recognition that we have to have a new government in South Vietnam. I'm not particularly concerned whether it is called a coalition or a fusion or a new government of some kind.
>
> And we have to recognize that the government would include the National Liberation Front. I think this is prerequisite to any kind of negotiations that may move on to talk about what the nature of that new government might be.

Immediately taking the offensive Kennedy suggested that McCarthy was willing to hand South Vietnam over to the Communists:

> I would be opposed to what I understand Senator McCarthy's position is, of forcing a coalition on the government of Saigon, a coalition with the Communists, even before we begin the negotiations.
>
> I would make it quite clear that we are going to the negotiation table, not with the idea that we want them to unconditionally surrender, and that we expect that the National Liberation Front and the Vietcong will play some role in the future political progress of South Vietnam, but that should be determined by the negotiators, and particularly by these people of South Vietnam.

McCarthy quickly replied:

> I didn't say I was going to force a coalition government on South Vietnam. I said we should make it clear we're willing to accept that. Now, if the South Vietnamese want to continue the fight, work out their own negotiation, that is well and good. But I don't think there's much point in talking about reform in Saigon or land reform because we've been asking for that for at least five years and it hasn't happened.

On some points the candidates agreed. They considered the administration's bombing policy in North Vietnam unsuccessful. Kennedy made a distinction between response to external aggression and to internal struggles and cautioned against intervention in places where foreign governments lacked popular support. The United States' commitment in Southeast Asia, said McCarthy, was "very limited" and must be balanced against the good "we might do there" and "our responsibilities in other parts of the world."

When Robert Clark raised the question of McCarthy's newspaper advertisements concerning Kennedy's role in his brother's decision to escalate American involvement in Vietnam, a spirited exchange took place:

> McCarthy: And I like to say the ad ran only one day, and that I had not seen it.

Kennedy: That I intervened in the Dominican Republic....

McCarthy: Well, I think what they did—

Kennedy: I hadn't even been in government at the time....

McCarthy: Well, you weren't out long.

Kennedy: But, it ran again today.

McCarthy: We stopped it. It did run in two pages, but I don't think it ran twice.[71]

McCarthy brought up the Kennedy literature attacking his voting record. Kennedy said, "I don't know what he is referring to." McCarthy replied, "I have it in my pocket," but the reporters persuaded him not to produce the evidence.[72]

While the two candidates agreed on the need to provide jobs to curtail violence and riot, they disagreed on how to solve the urban ghetto problem. Kennedy argued for rebuilding the ghettos and improving conditions for black persons in rural areas. McCarthy advocated breaking up the ghettos, rather than building low cost housing there. Kennedy said that McCarthy's proposal was not practical and would threaten the sanctuary of the white suburbs, and accused him of advocating the placement of 10,000 blacks into Orange County (a wealthy conservative county). McCarthy had never advocated moving 10,000 blacks into Orange County, but he let the remark pass.

William Lawrence asked Kennedy to comment on Drew Pearson's allegation that he had authorized a wiretap on Dr. Martin Luther King's phone. Kennedy said that discussing individual cases would violate the law. McCarthy did not challenge his answer. At this point, Frank Reynolds said that the debate appeared rather tame. He asked the candidates what they disagreed on? McCarthy said they disagreed over Dean Rusk and Robert McNamara. Kennedy said that he would not discuss cabinet appointments.

Lawrence pressed him: "Did Kennedy think Rusk had been secretary of state too long?" Kennedy answered, "I have made it quite clear that I think I disagree with him," and "I doubt very much that he would want to remain under those circumstances." McCarthy argued that cabinet members were given too much protection and ought to be held responsible for policy mistakes. "I think your brother was too kind to a number of people after the Bay of Pigs, myself." Kennedy ignored the remark, and the encounter ended.

Polls gave the debate to Kennedy, but newspaper sentiment was mixed. By two-and-a-half to one, a Los Angeles telephone poll gave Kennedy the debate, and an NBC Oliver Quayle poll reported that 45 percent of California's voters said that Kennedy won.[73] Studio newsmen gave Kennedy the edge. "It was like ball control in football," said one studio newsman. "Bobby got off more plays." "Of the two senators," reported the *Washington Post,* "McCarthy seemed to have the strongest views and gave the most direct answers."[74] "Neither candidate," observed the *San Francisco Chronicle,* "won a clean-cut decision."[75] "It was a conversation rather than a debate," said the *New York Times,* "and it demonstrated that the two rivals are in substantial agreement on every major issue."[76]

Kennedy and McCarthy agreed it was a draw. Kennedy's immediate reaction was that McCarthy "hadn't prepared himself adequately," and merely by holding his own, he had won.[77] "A stand-off," explained Schlesinger, "in the context of expectations was a Kennedy victory."[78] McCarthy staffer Sam Brown added, "There was a sense of egoism in the McCarthy camp: that McCarthy was a lot smarter than Kennedy and therefore pulling even was a loss."[79]

After the debate, McCarthy rejected Kennedy's offer to join with him in a post-California stop-Humphrey alliance. McCarthy said that he would make his own race and "see what happens." His staffers agreed that a post-California alliance was not in his best interest. If Kennedy could go into the national convention with 600 to 800 delegates and McCarthy with 500 to 600, they might deny Humphrey a first ballot victory, after which a move toward McCarthy might begin. In the event of a deadlock, they hoped that Johnson would use his influence to deny the nomination to Kennedy.[80]

The California Returns

Kennedy won a close race on June 4. He received 46.4 percent (1,472,166) of the vote, McCarthy 41.8 percent (1,322,608), and Lynch 11.9 percent (380,286). Blacks and Mexican-Americans contributed to Kennedy's margin. McCarthy cut into the independent and Republican vote while Kennedy did best among low-income voters. In the Central Valley, the Mexican-Americans helped Kennedy obtain a majority of the vote, but he did poorly in the ranching, agricultural and sparsely populated areas of the state. The state's Jewish voters divided about evenly between McCarthy and Kennedy.

On the same day, June 4, Kennedy won a resounding victory in the South Dakota primary. He won 59 percent of the vote to McCarthy's 20 percent, and Johnson-Humphrey's 30 percent. In addition, Kennedy ran strong with almost every segment of South Dakota's Democratic voters. He was pleased to learn that the state's Indians had supported him too. Beaming puckishly, he asked Newfield, "Do you want to hear about the Indians?"[81]

On the night of the returns, Kennedy motioned Goodwin and Soren-sen into the bathroom of his crowded Ambassador Hotel suite. He told them: "Even if McCarthy won't get out, his people must know after tonight that I'm the only candidate against the war that can beat Humphrey."[82] Shortly afterwards, Goodwin phoned John Galbraith and Allard K. Lowen-stein, the pro-Kennedy wing of the McCarthy movement. When Goodwin asked if they would now support Kennedy, they replied that they would first have to discuss it with McCarthy.[83]

Robert Kennedy's Assassination

Shortly after midnight, in the Ambassador's Embassy Ballroom, Kennedy gave a short victory statement to press and supporters. The crowd cheered, and many held up two fingers, signaling V for Victory. Kennedy then worked his way off the podium, through the crowd, and into the hotel's kitchen. According to eyewitness accounts, there was a single shot, a pause, and then a rapid volley: pop-pop-pop-pop-pop-pop-pop. "When I saw him lying on the floor," recalled Kennedy staffer Earl Graves," I thought he would shake it off."[84] But Kennedy was gravely wounded. His bodyguards Roosevelt Grier and Rafer Johnson and campaign aides Jack Gallivan and Bill Barry disarmed the gunman (identified as Sirhan Sirhan, an Arab nationalist who disliked Kennedy's pro-Israeli policies).

In the Embassy Ballroom, pandemonium broke out among Kennedy's supporters, and upstairs, in the Royal Suite on the fifth floor, the victory party turned into a vigil. "There was something close to acceptance in many of the dazed faces," recalled Newfield, "as if they all had a fatalistic pre-monition that he would end this way."[85]

At San Francisco's Fairmount Hotel, Edward Kennedy, just returned from a victory rally, was watching television in his room. He saw the commotion and turned to Senate aide Dave Burke: "We better get down there."[86] At the Ambassador, Goodwin was on the phone in Dutton's room when he heard Steve Smith's voice on television saying that help was needed. "I rushed into the bedroom and sat beside Ted Sorensen paralyzed watching the dread inevitability unfold on the television screen."[87] "A big commotion could be seen on the television screen," recalled O'Brien. "I slumped in my chair.... 'That's it,' and the television quickly confirmed our fears."[88]

In his seventh-floor suite at the Beverly Hilton Hotel, McCarthy was drafting a congratulatory telegram to Kennedy. Abigail, Clark, and Finney were present. David Schoumacher, a reporter, came into the room. "Sena-tor Kennedy has been shot," he said. McCarthy and the others looked at him in total disbelief, and McCarthy's face grew ashen. Abigail cried, and Clark and Finney stood staring at the television. McCarthy began to pace up and down his suite. When he learned that a bullet had lodged in Kennedy's brain, he wept.[89]

The scene at McCarthy's Los Angeles headquarters, the Westwood, an old Sears Roebuck building with three huge floors, was grim and tense. Because the first reports did not indicate the severity of the wounds, the staffs immediate reaction was that Kennedy would be a stronger candidate, but as the night wore on, anxiety and concern for Kennedy's life increased. Stavis was worried that the shooting might include a plot against McCarthy and his campaign. He asked the staff to vacate the headquarters and watch television in their motel rooms. "Many agreed with me and went home," he recalled. "Others stayed all night at the television set, which we moved away from all windows as a compromise for safety."[90]

Humphrey learned of the shooting while at the Air Force Academy in Colorado Springs, to give the commencement address. Badly shaken, he told the Academy's officials that he would not be able to speak. The next morning several generals, including Secretary of the Air Force Harold Brown and General John McConnell, urged him to reconsider. They emphasized its importance to the Academy and the morale of the air force. They were persistent, "almost threatening." Sleepless, depressed, overwhelmed by the tragedy, Humphrey recalled, "I barely remained civil as I repeated that I would not speak. I urged them to leave me as quickly as possible."[91]

In the shock following Kennedy's death, shops and offices throughout the country closed, and the presidential candidates from both parties cancelled their campaign activities. Calling Kennedy's death a tragedy, President Johnson asked that "divisiveness and violence be driven from the hearts of men everywhere." Humphrey went into retreat for almost two weeks. Rockefeller said that he was "stunned and appalled" and Nixon said, "My deepest sympathies go to the Senator's family, which already has known more than its share of tragedy."[92] "Our grief," editorialized the *San Francisco Chronicle,* "must concern itself with the apparent trend in this country toward politics of the trigger."[93] "For whatever reasons," said the *London Times,* "violence is a growing power in the United States, and in Paris" *Le Monde* remarked, "How many men are still to fail before the long and exacting efforts to furnish a sick and extremely tense society with new reasons for a soothing balance are successful?"[94]

Chapter VI

The Republicans Before Their Convention

O n April 2, Nixon won the Wisconsin primary by 79.4 percent to
Reagan's 11 percent. Although Reagan's name was on the ballot, he
did not campaign in the state nor did his supporters mount a significant
effort on his behalf. Consequently, Nixon's victory lacked the necessary
competition to erode his loser image.

Nelson Rockefeller Enters the Race

By late March, 1968, Rockefeller was reconsidering his decision to stay
out of the race. While observers pointed to Johnson's withdrawal and
King's assassination and the subsequent riots as the reasons for Rockefeller's reassessment, Emmett Hughes has discounted them. He pointed out
that a number of business leaders who were previously hostile to Rockefeller were courting him by March. They included John Hay Whitney, head
of Whitney Communications Corporation; Gardner Cowles, whose family
owned *Look* and newspapers in Minneapolis and Des Moines; Ralph
Lazarus, owner of department stores; H. J. Heinz II; Henry Ford II; and J.
Irwin Miller, owner of Cummings Engine Company firm in Indiana. They
were convinced Nixon would lose. Hughes recalled: "It was the first time in
Rockefeller's life that these big businessmen were asking him to run rather
than not run."[1]

On April 30, in Albany, New York, the 59-year-old Rockefeller announced his candidacy to reporters and well-wishers jammed into the Capital's Red Room. In the audience were the former chairman of the Republican National Committee Leonard W. Hall, and Meade Alcorn, William E. Miller, Senators Thruston Morton of Kentucky and Hugh Scott of Pennsylvania, and a few of Rockefeller's recent converts within the business community: Whitney, Cowles, Heinz, and Miller. Outside hundreds of state workers crowded the Capital's corridors to hear Rockefeller's announcement. He listed four reasons for entering:

> First, the dramatic and unprecedented events of the past week have revealed in most serious terms the gravity of the crisis that we face as a people.
>
> Second, in the new circumstances that confront the nation I frankly find that to comment from the sidelines is not an effective way to present the alternatives....
>
> Third, men and women in all walks of life within the Republican Party and outside it have urged me to take this step....
>
> Fourth, personally, I am deeply disturbed by the course of events the growing unrest and anxiety at home and the signs of disintegration abroad.[2]

The press favored Rockefeller's entry. "His party and our system will be the better for his offer of a wider choice," said the *Washington Post*.[3] According to the *Wall Street Journal*, his candidacy will be good "both for his party and for the political debate within and between the parties."[4] With Rockefeller in the race, editorialized the *Observer*, "there has begun to emerge the glimmering possibility of an American de Gaulle."[5]

But many commented that Rockefeller's prospects were not bright. "It seems doubtful," reported the *Indianapolis News*, "that Rockefeller's candidacy will make a great deal of headway."[6] "Realists in the Rockefeller camp," observed columnists Evans and Novak, "realize the deterioration of the past six weeks and that Nixon's lead is long."[7] "The only asset Mr. Rockefeller has," remarked columnist Tom Wicker, "is the widespread belief that he would make a stronger race against the Democratic nominee than would Mr. Nixon, the 'two-time loser.'"[8]

Republican reaction was mixed. According to Nixon, "It would have been more meaningful if he had entered earlier and entered the primaries."[9] Rockefeller's entry, said the Reagan camp, would not affect his own non-candidate position, nor "alter his determination to exclude entirely a vice presidential nomination from his considerations."[10] "It doesn't alter the picture," said Senator Karl E. Mundt of South Dakota.[11] "It is quite important," said Barry Goldwater, "that his philosophies be made clear."[12] It was said of Maryland governor Spiro Agnew that "He didn't know whether he would support Rockefeller."[13] "Rockefeller has an uphill struggle ahead of him," said Mayor Lindsay, "but there is a real chance he might make it."[14] "This is one case where an additional cook will improve the broth," said Maryland congressman Charles Mathias.[15]

On the day of his announcement, Rockefeller won the Massachusetts primary. In a write-in vote, Rockefeller received 30 percent, while Governor John A. Volpe as favorite son got 29.5 percent, and Nixon netted 25.8 percent also in write-ins. "The victory," said Nixon, "was embarrassing to Volpe, irritating to me, and a great boost to Rockefeller."[16]

The next day, at a luncheon of the World Affairs Council in Philadelphia, Rockefeller broke his long silence on the Vietnam War. He advocated reversing the "Americanization" of the war and turning more responsibility over to the South Vietnamese. But he cautioned against permitting opposition to the war to result in a new wave of "American isolationism." Peace negotiations, he said, should include nonacceptance of any solution dictated by force, and acceptance in South Vietnam's political life of any group that sought its objectives through the political process. "The speech," reported the *Oregon Journal,* "broke a lengthy and conspicuous silence by Rockefeller on U.S. policy in Southeast Asia."[17] "But," editorialized the *New York Times,* "the Johnson Administration should not find much to differ with in this analysis."[18]

Rockefeller's goal was to obtain high poll ratings and win over uncommitted delegates and favorite-son states. He planned to spend a large amount of money in key cities and states and then poll them to show that he was the people's choice. The plan, drawn up by the Jack Tinker and Partners Advertising Agency in New York, focused on 13 "Northern Tier" states plus Texas, which together contained 60 percent of the nation's population. Rockefeller also hoped to carry the favorite-son states of Ohio, Michigan, Pennsylvania, and Massachusetts. "The truth of the matter," said Joseph Alsop, "is that the New York Governor's embryo candidacy is more keyed to the public opinion polls and will be more affected by the pollsters' fugitive findings than any other candidacy in our recent political history."[19]

The Indiana and Nebraska Primaries

Since the May 7 Indiana primary did not permit write-ins, Nixon was the only Republican on the ballot. His large vote, 508,000 gave him a significant victory, but the May polls were inconclusive. Released on May 12, the Gallup poll gave Rockefeller a slight edge over Nixon in beating the three Democratic contenders, but a United Press International survey indicated that rank-and-file Republicans in 31 states preferred Nixon over Rocke-feller. The polls showed that Humphrey would be the strongest of the possible Democratic nominees and that Rockefeller would have a better chance of being elected than Nixon. But that was not good enough. Unless Nixon was a sure loser, the party was inclined to go with him. "What Rockefeller needs," remarked Wicker, "is a couple of good polls just before the Republican convention demonstrating that only he can beat the Demo-crats in November."[20]

Although he was the only candidate to campaign in the state, Nixon faced his first real test in Nebraska. Rockefeller's people bought 247 tele-vision spots and 564 newspaper ads, and Reagan's backers mounted a sub-stantial effort including several statewide prime-time showings of a half-hour television documentary. At the last minute, Nixon's staff countered with a Nixon write-in campaign on the Democratic side (mailing 220,000 letters to Democrats).[21]

Despite the opposition's efforts, Nixon won a resounding victory. On May 14, he polled 73 percent of the vote, with Reagan at 23 percent, and Rockefeller at 4. "This was the most competitive Republican primary so far," said Nixon, "and I was gratified by the results."[22] Reagan was pleased. He told reporters that he had expected "10 percent of the vote at most."[23] Rockefeller made light of his small showing. "When I'm not on the ballot, I don't expect to make a good showing." According to newsman Ward Just, "Nixon must be America's only major political figure who can win 70 per-cent of a state's vote and still have the analysts talking about his opponent's 23 percent."[24]

The Southern State Chairmen

As the candidates battled for position, the southern state chairmen were developing their own strategy. State chairmen Harry S. Dent of South Carolina, William Murfin of Florida, and Clarke Reed of Mississippi, were its main architects. "The original idea," recalled Murfin, "was to hang loose, but hang together so we could get something for the South."[25] "We southerners," recalled Reed, "wanted to build the GOP in the South, and the idea was to go with the nomination."[26] "The first step," said Dent later, "was to bargain with the candidates, make them come to me, and we would extract from them whatever we wanted."[27]

Although the southern chairmen leaned towards Reagan, his infrequent visits to the South lessened his appeal. In 1966, Reagan had declined Reed's invitation to speak on behalf of gubernatorial candidate Rubel Phillips.

"Reagan didn't come," said Reed later, "because he knew we were going to lose, and he didn't want to take on a loser."[28] In September, 1967, Dent had persuaded Reagan to speak at a statewide rally in Columbia to help clear up a $40,000 debt. "Reagan was magnificent," recalled Dent, "setting Republican hearts afire clearing up our debt."[29] But when Alfred Goldthwaite asked Reagan aides Tom Reed and Lyn Nofziger to persuade Reagan to visit Alabama to help clear up a debt, they told him that Reagan would remain in California for an indefinite period. "I don't know who sold him on that," said Goldthwaite, "but at that point is when he lost the nomination."[30]

By late May, Nixon had won over Goldwater and received private support from Senator John Tower of Texas, but Senator Strom Thurmond of South Carolina, a leading southerner who ran as a segregationist on the Dixiecrat's third-party presidential ticket in 1948), and the southern state chairmen were officially uncommitted. They leaned towards Reagan but feared he could neither unite the party nor win a national election. "If the Goldwater defeat had not occurred four years earlier," recalled Dent, "It might not have been possible to adopt the hang loose, but hang together strategy."[31] "There was a lot of people in the South," recalled Sears, "who as a matter of heart would have rather had Reagan but as a matter of mind would be with us."[32]

The New Orleans Meeting

Early in 1968, the 12-member Southern Republican Chairmen's Association invited Nixon, Rockefeller, and Reagan to meet with them in New Orleans on May 19 and 20. Reagan and Rockefeller agreed, but Nixon said that he would not be available to the chairmen until May 31, in Atlanta.

On the evening of May 19, Reagan and the southern chairmen assembled in the Rendezvous Room of New Orleans' Roosevelt Hotel. "I told Reagan to look out," recalled Goldthwaite; "that he could not trust a lot of these people and that he was playing into their hands by saying 'You shouldn't seek the presidency, the job seeks the man, not the man seeks the job.'"[33] But throughout dinner, Reagan kept emphasizing his noncandidacy position. Those present, repeated Evans and Novak, came out of that meeting convinced that Reagan was not a candidate. "Reagan, one chairman told us, 'killed the idea dead.'"[34]

At 7:30 a.m., Rockefeller paid an unexpected 37-minute call at Reagan's suite. Reagan told reporters, "Rockefeller dropped by for a cup of coffee," and Clifton White added, "It was just a friendly discussion."[35] According to Rockefeller, it was "an analytical discussion" and not centered on a Rockefeller-Reagan ticket.[36] But actually arranging such a ticket seems to have been the purpose of the Rockefeller visit. The meeting, wrote Richard Dougherty in the *Los Angeles Times,* was to minimize opposition if the convention should go beyond a first ballot and "the idea of a Rockefeller-Reagan ticket catches fire."[37]

The Oregon Primary

In the May 28 Oregon primary, where he faced far more opposition than he had in the Nebraska battle, Nixon considered a victory crucial to the nomination. Although Reagan and Rockefeller did not appear in the state, their political supporters mounted substantial efforts. The press and others had built up Oregon as a measure of whether Nixon could finally get rid of his "loser image." According to Sears, "To take a loss under those circumstances would have damaged us badly."[38]

Nixon made a nine-day whirlwind tour of Oregon. He attacked the "absentee" candidates, refused to spell out his Vietnam views, and emphasized his law-and-order and antiwelfare themes. As part of his strategy, he regularly underestimated the number of votes he expected to receive. Staffer Robert Ellsworth predicted that Nixon would obtain only 33 percent and claimed that receiving over 40 percent would "stop the 'Stop Nixon' drive in its tracks."[39] "To hear them tell it," wrote satirist Art Buchwald, "they're lucky to be in the race at all."[40]

On May 27, Nixon ended his campaign with an hour-and-a-half telethon from the television studios of KGW, Portland's NBC outlet. With Julie and Tricia Nixon among a score of young women answering telephones, former University of Oklahoma football coach Bud Wilkinson screened the questions. Nixon said that he would keep J. Edgar Hoover as head of the FBI, and that he did not want the nomination if he could not demonstrate in the Oregon campaign that he was the best qualified to head the nation."[41]

On May 28, Nixon won a decisive victory. He received 73 percent of the Republican primary vote to Reagan's 22 and Rockefeller's 5 percent. Rockefeller discounted the results and Reagan said that he was "pleased and gratified" by his 22 percent. Asked if Nixon's win locked up the nomination, Reagan responded, "Only time will tell."[42] Staffer Richard Kleindienst was more emphatic: "Oregon locked-up his nomination." But Nixon considered the national polls more decisive than Oregon. "If I run ahead of the Democratic candidates in the polls," he said, "even a Rockefeller-Reagan deal won't keep me from getting the nomination."[43]

The Atlanta Meeting

On the evening of May 31, 1968, Nixon and the southern chairmen assembled at Atlanta's Marriott Motor Hotel. They discussed Supreme Court appointments, busing, protecting textiles, law and order, communism, national defense, and party building in the South. "He gave us the right answers," recalled Dent. "I then called Thurmond to come on down."[44]

When Nixon and the chairmen reassembled, Thurmond was present. Nixon said that he supported the 1954 Supreme Court decision overturning the old separate but equal system of education for blacks and whites, promised to appoint strict constructionists to the Supreme Court, opposed busing, and sought a vice president "who shared his philosophy in the event he ascended to the presidency."[45] His remarks pleased everyone present.

"For those who had doubts that he could lead us to the White House," said Georgia Chairman G. Paul Jones, "he had laid them to rest."[46] "When Nixon left," reported Theodore White, "his nomination was secure."[47]

At the time Thurmond was more concerned over the defense posture of the country than civil rights and would give his support on that basis. On the way to the airport, Nixon assured him of his "commitment to a strong national defense." "He believed that America should be unquestionably first in the world in military power," recalled Nixon; "I agreed with him completely."[48] Apparently, this clinched Thurmond's support.

Nixon's Summer Campaign

In early June, Nixon and staff assembled at Key Biscayne, Florida, for a preconvention strategy meeting. In attendance were Mitchell, H. R. (Bob) Haldeman (West Coast manager of the J. Walter Thompson advertising agency), and Chapin, Buchanan, Price, Ellsworth, and Sears. The consensus was that Nixon had the nomination locked up. They agreed that he should avoid confrontations with Rockefeller or controversy over the issues. "I felt certain of defeating Rockefeller," recalled Nixon, "and I didn't want to let him draw me into internecine warfare that could only hurt my chances in the fall."[49]

Throughout June and July, Nixon's delegate strength increased, and he won important endorsements. The Illinois primary gave him an estimated 50 of 58 delegates, and state conventions in New Mexico, Montana, and Washington delivered another 34. On June 20, claiming that Nixon would end the war, Senator Mark Hatfield of Oregon endorsed him, and two days later Thurmond endorsed Nixon. On July 18, former President Dwight D. Eisenhower, recuperating from a heart attack in Walter Reed Hospital, endorsed Nixon. Although Eisenhower would have preferred to wait until after the convention, intermediaries had impressed upon him the importance of an early endorsement.[50] But the *New York Times* emphasized, "Nixon did not succeed when he last ran with the Eisenhower blessing.[51]

Rockefeller's Summer Campaign

On May 1, 1968, Rockefeller began a whirlwind three month campaign. He swept into 45 states, traveled more than 65,000 miles, talked personally with 1,000 delegates and spent millions on advertising. Rockefeller's staff targeted New York, Ohio, Oregon, Pennsylvania, Texas, California, Illinois, Maryland, Massachusetts, Missouri, New Jersey, Washington, and Michigan for advertising and polling. They placed 377 pages of ads in 54 newspapers in 40 cities and scheduled 462 television spots a week in 30 cities. Despite these efforts, Hughes was convinced that most Republicans would reject Rockefeller. "If the polls show you well ahead of Nixon, that's going to make you even less popular," Hughes told Rockefeller. "That might mean you could get elected, and the last thing the Republican convention wants is to see you elected."[52]

Rockefeller gained some of Kennedy's former followers. Michael Medved, chairman of Kennedy students for a New America, announced that 5,000 members had endorsed Rockefeller for the Republican nomination, and the Black Independents, made up of moderate and militant blacks, endorsed him "because we believe he is a reasonable man."[53] "As I joined him," recalled Theodore White, still mourning from the Kennedy campaign, "I felt at home again—the gaiety and zest of the campaign were the same."[54]

Rockefeller no longer appeared to be seeking Reagan as a running mate. "That's pretty well past now," explained a Rockefeller staffer in late June. "Reagan has made it clear that he isn't interested in the second spot, and we don't hear much Rockefeller-Reagan talk from the Republicans around the country."[55] But on July 4, Hughes secretly called on Reagan at his home in Palisades. Hughes wanted to know if Reagan was going to remain in the race. If he dropped out, a Nixon first ballot victory appeared inevitable. "Reagan assured me categorically that he would stay in the balloting and that he would not drop out," recalled Hughes. "No alliance, no coordination of strategies, or anything like that."[56]

On July 14, at a news conference at the New York Hilton Hotel,

Rockefeller announced a comprehensive four-stage plan to end the war. It was the most important foreign policy declaration of his presidential campaign. With help from Professor Henry A. Kissinger of Harvard and General James M. Gavin, Rockefeller staked out a middle position between Nixon and McCarthy. Rockefeller's four-point proposal called for (1) North Vietnamese troops pulling back toward the demilitarized zone and the borders of Cambodia and Laos, (2) North Vietnamese regulars and "fillers" in Vietcong units and most allied forces withdrawing from South Vietnam, (3) free elections under international supervision, (4) eventual reunification. "Rockefeller's plan," editorialized the *New York Times,* "is the direction in which U.S. military policy already appears to be moving under General Abrams."[57]

In midsummer, Rockefeller received his first important endorsement, that of Governor Raymond P. Shafer of Pennsylvania. It meant that he would get a substantial majority of Pennsylvania's 64 delegates. While he appreciated the endorsement, he told reporters that he needed to strike a delicate balance. If the governors of large states endorsed him and released their delegations, a small percentage of their delegates would go to Nixon and, perhaps, put him over the top. Asked whether the same thing would not happen at the convention, he replied, "I've got to assume that during the interim period the atmosphere is going to change."[58]

Reagan's Summer Campaign

Despite Nixon's success at Atlanta, Reagan knew that the South "adored" him, and during the summer months, he tried to convert his "natural constituency" into delegate strength. In late June, he flew southern delegates to California so he could make ideological appeals to them. Three weeks before the convention, he and Clifton White visited Texas, Arkansas, Virginia, Maryland, Indiana, Kentucky, Alabama, and North Carolina. "We were saying to the delegates," said White later, "don't commit yourself to anybody yet and we would come out of each one of those sessions with a certain few who would say, 'Well, you know Cliff, we're with you.'"[59] Jack Cox, Texas' 1962 Republican candidate for governor, shifted from Nixon to Reagan and began soliciting other pro-Nixon delegates to join him. In Alabama's 26 vote delegation, Reagan's vote rose from 10 to 12 and in Florida's 34 vote delegation from 8 to 9. Reagan partisans predicted that the Florida vote would rise as high as 18 by nomination night. Also, 6 of North Carolina's 26 delegates, including Chairman James C. Gardner, moved from pro-Nixon to pro-Reagan.

On their southern tour, Reagan and White persuaded numerous southern delegates, committed to vote for Nixon on the first ballot, to switch to Reagan on subsequent ballots. Governor Nunn of Kentucky, and 22 of the delegation's 24 delegates agreed to vote for Reagan if Nixon did not win by the third ballot.[60] Texas and South Carolina delegates agreed to go with Reagan on a second ballot.

In early July, Reagan faced a recall move by opponents at home. In California, the backers of the recall effort needed the signatures of 780,414 qualified voters by July 31. If the petition drive succeeded, the lieutenant governor would set a recall election date 60 to 80 days after the Secretary of State certified that the petitioners had collected enough valid signatures. "It's like a stone in your shoe," said Reagan, "you can live with it, but you'd be happier if it weren't there."[61] But his opponents failed to obtain the necessary number of signatures.

The Battle of the Polls

The final preconvention Gallup poll indicated that Nixon had overtaken both Humphrey and McCarthy. The June 29 poll had shown Nixon running five percentage points behind Humphrey and three points behind McCarthy, but the new July 29 poll reported Nixon beating Humphrey by 40 percent to 38 and McCarthy by 41 percent to 36. Rockefeller's standing had changed little. He again tied Humphrey at 36 percent, but unlike the earlier poll, where he ran two points behind McCarthy, Rockefeller now beat him by one point, 36 percent to 35. Hughes conceded that this poll "was a big psychological weapon for the Nixon people," and Nixon's staff said it "dramatically firmed up the situation."[62]

But two days later the Harris poll indicated that Rockefeller, not Nixon, was the strongest Republican candidate against the Democrats, leading Nixon in trial heats against both McCarthy and Humphrey. Rockefeller led both Humphrey and McCarthy 40 percent to 34 while Nixon trailed Humphrey 36 percent to 41 and McCarthy 35 percent to 43. On the same day, Rockefeller's private pollster Archibald Crossley reported Nixon leading Rockefeller by 2 percent nationally, but Rockefeller leading in most of the nine key industrial states: New York, New Jersey, Pennsylvania, Massachusetts, Maryland, Ohio, Michigan, Illinois, and California. "Rockefeller," insisted staffer Leonard Hall, "is the strongest man the party can nominate."[63]

Trying to clarify the disparities in their polls, Louis Harris and George Gallup issued a joint statement on August 1. Their figures, they said, along with those of Crossley, "firmly" showed that Rockefeller now led both of the Democratic opponents, but they added that a Nixon-Humphrey race "would be extremely close," with Wallace perhaps holding the balance. Fellow pollster Burns W. Roper countered, "All that could be concluded from the several polls at this point was that all four candidates had 'roughly equal' though shifting support among an electorate that shows something less than solid conviction." "This doesn't contradict the fact that Nixon is doing very well," said Herbert Klein, and "he is going to win."[64]

On the eve of the convention, Nixon was the most formidable candidate. He had acquired a string of primary victories, amassed a substantial delegate lead, and strengthened his position with the southern chairmen. But his lead was tenuous. If he did not win on the first ballot, his support might erode. And Rockefeller and Reagan were determined to deny Nixon that all-important first ballot victory.

Chapter VII

The Republican Convention

Arrangements

On August 5, 1968, 1,333 delegates, with their alternates, assembled at the Miami Beach Convention Hall. Of the delegates, 150 had been chosen in the primaries. The rest, mainly businessmen or lawyers chosen for loyalty and financial service to the party, were picked in state caucuses and conventions. Four out of five were Protestant, and 26 were black. The most colorful and leading senators of the party's two ideological wings were on hand: conservatives Thurmond, Tower, and Goldwater and liberals Hatfield, Percy, and Romney. Black leaders included Senator Edward W. Brooke of Massachusetts, temporary chairman of the convention, and Roy Wilkins, head of the National Association for the Advancement of Colored People (NAACP). But the party's most popular leader, former President Eisenhower, was still recuperating from a heart attack in Walter Reed Hospital.

The convention officers included Chairman of the National Committee Ray C. Bliss of Ohio, Secretary of the Convention Mrs. Consuelo Northrop Bailey of Vermont, Vice Chairman of the Arrangements Committee Donald R. Ross of Nebraska, Permanent Chairman of the Convention Gerald R. Ford, U.S. representative from Michigan, Chief Sergeant of Arms John T. Sherwood of Florida, and Parliamentarian H. Allen Smith of California. All leaned towards Nixon.

Miami Beach, a city of 80,000, was well equipped to host the first

Republican convention south of the Mason-Dixon Line. Tourism was the city's only industry, and it handled more than 500 conventions a year and 2.5 million tourists annually. On its seven square miles, the city crammed 369 hotels including such famous ones at the Marco Polo, Casablanca, Ivanhoe, Eden Roc, Twelve Caesars, Monte Carlo, and Moulin Rouge. It supplemented the city's 200 police with policemen from Miami, the Dade County Public Safety Department, the highway patrol, the conservation patrol, and even the state beverage department. Federal agencies, including the FBI, military intelligence, the Bureau of Narcotics, the Internal Revenue Service, and the Border Patrol, sent agents to Miami. The army sent bomb control experts. The Secret Service sent 100 agents to provide personal protection to the candidates.

As the Republicans assembled, political observers remarked that the Republicans appeared confident that the disarray in the Democratic camp would ensure a Republican victory in November, and they appeared ready to unite for that purpose. Newsman Marquis Childs observed, "They can almost taste the victory," and James Reston added, "Nobody is putting party ideology above party unity, not even Goldwater."[1]

The Candidates

Nixon was confident of the nomination. He had eroded his loser image in the primaries, impressed the southern chairmen at Atlanta, kept pace with Rockefeller in the polls, and acquired supporters like conservatives Thurmond and Tower and liberals Hatfield and McCall. In addition, a July 30 United Press International poll gave Nixon 684 delegates, Rockefeller 290, and Reagan 165, and a *New York Times* survey taken on August 3 showed Nixon 50 short of the 667 delegates needed to win. A *Newsweek* poll reduced that figure to 30.[2]

Despite the positive signs, Nixon's staff agreed on the importance of a first ballot victory. The convention was not locked up and the holding of the southern delegates was of paramount importance. According to Finch, "There were a lot of marginal votes," and Dent insisted, "Everything depended on a first ballot victory."[3]

High in the Hilton Plaza Hotel, behind chicken-wire barricades and squads of security policemen, Nixon's top staff directed an elaborate convention operation. They commanded 225 persons with access to about 125 automobiles, several speedboats, walkie-talkie radios, and other communication facilities to keep the main command post in touch with virtually every delegate. On the convention floor, Congressman Rogers Morton of Maryland monitored activities. In each delegation, Nixon's agents communicated policy and strategy to the delegates and kept the post informed of changing political sentiments.

Rockefeller's convention staff set up command posts on the fifteenth floor of the Americana Hotel, and fourteenth floor of the Octagon, a 16-story apartment building overlooking the convention hall. Leonard Hall coordinated the effort, and his field officers included Senators Thruston Morton of Kentucky, Mead Alcorn and Hugh Scott of Pennsylvania, John A. Love of Colorado, Harold LeVander of Minnesota, and former Governor William W. Scranton of Pennsylvania. Senator Brooke of Massachusetts and Mayor Lindsay monitored the sentiments of the state delegations. Campaign consultant John Deardourff and New York's Lieutenant Governor Malcolm Wilson coordinated the efforts of 16 field agents on the convention floor.

Rockefeller's main problems were his 1963 divorce and remarriage and the continuing resentment by party leaders of his failure to support Goldwater in 1964. His main hope for victory lay in persuading the delegates that he had a better chance of defeating the Democrats. He appealed to Democrats, independents, blacks, and the militant young, and Nixon was in trouble with all those critical groups.

Rockefeller and Reagan cooperated to deny Nixon a first ballot victory. While Reagan hoped to erode Nixon's southern strength, Rockefeller would try to keep favorite-son governors uncommitted past the first ballot.

Stassen, Romney, and Lindsay remained in the background. Stassen claimed to have 103 delegates and offered "to bet a good steak dinner" that his estimate was better than that of skeptical newsmen who credited him with the sole vote of his nephew J. Robert Stassen of Minnesota. In case of a deadlock, Romney and Lindsay hoped that the convention would turn to them. Shortly before the convention, Romney told reporters that he was uncommitted, leaning "nowhere" and likely to remain in that posture for some time. Lindsay publically supported Rockefeller, but his advisers had been working quietly for months to gain late-ballot supporters. If Rockefeller fell behind, they hoped that public pressure would force him to throw his support to Lindsay. Likewise, if Nixon fell behind, he would back Lindsay because, as one Lindsay man put it, "Nixon would do anything to keep Rockefeller from being President."[4]

Credentials and Rules

In preconvention hearings, two complaints came before the seven-member preconvention Contests Committee. The Committee rejected the petition from a group of blacks seeking representation on the all-white

Florida and Louisiana delegations on the grounds that they had failed to submit their position by the required 25 days before the convention deadline. Also, Joy Rohm, a moderate who headed the Iowa Republican Workshop, complained that Iowa's Republican convention (April 17, 1968) improperly dropped her from an at-large delegation list because she failed to commit herself to a presidential candidate. At the national convention, the Committee ruled against her, and the Republican National Committee upheld its decision.

The Rules Committee approved an antidiscrimination resolution which forbid any discrimination "for reasons of race, religion, color, or national origin" in the selection of future delegates.

The Platform Committee

Between July 29 and August 1, the 102-member Platform Committee, under the leadership of Senator Everett Dirksen of Illinois, heard representatives from the party's two ideological wings advocate different positions on the major issues of Vietnam and law and order. John H. Chafee said that the platform should say that America is not the policeman of the world, and Romney insisted that the plank outline "a positive peace program that will enable us to take the peace offensive." Lindsay said that the root cause of most crime and civil disorder was poverty, but Reagan blamed an all-pervasive permissive attitude for crime and disorder. He said that disengagement would open the way to greater aggression and weaken the credibility of American commitments everywhere.[5]

From August 2 to August 4, the Platform Committee hammered out the platform. As originally written, the Vietnam plank criticized Johnson for not leaving key decisions to the military, and attacked his policy of military gradualism. The Nixon and Rockefeller forces agreed that the plank sounded too hawkish and offered a compromise plank, drafted by Congressman Peter H. B. Frelinghuysen of New Jersey, which was adopted by a vote of 100 to 1. "I don't recall any strong dissent down the line on the platform," recalled Governor Louie B. Nunn of Kentucky, vice chairman of the Platform Committee.[6] Emmett John Hughes added, "Nobody was paying any attention to the platform, everybody's mind was on the delegate count."[7]

The Platform

Released to the press on Sunday afternoon, the 11,500-word platform took a careful middle course between conservatives and liberals on domestic policy, and doves and hawks on the Vietnam issue. It was ideologically correct for either Nixon or Rockefeller but well to the left of Reagan's most frequently voiced opinions.

On domestic policy, the platform endorsed the traditional Republican philosophy of sound monetary policies and reliance on local government and private industry rather than on the federal government to solve problems. It would enlist the "vast private enterprise resources" to improve urban life, and it pledged to apply federal funds only to priority needs and "to eliminate and prevent improper federal competition with private enterprise." While praising organized labor's contribution to the economic strength of the country, it emphasized the protection of individual liberty and reduction of government intervention in labor-management disputes. It called for a strong, all-out federal, state, and local crusade against crime.

The Vietnam plank was vague. It advocated a progressive de-Americanization of the war while encouraging the South Vietnamese to assume more responsibility for the fighting. But it remained silent on the issue of a bombing pause and a coalition government that would include National Liberation Front participation.

Also on foreign affairs, the platform hoped to further efforts to strengthen international law and called for a strong national defense and promised to press for greater international participation to encourage regional approaches to defense, economic development, and peaceful adjustment of disputes. It accused the Democrats of allowing the Soviets to narrow the defense gap and pledged to restore the preeminence of American military strength.

The press favored the platform's moderate tone and balance. The thrust of the platform, said Drummond, leaned towards the political center, and Evans and Novak called it "a measurably more liberal platform than the 1964 document but still conservative enough to please the South."[8] "Happily," said the *Los Angeles Times,* "the GOP's policy statement does not turn back the clock on such pressing matters as education, housing, jobs, welfare, and social security."[9] But according to the *Indianapolis News,* "It is mostly just indecisive, skirting the hard issues, with careful phrases designed to anger few and excite nobody."[10]

Reagan's Candidacy

As the convention assembled, the real center of interest concerned Reagan's intentions.

On Monday, August 3, Dent, Goldthwaite, Reed (the only Reagan-committed southern chairman), Reagan and Clifton White assembled over lunch in Reagan's suite at the Deauville Hotel. "It was a most embarrassing type of luncheon," recalled Goldthwaite. "Dent and Reed tried to say that they loved Reagan but they had to go with Nixon, but they were squirming because at one point they let Reagan think they were for him."[11] "To a certain extent," recalled White, "Goldthwaite and Reed were still sympathetic to us but didn't think we could make it."[12]

Reagan's advisers had agreed that delegate sentiment was polarizing rapidly toward avowed contenders and that Reagan would have to act quickly. (He had originally decided to announce on Wednesday, August 7.) At four o'clock in the afternoon, former California Senator William F. Knowland informed reporters in the Deauville's Napoleon II room that the California delegates had adopted a resolution endorsing Reagan's candidacy. As if it were planned, Reagan walked in from a nearby room and announced his entry.

Rockefeller welcomed Reagan's announcement, but the Nixon camp appeared undismayed. "The Reagan move," said Rockefeller, "will help bring the situation into sharper focus."[13] A Nixon staffer said, "The Reagan declaration changes nothing," and Senator Tower exclaimed, "It's too late."[14] "We believed a Rocky-Reagan alliance would now come into play," recalled Finch, "but nobody felt it would be very solid."[15]

When Nixon arrived at the convention late Monday afternoon, he appeared confident of winning. He was, reported the *Washington Post,* "smiling and beaming confidence that victory will be his in the final thirty-six hours of the nomination battle."[16]

Agnew had endorsed Nixon and released his convention delegates to "cast their votes as they see fit." But Governor Rhodes, heading Ohio's 58 delegates, and Romney, heading Michigan's 48 delegates, continued their favorite-son roles.

Southern Rumblings and Nixon's Reassurances

On Monday, Nixon's southern support began to weaken. Former congressman Jim Martin, boss of the Nixon faction in the Alabama delegation, told a Nixon contact man, "If Alabama did not show at least token support for the one true conservative in nomination, we could get lynched when we get home."[17] A Nixon man, John W. Gardner of North Carolina, came out for Reagan. "Strategically, we needed some competition in there," he explained. "We would be in a much stronger position if we didn't go the first round with Nixon."[18] Gardner's defection, recalled Dent, "created the most traumatic shock wave we Nixonites had felt, and delegates from all over the convention floor were telling of more and more possible defections from Nixon to Reagan."[19]

On Monday evening, at 10:00 p.m., Dent, John Buzhardt, Thurmond, Nixon, Mitchell, Haldeman, and John Ehrlichman assembled in Nixon's Hilton Plaza suite to discuss the southern situation. "Nixon felt we had the South secured and that he could make it on the first ballot," recalled Dent. But when he mentioned that Reagan's announcement had "stirred" the southern delegates and that Gardner had switched to Reagan, Nixon became concerned and asked what he could do to help. Thurmond replied that Nixon should repeat his Atlanta statements to the southern delegates.[20]

On Tuesday morning, August 6, over coffee and buns at the Hilton Plaza, Nixon met separately with two different groups of southern delegates. He first met with delegates from Alabama, the District of Columbia, Georgia, Kentucky, Louisiana, Mississippi, Texas and the Virgin Islands. He told them that he was a strict constructionist and that his vice presidential choice would "be acceptable to all."[21] Then he met with delegates from Arkansas, Florida, North and South Carolina, Tennessee, and Virginia. "I stood on the front row and prompted Nixon or asked questions that brought out the key points I wanted made," recalled Dent. "And sure enough every time Nixon spoke, his words were the right ones."[22] He opposed the busing of students and said that the job of the courts is "to interpret the law and not make the law" and that he knew of no court in the nation "qualified to be a local school district and to make the decision as your local school board."[23]

The southerners were pleased with Nixon's performance. National committeeman Tom Stagg of Louisiana exclaimed, "It was the greatest standup performance by a politician I've ever witnessed," and to Alabama's Jim Martin, Nixon's message was clear: "He's not going to write off the South to George Wallace."[24]

The Tuesday Delegate Hunt

On Tuesday, Thurmond, Goldwater, and Tower worked feverishly to keep the southern delegations in line. "Everywhere that Reagan went," recalled Dent, "We had Thurmond right behind him. We didn't sleep."[25] With Nixon, Thurmond told the delegates, the South "need not worry about a pesky northern liberal being installed a heartbeat from the Presidency."[26] "Thurmond called on all of his IOUs all over the South to vote for Nixon," said Goldthwaite.[27] "We had the pledges," said Sears later, "but it was a matter for Thurmond, Goldwater, and Tower to make sure everybody kept their word."[28] To the delegates, recalled Finch, Nixon was more predictable than Reagan.[29] White was frustrated, "I couldn't get my hands on the southern delegates."[30] After Congressman Donald Lukens of Ohio, Reagan's southern operative, gave "a real firebrand pitch" to the Louisiana delegation, a delegate stood-up and summed-up their feelings:

> In the last twenty-four hours this delegation has seen Barry Goldwater, Strom Thurmond, and John Tower. Now, as much as we respect you, where the conservative movement is concerned that is the Father, the Son, and the Holy Ghost.[31]

While Nixon's men were busy trying to hold the South, Rockefeller made some headway. By Tuesday, he had won endorsements from Governor Daniel J. Evans of Washington, Congressmen Gary E. Brown, Jack H. McDonald, and Marvin L. Esch of Michigan; and Alphonzo Bell of California and Charles Mathias of Maryland. After Rockefeller spoke to the 26-member Minnesota delegation, a Nixon backer and four uncommitted delegates endorsed him. Governor LeVander of Minnesota told reporters that he expected 16 or 17 first ballot votes for Rockefeller to 9 or 10 for Nixon.[32] Rockefeller also talked with delegates from Utah, Puerto Rico, Hawaii, the Virgin Islands, and Iowa. Meanwhile, Mayor Lindsay was circulating around hotels and swimming pools urging delegates to vote for Rockefeller.

Because of New Jersey's critical position midway through the roll-call, Rockefeller depended heavily on favorite-son candidate Clifford P. Case, a highly respected liberal senator, to keep his delegation uncommitted for at least one ballot. A Rockefeller staffer explained, "We had a lot of people in other states who promised they would stick with us if Jersey held."[33] Prior to the convention, the delegation had voted 33 for Case and 7 for Nixon, but by Tuesday, the vote had changed to 24 for Case and 11 for Nixon with 5 uncommitted. On Tuesday, Nixon met with Nelson Gross, a young attorney who controlled Bergen County's five votes. Flattering Gross, Nixon recalled how in 1956, Bergen County had supported Eisenhower, the winner, and Gross could now do the same for him. Upon leaving the meeting, Gross exclaimed, "It's time Bergen took the lead."[34] Subsequent caucuses showed the New Jersey vote split down the middle, 20 for Case and 20 for Nixon.

On Tuesday evening, Reagan and staffers Thomas Reed, a California nuclear physicist, and Lyn Nofziger, a former newspaperman, called on Thurmond and Dent at the Versailles Hotel. While Reagan talked to Thurmond, Reed and Nofziger herded Dent into a separate room and locked the door. "They figured I was the evil one," he recalled, "but when Thurmond's mind locks in place, you can't get it unlocked."[35]

After an unsuccessful hour with Thurmond, Reagan met with the South Carolina delegates downstairs. The session with Thurmond had "drained and distressed him," and Reagan was not at his best. Although Reagan "answered right on all the questions of the delegates," recalled Dent, "when Reagan failed to unlock Thurmond, he failed to unlock the South Carolina delegation."[36] But seven South Carolina delegates had secretly promised White to vote for Reagan should a second ballot occur.[37]

Mississippi, Florida, and Alabama

Reagan also sought to cut into Nixon's strength in three other southern state delegations. If Reagan cracked them, he could deny Nixon a first ballot victory.

Reagan had an excellent team. Besides White, Reed, and Nofziger, Reagan's top staff included Tom Van Sickle, former chairman of the Young Republicans, and Frank Whetstone, a newspaper publisher from Montana.

Reagan's southern operatives included Lukens, William Rusher, publisher of the conservative *National Review,* and Margaret Maytag, a long-time conservative activist.

On Tuesday evening, Nofziger urged Reed to release Mississippi's 20 delegates from the unit rule, apparently unaware of Reed's grudge against Reagan for failing to visit Mississippi during Reed's 1955 gubernatorial race. Nofziger threatened, "Look, if you want Reagan to come to Mississippi, you better let your delegates go." "Listen," replied Reed, "don't threaten me that you are not going to come. You never came to Mississippi when we needed you." But Reed was also pragmatic. He recalled, "I just didn't see Reagan ever getting the thing. It was Nixon's convention, and I'd rather he owe us than the liberals."[38]

Martin feared that Nixon's strength in the Alabama delegation might slip below the breakeven mark of 13 out of 26 and the whole delegation break loose. Because Alabama was the first state to be called, both for nominating and balloting, Thurmond reasoned that its vote would have some psychological impact on subsequent events. Earlier, Thurmond had asked Martin to persuade Alabama to yield to South Carolina in the nominating session. (A delegation could yield its privilege to nominate to another delegation of its own choice lower down the alphabet). But Martin demurred. "By forcing a vote," he argued, "we Nixonites would risk alienating some pro-Nixon delegates in the Alabama delegation."[39]

Florida was the key delegation. If Reagan took it, a Nixon first ballot victory was doubtful. Murfin, whose 34-member delegation operated under the unit-rule, was unofficially committed to Nixon. But shortly before the convention assembled, he and White made a deal. "If I get sixteen votes for Reagan," asked White, "will you make it seventeen and go with us?" "Yes," replied Murfin.[40] When Lukens learned that Murfin was trying to hold the delegation in line for Nixon, Lukens informed White, "Murfin double-crossed me!" declared White. He immediately assigned Lukens to cover the Florida delegation.

Nixon's base within the Florida delegation was not secure. Surprisingly, Murfin had picked a large number of pro-Reagan delegates. "I knew they were Reagan people when I picked them," he explained. "They were good party workers, and I would have been a very unpopular person had I not selected the real workers in the party." "But they were honorable people," he added, "and we agreed to abide by the unit rule."[41]

On Tuesday evening, Reagan began calling the Florida delegates off the convention floor to his trailer behind the convention hall. Half the delegation, as stipulated by Florida law, were women. "They were emotionally and philosophically for Reagan," recalled Lukens, "but they wavered back and forth virtually every four or five hours.[42] Murfin informed Dent that Reagan was attracting the women delegates and that

Knowland and Max Rafferty, the outspoken superintendent of education in California, were coming to nail them down for Reagan early Wednesday morning.[43] Dent agreed to have Thurmond speak to the delegation before the Reagan people arrived.

On Wednesday morning, Thurmond and Dent arrived at the Doral Country Club, where the Florida delegation was staying, just ten minutes before Knowland and Rafferty. Dent told the delegates that Nixon had given Thurmond veto power over the vice presidency. Nixon had not given Thurmond such a veto, but the tactic worked and it scuttled the strategic Reagan move.[44]

At 2:00 p.m., the Florida delegates caucused at the Doral Country Club. They were in a highly emotional state. Most wanted Reagan. "That will only get Rocky nominated," said Murfm.[45] Mitchell phoned, "Look, we almost feel it would be better to release the delegates from the unit rule." "No, we've got it," replied Murfin, "we're all right, we're going to stay with it."[46] They would not go against him. They voted to hold for Nixon on the first ballot.

Shortly before the nominations on Wednesday morning, the Reagan camp assembled in their communications trailer. By White's reckoning,

Reagan had 180 to Nixon's 682 votes. Hoping for a break, Reagan began calling Alabama, Florida and Mississippi delegates to the trailer. According to White, "I had to mop up after every delegate because they set there and wept about how much they wanted Ronald Reagan, but they argued that Nixon had the nomination: why go ahead and put themselves in trouble with the nominee when they could get the credit for his victory."[47]

Nominations and Balloting

Nominating speeches began at five-thirty on Wednesday evening and ended shortly after midnight. California's Treasurer Ivy Baker Priest nominated Reagan; Governor Shafer nominated Rockefeller; and Agnew nominated Nixon. J. Robert Stassen, a Minnesota delegate, nominated his uncle, Harold Stassen. Favorite sons placed in nomination included Governors Winthrop Rockefeller of Arkansas, Romney of Michigan, James A. Rhodes of Ohio, and Walter J. Hickel of Alaska, and Senators Frank Carlson of Kansas, Hiram L. Fong of Hawaii, Case of New Jersey, and Thurmond of South Carolina. Thurmond withdrew in favor of Nixon.

Balloting lasted only 33 minutes. The A's through D's went as expected. Alabama awarded Nixon 14 votes, Reagan 12. Alaska and Arizona went for Nixon, and Arkansas and California stayed with their governors. But when Florida cast 32 of its 34 votes for Nixon, Hughes said, "I knew it was all over. I turned off the television set."[48] "That's it," Nixon told staffers, "we've got it."[49] In addition, he picked up 50 of the 58 Illinois and 18 of the 22 New Jersey delegates. In New York, Rockefeller obtained 88 votes, Nixon 4. Ohio held: 56 votes for Rhodes, 2 for Nixon. Nixon's agents had raided the Pennsylvania delegation with considerable success: Rockefeller 41 votes, Nixon 22, Reagan 1. Mississippi held firm: all 20 votes for Nixon. And Wisconsin put Nixon over the 667 votes required for the nomination. The final count: Nixon, 692; Rockefeller, 277; Reagan, 182; Rhodes, 55; Romney, 50; Case, 22; Carlson, 20; Winthrop Rockefeller, 18; Hiram Fong, 14; Stassen, 2; Lindsay, 1.[50]

Reaction to Nomination

Rockefeller and Reagan called Nixon's nomination a "spectacular success," and Humphrey and McCarthy agreed that Nixon was well qualified to represent Republican philosophy. The American people now have a clear choice, said Humphrey, and McCarthy added, "Nixon is truly a Republican candidate."[51]

Newspaper reaction varied. The *Los Angeles Times* congratulated Nixon on "winning this great and provocative opportunity."[52] According to the *Chicago Tribune,* "If courage, unwavering perseverance, and the gift of considered and stable judgment are the qualities that make a President, Richard Nixon has them in ample measure."[53] "Nixon showed," editorialized the *Miami Herald,* "a superbly scheduled unfolding of a master strategy."[54] "By conferring this year's presidential nomination on Richard Nixon," observed the *Indianapolis News,* "the Republican Party chose the man who had done the most to earn its allegiance."[55] "We are delighted," declared the New York *Daily News.*[56]

But many were less sanguine. "The name of the game was party unity," editorialized the *Washington Post,* "and the great question that grows out of the Republican Convention is whether, for a distinctly minority party, this can be a winning game."[57] "The basic reason for Mr. Nixon's nomination," said the *St. Louis Post-Dispatch,* "was a serene confidence on the part of the delegates that change is precisely what he does not stand for."[58] "The Republican Party," editorialized the *New York Times,* "again demonstrated that lack of imagination which so frequently characterizes the professional politician of both parties."[59] "The Republican Party," said *Le Monde* in Paris, "preferred a return to the past," and said Sweden's liberal *Expression,* "Nixon represented most of what is repellent in American politics."[60]

The press reported that Thurmond's role was crucial in holding the South for Nixon, but convention participants split on this question. Some, like Dent and Gardner, argued that "Thurmond literally held the South for Nixon."[61] But others felt there was more than Thurmond involved. "The southerners were very anxious and nervous about picking the right one," said Sears later, "in picking a winner."[62]

In retrospect, 1968 was Nixon's year. He had supported Goldwater in 1964, campaigned hard for congressional candidates in the midterm elections, raised money, and helped Republicans in local and state elections. In the process, he had acquired numerous political IOUs, enhanced his prestige among party leaders, and stayed in the national limelight. He had overcome his loser image in the 1968 primaries, impressed the southern chairmen at Atlanta, kept pace with Rockefeller in the polls, and obtained Eisenhower's support. The bitter split at the 1964 convention as well as Goldwater's disastrous defeat persuaded party leaders to seek a candidate who could both unite the party and win a national election. They considered Reagan too conservative to obtain a national following and Rockefeller too liberal to hold the party together. That left Nixon, the man of the middle, and the convention's choice to challenge the Democrats for the presidency.

The Vice Presidential Choice

Nixon first began to consider Governor Spiro Agnew of Maryland as a running mate in the spring of 1968. On May 16, he told the press that Agnew was one of the five men on his list of vice presidential choices. While repeating that Rockefeller would be the best candidate, Agnew admitted that he was looking Nixon over carefully. On two occasions, June 20 and July 17, the two men met privately, Nixon did not bring up the question of the vice presidency, but he found Agnew's political credentials impressive. "With George Wallace in the race," explained Nixon, "it was absolutely necessary ... to win the entire rimland of the South—the border states—as well as the major states of the Midwest and West," and "Agnew "fit the bill" geographically, and "as a political moderate, he fit it philo- sophically."[63] But it was a tentative choice and still reversible.

Born in 1918, Agnew was the son of a Greek immigrant who had changed his name from Anagnastopoulos. He served in the army during World War II, earned a law degree in night school from the University of Baltimore, and in 1962, was elected county executive of Baltimore County. Four years later, he defeated segregationist Democrat George P. Mahoney to win Maryland's governorship. In his first few months in office, he helped pass Maryland's first fair housing law, pushed through a tough antipollution law, and opened up personal communication with the state's black com- munity. After Rockefeller's March 21 withdrawal, recalled statehouse colleagues, Agnew's mood changed from liberal to "angry, illiberal out- bursts, and contradictions." During the Baltimore riots in early April, 1968, he called 100 moderate black leaders to his office and accused them of surrendering to the demands of black militants. They walked out in a rage. Shortly thereafter, he declared that "policemen ought to shoot looters who fail to halt when ordered," and argued that the cause of riots was "this per- missive climate and the misguided compassion of public opinion."[64]

In the early morning hours on Thursday, August 8, Nixon held four meetings with staffers and party leaders to discuss a vice presidential choice. He gave no clue that Agnew was his tentative choice. "That's the way Nixon always was," recalled Sears. "He didn't like meetings to decide any- thing. The meetings were to let people think they were in on something."[65] The participants did not agree on any one candidate. Those mentioned in- cluded Romney, Reagan, Lindsay, Percy, Hatfield, Tower, Rockefeller, Con- gressman George Bush of Texas, and Governor Volpe of Massachusetts.

Thirteen staffers and 11 outside political advisers attended the first meeting in Nixon's suite at the Hilton Plaza. Nixon rejected the more well-known figures, Lindsay, Percy, and Reagan, and kept mentioning Agnew and Volpe. "When I left that meeting," recalled Patrick Buchanan, "I felt sure that it would be either Agnew or Volpe."[66]

Twenty-four of the party's top leaders, including Thurmond, attended the second meeting. "There was a good cross-section of liberals and conservatives," recalled Murfin.[67] Nixon went around the room asking each one who he thought would be the best candidate for his area. Agnew's name was brought up, but it did not cause much of a stir.[68] Afterwards, Thurmond handed Nixon a small piece of paper with three columns of names: the acceptables, Reagan, Tower, Bush, Congressman Rogers Morton of Maryland, and senators Robert P. Griffin of Michigan, and Howard H. Baker of Tennessee; the no objections, Agnew and Volpe; and the unacceptables, Senator Mark O. Hatfield of Oregon, Lindsay, and Rockefeller. According to Dent, "This was Thurmond's way of casting his veto."[69]

The third meeting took place at 9:00 a.m., in the Hilton Plaza's Jackie of Hearts room. Nixon, his eyes now puffy with fatigue, met with prominent Republican political strategists. They included Finch, Ford, Tower, Ray Bliss, Rogers Morton, Wisconsin's Chairman Ody Fish, Texas' chairman Peter O'Donnel, Congressman Bob Wilson of California, Senator George Murphy of California, and Senate Minority Leader Everett Dirksen of Illinois. They split along liberal and conservative lines, and like the previous meetings, resolved nothing.

At midmorning, back in his suite, Nixon assembled with staffers Mitchell, Haldeman, Ellsworth, Tower, Finch, and Rogers Morton. Nixon was disturbed by the lack of enthusiasm shown for Agnew and asked Finch if he would consider the vice presidency. "Nixon was dead serious," said Finch later, "and I was equally serious in saying I wouldn't even think of it."[70] "He was deeply moved by my suggestion," recalled Nixon, "but he strongly rejected it, arguing that the leap from lieutenant governor to Vice President would be perceived as too great." Nixon next turned to Morton: "Rog, maybe you would be the better choice for me." But Morton insisted that he lacked the credentials. "That pretty well clinched it for me," recalled Nixon. "Had Morton said that he wanted it, even at that late moment I might well have picked him."[71] Nixon asked Morton to telephone Agnew. Before announcing his decision, Nixon had Tower phone Thurmond to ask whether he preferred Volpe or Agnew. Thurmond replied that he favored Agnew. Nixon knew that Thurmond would prefer the more southerly of the two.

Reactions to the Vice Presidential Choice

Although surprised that Nixon had picked an unknown, the conservative wing appeared satisfied. "He looked like he was our guy," recalled Reed.[72]

Murfin would have preferred someone better known. But he said later, "You don't make waves, you would be afraid it would get back to Nixon and he would say, 'Well, we'd better stay away from you.'"[73] "We could sell Agnew," said Dent afterwards, "and our major job was selling Nixon over George Wallace in the South."[74]

But liberals and moderates expressed serious reservations. "We'll have a difficult time in Michigan," declared Romney, and Senator Jacob Javits of New York added, "This is not the strongest ticket."[75] "We are not going to win nationally with a candidate beholden to Southern delegates," said Rockefeller.[76] "Nixon," insisted Hughes afterwards, "went out of his way to pick an early Rocky supporter to stick a finger in Nelson's eye."[77]

Democratic candidates expressed mixed reactions. Wallace complained that Nixon had picked Agnew to erode his southern support.[78] "The Republican ticket won't change my strategy," said McCarthy.[79] Barely able to conceal his pleasure, Humphrey declared, "We now have a Republican ticket we can go to the mat with."[80]

Press reaction was mixed. "Agnew was chosen," editorialized the *Washington Post*, "on the assumption that he would not be offensive either to the Southern vote or to the big cities of the North."[81] A candidate, said the *Wall Street Journal*, with more substantial national standing would "be highly desirable for someone who might become President."[82] "Though the naming of Agnew may not have been a 'sellout' to the South," wrote John Knight in the *Miami Herald*, "it was most certainly contrived to appease the South."[83] According to the *Chicago Tribune*, "There is nothing dishonorable in trying to bind up party wounds."[84] "He was the best northerner," said Joseph Alsop, "that Nixon could name for his special purposes."[85] "Any other choice," said James Kilpatrick, "would have provoked louder howls," and William White added, "He was simply and obviously a moderate accommodation between North and South."[86]

Nixon described Agnew as "one of the most underrated political men in America," and Nixon's staff insisted Agnew was not "a bone to the Southerners."[87]

On Thursday afternoon, a liberal faction, led by Chafee, Scranton, and Congressman Charles E. Goodell of New York, began looking for a candidate to challenge Agnew. They first asked Lindsay, but he had already agreed to support the ticket and second Agnew's nomination. They turned to Romney who made no effort to either head off or assist the movement. Nixon considered it a challenge to his leadership. "If the sore losers get away with something like this now, they'll do the same damn thing during my presidency."[88] He told Mitchell to impose whatever discipline necessary to keep the delegates in line.

But the vice presidential nomination was never in doubt. Agnew obtained 1,119, Romney 186, Lindsay 10 votes. And Governors Rockefeller, Chafee, Rhodes, Evans, Love, and LeVander endorsed Agnew. Thruston Morton signed on as a campaign traveling companion, and Shafer, a top Rockefeller booster, declared, "I am wholeheartedly behind Nixon's campaign."[89] Romney said he would plug the ticket on national television and told Nixon that the revolt was "like a good burp! It relieved the tension and united your support."[90]

Nixon's Acceptance Speech

Nixon's speech accepting the nomination took 40 minutes and was interrupted by applause 47 times. Now that the conservative vote was tied down, Nixon sounded moderate and liberal. He moved straight into a definition of his constituency:

> As we look at America we see cities enveloped in smoke and flame.
> We hear sirens in the night.
> We see Americans dying in distant battlefields abroad.
> We see Americans hating each other, fighting each other, killing each other at home.
> And as we see and hear these things, millions of Americans cry out in anguish.
> Did we come all this way for this?...
> Listen to the answer to those questions.
> It is another voice. It is a quiet voice, in the tumult of the shouting. It is the voice of the great majority of Americans, the forgotten Americans—the non-shouters, the non-demonstrators....
> They're good people; they're decent people, they work and they save and they pay their taxes and they care.

On the plight of the poor, Nixon criticized government programs and advocated private enterprise solutions. On law and order, he promised to appoint a new attorney general and wage a war against organized crime. Also, "our goal is justice," he said, "If we are to have respect for law in America, we must have laws that deserve respect."

In foreign affairs, he appealed to both hawks and doves. On Vietnam, he called for new leadership "not tied to the mistakes and the policies of the past," and he pledged to end the war. For those of militant temperament, he said:

And I say to you tonight that when respect for the United States of America falls so low that a fourth-rate military power, like North Korea, will seize an American naval vessel on the high seas, it's time for new leadership to restore respect for the United States of America.

And for the more dovish:

We believe this should be an era of peaceful competition, not only in the productivity of our factories, but in the quality of all people. To the Russian people. To the Chinese people. To all people in the world. And we work toward the goal of an open world, open sky, open cities, open hearts, open minds.

Nixon said that he believed in the American dream and that his had come true. He concluded:

It seems like an impossible dream.

But he is helped on his journey through life. A father who had to go to work before he finished the sixth grade sacrificed everything he had so that his sons could go to college.

A gentle, Quaker mother, with a passionate concern for peace, quietly wept when he went to war, but she understood why he had to go.

A great teacher, a remarkable football coach, an inspirational minister encouraged him on his way.

A courageous wife and loyal children stood by him in victory and also in defeat.

And in his chosen profession of politics, first there were scores, then hundreds, then thousands, and finally millions who worked for his success.

And tonight he stands before you—nominated for president of the United States of America.

As the convention ended, observers noted that the Republicans had avoided the mistake of the 1964 convention. They picked Nixon, the man in the middle, who could both unite the party and obtain a national following. Unlike Goldwater in 1964, Nixon would begin the general campaign with both a large war chest and a united party.[91]

Chapter VIII

The Democrats Before Their Convention

After Kennedy's Assassination

E ven before the assassination, political indicators pointed to Humphrey's nomination. In early May, *Time* reported that a poll of Democratic senators and congressmen showed Humphrey favored as the party's candidate by a four-to-one margin over both Kennedy and McCarthy. The Gallup poll reported Humphrey with 40 percent, Kennedy 31, and McCarthy 19 percent, and the Harris poll showed Humphrey with 38 percent, Kennedy 27, and McCarthy 25 percent. In the 36 states and four territories with no primaries, which had 1,568 of the 2,622 delegates, Humphrey had acquired almost enough delegates to win the nomination. A late May *Newsweek* survey indicated that Humphrey was only 32½ percent delegates away from the nomination.[1]

Despite Humphrey's strength, Kennedy's supporters insisted that their candidate would have been a formidable opponent by convention time. They argued that the California and South Dakota victories, combined with a probable victory in New York, would have assured him the nomination.[2] Some disagreed. William Vanden Heuvel considered Kennedy's chances "remote," and O'Brien admitted, "even if Bob had won New York, Humphrey might still have been the nominee."[3]

After the assassination, most of Kennedy's delegates and staff either switched to Humphrey or remained neutral. According to a June 10, *New York Times* survey, Humphrey gained 400 former Kennedy delegates to

McCarthy's 75. California's 174 Kennedy delegates remained uncommitted. Sorensen observed, "old wounds from the Kennedy-McCarthy primary fights were still unhealed."[4] "We much preferred Humphrey," said a Kennedy staffer. "Maybe, even Nixon."[5] "McCarthy does not really want them," reported Halberstam, and *Commonweal* insisted, "The rancor between the two camps is probably worse than ever."[6]

The New York Primary

McCarthy's New York effort was led by the Coalition for a Democratic Alternative (CDA), a local group. Its leaders included Sarah Kovner, a former Democratic state committeewoman, Eleanor Clark French, former vice-chairman of the Democratic State Committee, and Harold Ickes. Another group, Citizens for McCarthy, appealed to moderates and liberals uncomfortable with CDA's leftist tendencies.

The McCarthyites' main problem was New York's intricate ballot laws. The voters selected 123 of the 190 delegates in the primary; the Democratic State Committee chose 65; and two votes automatically went to the national committeeman and committeewoman. Voters elected 3 delegates and 3 alternates from each of the 41 congressional districts, but the ballot did not list the names of the candidates the delegates supported. Because delegates stood for election in congressional districts, McCarthy's supporters could not publicize a statewide slate. To meet these difficulties, they tailored campaign strategy to each district and prepared a standard tabloid explaining McCarthy's record and objectives but changed the last page in each district to identify the local candidates supporting McCarthy.

Another problem was McCarthy's refusal to take an active role in the New York campaign. It was too close to Kennedy's death, argued McCarthy. Staffers agreed that it would be in poor taste to campaign circus style, but he could still make appearances and talk on the issues. Kovner repeatedly tried to reach him to explain the staff's position, but her calls went unanswered. When McCarthy finally returned a call, Kovner, now furious, refused to speak to him. "Tell him," she told McCarthy's secretary, "that I'm too busy trying to win the election."[7]

When McCarthy cancelled a fundraising speech for the Poor People's Campaign, a black organization, staff morale hit a dangerous low. They had carefully billed the event as a benefit rather than a rally and sent out advertising announcing his presence. They insisted he attend. In support of their efforts, his Washington staff held an informal sit-down strike, and black supporters questioned his commitment to civil rights.[8] The intense pressure had the desired effect, and he spoke at the benefit.

Despite McCarthy's inactivity, he won the majority of delegates on June 18. He obtained 62 delegates, Kennedy 30, and Humphrey 12. Senate candidate Paul O'Dwyer, an uncompromising McCarthy supporter, came in first in the Democratic primary. (On June 28, the New York State Democratic Committee awarded McCarthy another 15½ of the remaining 65 delegate-at-large votes.) "The New York primary results," editorialized the *New York Times,* "when added to the results of every other primary represent a mandate for national political change."[9] But the *Wall Street Journal* observed that the total vote was only about 20 percent of the state's registered voters `[10]

McCarthy's Summer Campaign

Over the summer, McCarthy kept up a continuous round of public appearances and met with 25 delegations. His delegate-approach was low key. "I will simply ask them to be responsible delegates," he told reporters, "and to make the judgment that has to be made in August."[11] Despite pleas from staffers, he refused to change his style or make concessions.[12] "I'm not going to 'corral' or 'round up' delegates," he insisted. "That's Texas language."[13]

The impression persisted that McCarthy was not comfortable in dealing with blacks. We are a people of emotions, said one black leader, but he did not "appeal to us emotionally."[14] This "was a significant failure of his campaign," reported Halberstam.[15] He had experienced so little personal contact with black people, recalled Stavis, "that he may have felt uncomfortable."[16]

Throughout the summer, sharp policy disputes emerged over strategy. One faction, led by Gans, Brown, Stavis, and Clark, advocated petition drives, door-to-door canvassing, rallies, letter writing campaigns, local delegate lobbying efforts, and radio and television appearances by McCarthy and prominent supporters. This would, they said, generate grassroots support and persuade delegates that McCarthy would make the party's strongest candidate in the fall. Finney argued for an individual delegate approach. "The main thrust now," he said, "should be to win over non-elected delegates within the political system in accord with Senator McCarthy's promise that the whole campaign would be fought within the system." Newcomers Stephen Mitchell, a Chicago lawyer, and his associate Marty Gleason, a Chicago industrialist, advocated an aggressive convention approach. They argued for sustained challenges of the unit-rule, credentials, and Vietnam plank. "Our only chance," insisted Mitchell, "was to fight every damn thing we could, and bring the public to the point where they would bear on the delegates."[17]

By early July, the different factions came to an uneasy accommodation. Mitchell and Gleason took charge of convention planning; Clark continued as campaign manager; Finney became campaign coordinator; Gans accepted a reduced field program involving about fifty staffers; and Stephen Quigley became campaign comptroller with power to fire Gans' staff.

But the accommodation soon broke down, and factional disputes and personality conflicts continued to weaken the campaign. "The summer was few steps forward and many steps backward," explained a young staffer.[18] "A lot of the dissension," recalled Sam Brown, "was personality and a lot of it was a highly charged situation in which somebody needed to be found as a scapegoat for what was then a floundering campaign."[19] According to Stavis, the continued infighting was "fatal."[20]

The Coalition for an Open Convention

On June 29, at Chicago's Sherman House Hotel, over a thousand persons set up a broadly-based nonpartisan group called the Coalition for an Open Convention led by Allard K. Lowenstein. Participants included middle-level Kennedy and McCarthy people, between 85 and 100 delegates to the Democratic convention, and black and student leaders. They did not bill the meeting as pro-McCarthy because they hoped to attract as many opponents of the administration as possible. "The attempt was to find issues other than the personalities," recalled Sam Brown.[21] The participants charged many state delegations with violating the "one man, one vote" principle and the rules of the Democratic Party guaranteeing equal participation to all groups.

McCarthy's top staffers refused to participate in the new organization. They feared it would further factionalize the insurgent movement and make the anti-Humphrey forces look "pitifully weak." "The McCarthy people at the top are dubious," observed Halberstam, "regarding it as an attempt to take McCarthy's campaign and hand the work over to some other candidate."[22] "McCarthy's basic view," recalled Sam Brown, "was that the Kennedy people should be for me, and I don't know why we have to discuss other things beyond that."[23]

Humphrey's Summer Campaign

Throughout the summer, Humphrey encountered a number of serious problems. Despite his pro-civil rights record, he failed to generate much black support. An early June state-by-state survey indicated that many voters considered Humphrey too soft on the law and order issue. When staffer Eiler Ravnholt told Humphrey that he "should make it clear that he can provide the leadership to put an end to all this turmoil," Humphrey replied, "I would rather not be nominated as the Presidential candidate then depend on a racist vote to get the nomination or the election."[24] Humphrey also lost much of his business support. "A large share of the money pledged to me," he recalled, "came from New York business leaders who feared and distrusted Bob. With his death, their interest in me waned."[25] "The business community," recalled Schlesinger, "opposed Kennedy because he stood for reform and change, and after his death, they shifted support from Humphrey to Nixon."[26] The resulting loss in contributions forced him to reduce his staff by 25 percent and to cancel $277,000 worth of television and newspaper advertising.

Hecklers were another problem. Humphrey encountered them everywhere he campaigned. They chanted "Bring the boys home" or "Dump the Hump" and held signs "HHH is LBJ," and "Why Change the Ventriloquist for the Puppet." In Salt Lake City, he angrily told sign wavers, "There is plenty of room for spirited debate but no room for bigotry, hatred or demagoguery." In Minneapolis, he called on McCarthy to join him in denouncing tactics "characteristic of totalitarian politics."[27]

Humphrey's biggest problem was the Vietnam War. He realized that he needed to stake out an independent position to win over the dissidents, but he feared that a bad word from Johnson might cost him support from the regulars and the nomination. When John J. Gilligan, Ohio's senatorial contender, advised Humphrey "not to campaign in a defensive crouch," he insisted that he would not "attack the administration or even hint at such a thing."[28] "I wanted to speak out on what had gone wrong," he said later, "to raise my hopes as national hopes, yet, I was still part of the administration."[29]

Humphrey's staff split on whether he should break with Johnson on the war. O'Brien, Berman, Harris, and Mondale quietly argued that an open break would place Humphrey in a better position to unite the party. O'Brien, who became Humphrey's campaign manager in July, said that he should soften his Vietnam position, and Welsh said that he should "appeal to both those who support past policies and those who do not." But Connell, Freeman, and Rowe argued that "any attempt by Humphrey to fudge up that record might expose him to charges of hypocrisy."[30]

In late July, Humphrey considered adopting an independent bombing halt position. He discussed it with the president. According to O'Brien, Johnson advised him of a major new development on Vietnam and indicated that he was about to take a step that would please the antiwar people. "That was the last I heard of Humphrey's statement," recalled O'Brien.[31]

"He feared Johnson would denounce him," recalled Rowe; and Kampelman insisted, "I don't believe he ever really seriously considered doing it."[32]

As the convention neared, Humphrey began taking a softer line on Vietnam. "Although the plank must not repudiate our policies of yesterday," he declared to a group of Washington journalists, "it might have something in it about a further cessation of bombing." Also, he insisted that he had agreed with the late Robert Kennedy on most Vietnam issues. "His last statements on Vietnam," said Humphrey, "were so close to the ones I was making that I wasn't sure that we'd even be able to have a discussion." "The truth," replied Adam Walinsky, Frank Mankiewicz, Arthur Schlesinger, and Richard Goodwin in a letter to the *New York Times,* "is that the two men were fundamentally opposed in their entire view of the war."[33]

On the eve of the convention, Humphrey was still the frontrunner. His support included the white South, established black organizations, the mayors in the large northern cities, farm groups, President Johnson, the federal bureaucracy, and the AFL-CIO. An early August Gallup poll gave Humphrey a 53 to 39 percent lead over McCarthy as the choice of the Democratic rank-and-file. A week before the convention, *Newsweek* counted Humphrey's delegates at 1,246 (66 short of the 1,312 needed to win) to McCarthy's 800; similarly, a *New York Times* survey gave Humphrey 1,249 to McCarthy's 619. On August 20, O'Brien claimed 1,400 hard votes to McCarthy's 600 with the rest divided between favorite-sons and the uncommitted. "Humphrey had the delegates locked-up," insisted Rauh. "Most of them were chosen even before McCarthy had entered the race."[34]

George McGovern's Entry

In early June, as Kennedy's funeral train slowly inched its way from New York to Washington's Union Station, Gerald Dougherty, family friend and lawyer, approached George McGovern to enter the race. The rift between McCarthy and Kennedy during the primaries, argued Dougherty, ruled out a shift of Kennedy delegates to McCarthy nor could they support Humphrey because of his war policy. Before the train ride was over, McGovern heard the same argument from Adam Walinsky and Peter Edelman; and later, he received telephone calls from Frank Mankiewicz and Joe Dolan urging him to run. But McGovern considered their pleadings premature. If anyone was to enter the race at that point, he told them, it should be Bob's surviving brother, Ted, and he should be given the time to compose his thoughts.[35]

Like McCarthy and Humphrey, McGovern was a liberal from the Midwest. Born on July 19, 1922, McGovern grew up in the small farm town of

Avon, South Dakota. His father was pastor of the Wesleyan Methodist Church and received part of his salary in potatoes and cabbages from a congregation too poor to pay in cash. In World War II, McGovern flew 35 bombing missions over Germany, Austria, and Italy. After the war, he received degrees in political science and history from Dakota Wesleyan and Northwestern University. He won a seat in the United States House of Representatives in 1956, and the Senate in 1962. Standing six feet tall, McGovern was shy and spoke softly with a Midwestern twang. Just before he went overseas in the war, he married the former Eleanor Stegeberg, and they had four girls and a boy.

Throughout the summer, Dougherty, Jesse Unruh, Goodwin, and others continued to urge McGovern to run. His candidacy, they hoped, would provide an outlet for the Kennedy delegates who were uncomfortable with McCarthy and Humphrey. "There was," recalled Goodwin, "a lot of animosity built up in the campaign which hadn't had time to die."[36]

By late July, McGovern had decided to enter the race. First, he called Steve Smith to ask if Edward was planning to enter as Robert's stand-in. "I see no chance of that," replied Smith. "Do you think I should?" asked McGovern. "Well," answered Smith hesitatingly, "I'm not sure. I think I would stop short at the favorite-son role."[37] McGovern then asked Carl Burgess, a Republican friend, whether he should make a bid for the nomination. Instead of answering, he pulled out his checkbook and wrote, "McGovern for President-$5,000." "That was it," recalled McGovern. "I knew I would be in the race."[38]

On August 10, McGovern called a press conference in the Caucus Room of the Old Senate Office Building, and announced his entry. He made no claim "to wear the Kennedy mantle." He said:

> But I believe very deeply in the twin goals for which Robert Kennedy gave his life—an end to the war in Vietnam and a passionate commitment to heal the divisions in our life here at home....
>
> Senator McCarthy has with great dignity and nobility given us a new hope for peace in Vietnam while Vice President Humphrey has long championed the cause of social justice and a progressive America. And if either of these men win the Democratic Presidential nomination, he will have my active support not only for his own considerable merit but because a victory for Mr. Nixon is a disturbing prospect for America....
>
> Whether or not I secure the nomination at Chicago, I would hope that my words and my candidacy may strengthen both the platform and our leadership in those inseparable aspirations of peace abroad and social justice in our own troubled county."[39]

Liberal editorial sentiment ran against McGovern's entry. "If he does see McCarthy as worthy of endorsement," editorialized the *New Republic,* "and does see clearly and sharply that the blocking of the Vice President is imperative, would he not have done better to have come out for McCarthy earlier?"[40] "McGovern's entry," reported the *New York Times,* "was a pincer attack on McCarthy's position by sorehead elements in the party's Kennedy wing and a kind of emotional stand-in for those who nurture the wild hope that the convention may draft Senator Edward M. Kennedy."[41] However, he got some backers. "The vital need is to stop Humphrey," said the *Progressive.* "The McGovern candidacy makes that much more possible because Kennedy supporters who might have gone for Humphrey, for whatever reasons, will now vote for McGovern."[42]

McGovern and supporters, mostly former backers of Robert Kennedy, denied rumors that his candidacy was a holding action for Edward Kennedy. McGovern "did not expect a Kennedy endorsement," "or any attempts by the Kennedy people to use his candidacy to promote a draft movement for the Massachusetts Senator," but if Kennedy entered the race, he admitted that he would withdraw.[43] According to Sorensen, Kennedy did not regard McGovern's candidacy as a "holding action" for his own, but Gans recalled, "It became a convenient place for Kennedy people to hang their hats."[44]

Lester G. Maddox

On August 17, while a high school band played the "Battle Hymn of the Republic" on the capitol steps in Atlanta, Georgia, Governor Lester G. Maddox, a former proprietor of a "whites only" cafe, strode into the statehouse and announced his candidacy to newsmen and supporters. In a twenty-three minute speech, he declared:

> No one is above the law, below the law or beyond the law.... We have been chained by riots and senseless destruction which have turned our cities into battlegrounds and reduced large portions of them to rubble and ashes....
>
> Law enforcement officials must be supported and given the authority to protect themselves and us....
>
> We are in Vietnam because we surrendered to Communism in Cuba and compromised with it in Korea. We are in Vietnam because we have helped to feed, clothe, house, encourage, yes, and strengthened and financed Communism throughout much of the world.
>
> As that great American, General Douglas MacArthur said, there is no substitute for victory.

Few took Maddox's candidacy seriously. Southern observers agreed that he had only fifty or sixty delegates. "Many saw today's announcement," reported the *New York Times,* "as simply a brilliant move to avoid voting in Chicago for one of the 'Socialist' candidates," and to the *Atlanta Constitution,* "Maddox's decision has its cheering aspects. Georgia will have to manage without him if he wins the Presidency."[45]

New frenzy in the war
Vietcong terrorize the cities

SUICIDE RAID ON THE EMBASSY

A guerrilla is
taken alive during the
Embassy battle

FEBRUARY 9 · 1968 · 35¢

The cover of *Life* on February 9, 1968 graphically depicted the daring of the Viet Cong Tet offensive.

The Tet Offensive begins on January 31 and reaches deep inside the U.S. Embassy in Saigon.

U.S. Marines holding the line in Hué during the Tet fighting.

General Westmoreland claimed victory after Tet but the American public thought otherwise.

Eugene McCarthy campaigning for the New Hampshire primary.

George Romney claimed he'd been "brainwashed" in Vietnam and that ended his career.

Anti-war protests grow in the U.S.

War weary LBJ gets ready to throw in the towel.

Martin Luther King just before his murder in Memphis, TN.

Robert F. Kennedy minutes before his assassination at the Ambassador East hotel in Los Angeles.

Deserted *RFK for President* Office in Manhattan the day after his death.

George McGovern made a short bid for the nomination as an anti-war candidate and withdrew.

The 'police riot' outside the Democratic party Convention in Chicago.

Hubert Horatio Humphrey (HHH) and Edmund Muskie: the Democratic Party ticket in 1968.

General Curtis LeMay had the reputation as a super hawk on Vietnam.

George C. Wallace and running mate Curtis Le May the third party candidates.

Hubert Humphrey campaigning in New York City.

"Then there was Nixon and he was a pro." David Broder

"All the News That's Fit to Print"

The New York Times

LATE CITY EDITION

VOL. CXVIII..No.40,465   NEW YORK, THURSDAY, NOVEMBER 7, 1968   10 CENTS

NIXON WINS BY A THIN MARGIN, PLEADS FOR REUNITED NATION

NIXON'S ELECTION EXPECTED TO SLOW PARIS NEGOTIATION

Allied Diplomats Suggest All Sides May Adopt a Wait-and-See Stance

By HEDRICK SMITH

GOAL IS HARMONY

President-Elect Vows His Administration Will Be 'Open'

By ROBERT B. SEMPLE Jr.

ELECTOR VOTE 287

Lead in Popular Tally May Be Smaller Than Kennedy's in '60

By MAX FRANKEL

Soviet Bids U.S. Confer; Calls for 'Normalization'

By RAYMOND H. ANDERSON

REPUBLICANS GAIN SAFE ALBANY EDGE

Lead in Assembly Put at 77-73 and in Senate at 33-24 Unofficially

By JAMES F. CLARITY

Senate's Liberal Coalition Survives Gains by G.O.P.

By DAVID E. ROSENBAUM

Election Tables

POSITION ON SINAI DEFINED BY ISRAEL

Note to Jarring Links Issue of Boundaries to Security Needs and Tiran Rights

By DREW MIDDLETON

The New York Times announces Nixon's 'thin margin' victory.

Lyndon B. Johnson hands over the White House to Richard M. Nixon.

Chapter IX

The Democratic Convention

Arrangements

In 1968, Chicago, once known as the world's largest center for grain, live-stock, and meat packing, had a population of over 3,500,000. The great Chicago industries attracted thousands of unlettered, semiskilled immigrants in the latter half of the nineteenth and early twentieth century. The city developed into a loose conglomeration of ethnic and racial neighborhoods. Regular newspaper and magazine publications could be found in Yiddish, German, Greek, Polish, Swedish, Italian, and Czech. Most of the city's large black population (30 percent of the total) lived in the South Side's "Black Belt" which extended for almost ten miles along Lake Michigan. After Martin Luther King's assassination, arson and looting broke out in this area, and racial tension was still high.

Between August 26 and 29, 3,099 delegates and alternates assembled in Chicago to attend the Democratic National Convention: 2 percent were under 30; 14 percent were women; and 5 percent were black.[1] The primaries produced 966 delegates; the rest were chosen by state conventions, local caucuses, and party appointments. Among prominent Democrats present were governors Harold Hughes of Iowa, Buford Ellington of Tennessee and John Connally of Texas, Senators Daniel Brewster of Maryland, Philip Hart of Michigan and Gale McGee of Wyoming, and Speaker of the California Assembly Jesse Unruh. Convention officers were House Majority Leader Carl Albert, permanent chairman, Senator Daniel Inouye of Hawaii, giver of the keynote speech and temporary chairman, Congressman Hale Boggs of Louisiana, chairman of the Platform Committee, and Governor Samuel Shapiro of Illinois, chairman of the Rules Committee. All were Johnson administration men.

Hotel accommodations appeared adequate, but Democrats were not entirely satisfied with the convention building. They chose the Conrad Hilton, which faced Grant Park and lay between Michigan Avenue and Lake Michigan, as headquarters for the Democratic National Committee and the presidential candidates. Because fire had destroyed the McCormick Place, Chicago's giant lakefront convention hall, the convention was held in the International Amphitheatre, a huge, ugly building near Chicago's stockyards. It was over five miles from the major hotels and close to one of the city's ghettos.

Hosting the convention was Mayor Richard J. Daley, a colorful and powerful figure then in his fourth four-year term. He controlled 38 of the 50 city council members, the school board, the park board, the housing authority, two-thirds of the county board, many suburban offices, and much of the state apparatus. He attended mass daily, abstained from drink, and was known for his personal modesty and honesty. He was also nationally prominent.

John Kennedy owed his close 1960 victory to Daley's Cook County machine, and he had obtained large federal grants from the Kennedy and Johnson administrations. President Johnson ordered the White House switchboard to put all of Daley's calls directly to him. At the convention hall, from his command post facing the podium, Daley would use hand signals to make his desires known to the convention managers. When he approved of their actions, he would clasp his hands like a prize fighter, and when he wanted to drown out the opposition, he would pantomime playing a trombone and the band would play "It's a Grand Old Flag," or "Happy Days Are Here Again."

Since Johnson's men held key control positions at the convention, political observers speculated that he was guiding the proceedings. His most trusted aide, Postmaster General Marvin Watson, oversaw credentials, schedules and arrangements with a staff that included Johnson men Valenti, Joe Califano, and Bill McSweeney. Another Johnson man, John Criswell, the convention's executive director, handled the sound apparatus and could turn the floor microphones on and off at will, "There was plenty of evidence," observed Weaver, "that the convention has been planned by a group of people who would like very much to run it the way they believe Lyndon Johnson wants it run."[2]

Antiwar Protesters

Before the convention assembled on August 26, thousands of antiwar activists and various dissident groups had converged on Chicago to stage demonstrations against the Vietnam War. While the supporters of senators McCarthy, Robert Kennedy, and McGovern would participate, others, often more radical and numerous, included communists, anarchists, hippies, pacifists, poor people's campaigners, civil rights workers, and moderate left-wingers.

The National Mobilization Committee to End the War in Vietnam, a left-leaning coalition, was the principle organization behind the planned demonstrations. Its leaders were David Dellinger, chairman and long-time antiwar activist and Quaker who had served two prison terms in World War II for his pacifist beliefs, and Tom Hayden and Rennie Davis, both former leaders in the Students for a Democratic Society (SDS). In late 1967, they decided to demonstrate at the convention against Johnson's Vietnam policy. If the Democrats wanted to end the war, said Dellinger later, "the protests would force them in that direction."[3] Hayden had a different view. "Our goal is not to influence the delegates in the convention," he told reporters, "but to re-assert the presence and vitality of the anti-war movement."[4]

The National Mobilization was unsuccessful in recruiting black support. Many blacks viewed it as a white-run organization remote from their problems. National groups like the Poor People's Campaign, the Southern Christian Leadership Conference, the Congress of Racial Equality, and the Student Non-Violent Coordinating Committee sought to make their views known inside the convention. Chicago's black organizations, the Woodlawn Organization, the Black Consortium, and Operation Bread-basket, urged the black community to "stay cool" and not get involved in the demonstrations. The violence and upheaval that had occurred during the April 1968, riots, and Daley's remark that in future riots the police would "shoot to kill arsonists and shoot to maim looters" was still fresh in their memory.

Known as the Yippies, the Youth International Party, founded in December, 1967, in an effort to unite the hippies with the new left, also planned a number of protests for the Democratic Convention. Led by former civil rights workers Abbie Hoffman and Jerry Rubin, the Yippies planned to hold workshops, exhibits, demonstrations, rock concerts, and nominate Pigasus, a pig for president. Their literature stated that Yippie males would seduce the wives and daughters of convention delegates, swim nude in Lake Michigan, and insert LSD into the city's water supply. "We did all of this with one purpose in mind," recalled Rubin, "to make the city react as if it were a police state and to focus the attention of the whole world on us."[5]

City officials were reluctant to issue parade and rally permits to the demonstrators. Initially, they had offered the National Mobilization parade permits if its leaders agreed not to carry the march near convention hall, but this offer was refused. The only permit the city issued was for a rally on Wednesday, August 28, in Grant Park. "The authorities," charged Lowenstein, "seem determined to have a confrontation that can only produce violence and bloodshed."[6]

Police, Military, and Convention Security

Daley prepared for trouble. He placed the entire 11,900-man police force on 12-hour shifts, the Cook County sheriff commanded two armored trucks outfitted with heavy weapons, tear gas and mace, and Governor Samuel Shapiro activated 5,600 National Guardsmen, including detachments of infantry, artillery, cavalry, and military police. Guardsmen carried .30-caliber rifles, bayonets, riot-control shotguns, tear gas and orders to shoot to kill if unable to prevent looting and arson. The government mobilized some 7,500 regular army troops equipped with rifles, flame throwers, and bazookas in Texas, Oklahoma, and Colorado and assembled 250 Air Force C-141 jet cargo planes which could airlift the troops to Chicago within 24 hours. A giant serial photograph of Chicago hung in the army's command post in the Pentagon.

Tight security prevailed at the Amphitheatre. With the help of FBI agents, narcotics investigators, military intelligence men, and the Andy Frain private security agency, 1000 Secret Service men coordinated convention security. To enable the Secret Service to monitor all traffic in and out of the Amphitheatre, only one door, a narrow entrance adjacent to the Stockyards Inn, was in use, and convention officials issued plastic cards to the delegates to insert into hip-high electronic validation machines which flashed green for pass and red for stop. Inside the Amphitheatre, security guards armed with rifles, binoculars, and walkie-talkies manned a cat-walk stretching 95 feet above the convention floor; outside, city officials installed a half-mile of linked chain fence topped by a triple strand of barbed wire, sealed all manhole covers in the area with tar, and restricted planes from flying below 2,500 feet over the Amphitheatre.

The Candidates

Humphrey and McCarthy were the leading contenders. If Humphrey could keep his coalition of supporters intact, he would win the nomination. The McCarthyites hoped to "shake things up" by provoking fights on credentials, rules, and platform. Their goal was to force Humphrey to side with the southerners and alienate his northern supporters. "The peace plank is obviously crucial," said McCarthy staffer Jeff Pressman. "The best strategy is necessarily one which provides a stand which Humphrey cannot support, [but] which Kennedy-McCarthy forces can."[7] McCarthy's biggest handicap, however, was his inability to win over the party regulars. To them, observed Halberstam, McCarthy "is just too irregular, too unpredictable, he does not know the language."[8]

On Monday, August 26, Maddox visited with delegates from Alabama, Arkansas, Alaska, and Florida. He explained that his campaign was similar to that of Republican Wendell L. Wilkie's 1940 bid. "Mr. Wilkie," said Maddox, "had few supporters when he arrived at the Republican convention in 1940, but won the nomination." But most of the delegates ignored Maddox, and on Tuesday morning, he withdrew from the race. Before departing for Atlanta on a noon flight, he assailed the Democrats as the party of looting, burning, killing and draft card burning. "What's more," he declared, "I denounce them all."[9]

On Tuesday, Channing E. Phillips, a 40-year-old black minister and the District of Columbia's favorite-son candidate, entered the race. This was the first time a black had ever run for nomination by either major party. He immediately picked up support from the 300 delegates and 6 alternates (out of 337 black delegates and alternates) of the Democratic Black Caucus, but its members privately admitted the gesture was symbolic, and they were committed to other candidates. "We're trying to act in a constructive sense," said Mayor Richard T. Hatcher of Gary, Indiana, "to build a party that will be relevant to a nation made up of many minorities."[10]

Edward Kennedy's attitude towards a run for the nomination was uncertain. After the assassination of his brother Robert, he refused to endorse either Humphrey or McCarthy. In mid-July, two Chicago newspapers, the *Sun-Times* and *Daily News,* advocated a Humphrey-Kennedy ticket. In addition, Humphrey, Governors McKeithen of Louisiana, Hughes of New Jersey, Robert E. McNair of South Carolina, and Samuel H. Shapiro of Illinois, urged Kennedy to consider the vice presidency. Louis Harris reported that a Humphrey-Kennedy ticket would add three to five million more votes for the Democratic Party in the fall.

Kennedy firmly rejected the vice presidency but said nothing about the presidency. Political observers agreed that Kennedy needed to make sure "the votes were there" before making even a private declaration of candidacy. "It didn't seem possible to me," remarked O'Brien, "that Ted, less than three months after Bob's death, could be in any emotional state to run for president."[11] "Conversations with his closest associates in Chicago," reported a McCarthy staffer, "re-affirmed the conviction that Kennedy was not a candidate and would do nothing to stimulate or encourage a draft."[12] But the *New York Times* reported that a number of his friends and associates believed that Kennedy would accept a draft if the National Convention became deadlocked.[13]

The Credentials Committee

Chaired by Governor Hughes of New Jersey, the 110 member Democratic Credentials Committee met at Chicago's Conrad Hilton Hotel from August 19 to August 23. It heard a total of 17 challenges from 15 states and decided in favor of the regulars in all but 3 instances. Two provisions in the Official Call laid the basis for the challenges: the first that each delegate be a loyal Democrat who would participate in "good faith" at the convention, and the second that the delegates be selected without regard to race, creed, color, or national origins. Southern black activists and northern white civil rights workers at the 1964 Democratic convention had obtained a special committee on equal rights to investigate state selection procedures. Its findings and recommendations influenced the outcome of the credential challenges.

The most important battles took place over the Mississippi, Georgia, and Alabama challenges. In the Mississippi case, the Loyal Democrats, a biracial delegation of 22 blacks and 22 whites charged that the regulars denied black participation in precinct, county, and state conventions. The Credentials Committee voted to seat the challengers, and the decision passed the convention by voice vote. Headed by Julian Bond, a 28-year-old black state legislator, Georgia's Loyal National Democrats pointed out that only five of the state party's 100-member executive committee and 7 of the 107 delegates and alternates were black. The Credentials Committee split Georgia's 43 delegates equally between the insurgents and regulars, and the convention adopted the plan by 1,413 to 1,014. In the Alabama case, the insurgents hoped to replace regulars who might refuse to take the party's loyalty oath, but all did take it.

The Platform Committee

Between August 19 and August 21, the 110 member Platform Committee, chaired by Hale Boggs of Louisiana, the House Democratic whip, met in Washington's Statler Hotel and reassembled August 22 to August 25 at the Amphitheatre. About 40 of the 110 members leaned towards the dovish side. (A minority report required only 11 dissenting votes.) The Vietnam War was the foremost issue.

Through Boggs and unofficial platform adviser Charles Murphy, President Johnson exerted considerable influence over the Platform Committee. He wanted to make sure his Vietnam policy was approved by the convention. The wording of the Vietnam plank was crucial. He had picked Boggs for chairman because he was on the hawkish side and, along with Murphy, had direct phone communication with Johnson.[14]

On August 17, two days before the Platform Committee assembled at Washington's Statler Hilton, McCarthy had submitted a Vietnam plank. It advocated a general de-escalation of the war, an unconditional bombing halt, and establishment of a coalition government in South Vietnam that would include substantial participation by the National Liberation Front. "If the present leaders of South Vietnam refuse to agree to such a broadly based coalition," the plank read, "we will then withdraw our support and our forces since an honorable peace will no longer be possible."[15]

On Monday, August 19, the first day of the platform hearings, Senator Edmund S. Muskie of Maine, presenting Humphrey's position, called for a conditional bombing halt. He would not insist, as McCarthy did, on initial NLF participation in a coalition government. Also, he said that the Democratic platform should not prescribe tactical military and diplomatic moves.[16]

The Unity Peace Plank and Rusk Testimony

On August 1, some McCarthy staffers, former Kennedy aides and McGovern advisors assembled at Washington's Carroll Arms, a restaurant just behind the Old Senate Office Building. The group included Clark, Rauh, Mankiewicz, Dutton, O'Connell, Gilligan, Sorensen, and dovish senators Claiborne Pell of Rhode Island and Wayne Morse of Oregon. They agreed on the need for a single peace plank not tied to any one candidate. They were not anti-Humphrey, believed that Humphrey was going to be nominated and wanted to provide him with a peace plank that he could win on.[17]

On Tuesday, August 20, the unity plank, written by Dutton, Goodwin, Sorensen and Gilligan, was submitted to the Platform Committee. It called for a halt to the bombing of North Vietnam, a cease-fire, and negotiations between the Saigon Government and the National Liberation Front. McCarthy partisans called it weak.

That evening Boggs called in Secretary of State Dean Rusk to defend the administration's position. Rusk advised committee members not to outline tactics and strategy, and he said that to offer an immediate bombing halt without a response from Hanoi would be a dangerous concession. When he finished, Galbraith narrowly beat Gilligan in a race to the questioner's microphone, but Boggs halted the proceedings. He just learned, he said, that the Soviets had invaded Czechoslovakia. Rusk excused himself: "I think I ought to see what this is all about."[18]

The Soviet Invasion of Czechoslovakia

On August 20, in response to the liberalized regime of Alexander Dubček, 200,000 Soviet troops invaded Czechoslovakia. The Soviet invasion frustrated Johnson's hopes for a summit conference, the main intent of which, said George Christian, "was to get the Soviets to pressure the North Vietnamese for a negotiated settlement."[19] "From a successful summit in Europe," observed Theodore White, "a quick flight would bring him as peacemaker to a cheering convention in Chicago—and then, who could guess what might happen?"[20]

Of the Soviet invasion, McCarthy said it was not a major world crisis, and the United States could have done little to stop it. To some, he appeared to have underreacted. His response, insisted Governor Connally, only hinders the Paris negotiations."[21] "He has weakened his position," editorialized the *New York Times;* the *Los Angeles Times* added, "He has pretty well forfeited any right to serious consideration for his candidacy."[22]

A Minority Vietnam Plank

On Friday, August 23, the doves united behind a Vietnam plank. The various Vietnam planks had produced three main areas of friction with the Humphreyites: (1) the word "unconditional" in relation to a bombing halt, (2) the description of the conflict as a civil war, (3) the imposition of a coalition government on South Vietnam. The new plank, drafted by Goodwin, Salinger, Sorensen, Gilligan, and William Clark of Illinois, and released to the press on Friday evening, compromised on points two and three, but the doves would not compromise on an "unconditional" bombing halt. "Otherwise," insisted Sorensen, "it was deliberately mild."[23] It said:

> That war must be ended now. It will not be ended by a military victory, surrender or unilateral withdrawal by either side; it cannot be ended by further United States escalation, either increasing our troops, introducing nuclear

weapons, or extending the conflict geographically: it must therefore be ended by a fair and realistic compromise settlement....

We will then negotiate a mutual withdrawal of all United States forces and all North Vietnamese troops from South Vietnam. This should be a phased withdrawal over a relatively short period of time....

The South Vietnamese will assume increasing responsibility for the resolution of the conflict, and full responsibility for determining their own political destiny....

We will lower the level of violence by reducing offensive operations in the Vietnamese countryside, thus enabling an early withdrawal of a significant number of our troops.

In this way we can eliminate all foreign forces from South Vietnam. Our troops will leave and those of North Vietnam will also depart. It will be up to the South Vietnamese to achieve a political and social reconciliation among their warring peoples.[24]

Around midnight, Gilligan and Ginsburg joined William Geoghegan in his room at the Conrad Hilton. Hoping to find common ground, they compared the minority plank to Ginsburg's plank, favored by Humphrey. "Every word, every nuance became significant," said Geoghegan later, "but the basic question was over adoption of a conditional or unconditional bombing halt."[25] "There were substantial differences," recalled Ginsburg. "everybody was locked in."[26]

Johnson Influences the Vietnam Plank

At the White House the next morning, Saturday, August 24, Johnson met with Boggs, Albert and Senator Jennings Randolph of West Virginia. Officially, Johnson had summoned them back from Chicago to explain the Czechoslovakian crisis, but his real motive was to influence them on the Vietnam plank, and he had Westmoreland present. "If the bombing were stopped," said Johnson, "the enemy's capability in the area of the DMZ would increase by 500 percent." "A bombing halt," General Westmoreland told them, "would endanger the lives of American troops."[27] "If the President would not accept the plank," replied Boggs, then he would send out the word that the plank was unacceptable.[28]

On Sunday evening, Ginsburg and Murphy joined Boggs at his hotel suite. "The language of Ginsburg's draft was unacceptable to the President," recalled Murphy, "particularly on the issue of the bombing halt."[29] Boggs was "unwilling to serve as chairman of the platform committee if substantial differences existed between the president and the probable nominee of the party."[30] Ginsburg's bombing halt clause read: "Stop the bombing of North Vietnam. This action and its timing shall take into account the security of our troops and the likelihood of a response from Hanoi." But Murphy said Johnson preferred to: "Stop all bombing of North Vietnam when this action would not endanger the lives of our troops in the field; this action should take into account the response from Hanoi."[31]

When Ginsburg told Humphrey that the President was not satisfied with the plank, he called Johnson. Humphrey stressed that Rusk and Rostow supported it, but Johnson was not persuaded. "In the gentlest words I could muster," recalled Humphrey, "I told the President that I thought the plank was acceptable and not offensive." Johnson replied that the plank undercut his whole policy, and he would have no part of it. He was immovable.[32]

The next morning Humphrey made the demanded changes in Ginsburg's plank. He feared Johnson's anger. "Johnson enraged," recalled Humphrey, "would have been a formidable foe."[33] Apparently, he feared that Johnson would have denied him the nomination.[34] "But who would it have gone to?" asked Goodwin later.[35] "Johnson was not going to have the convention or the party publically repudiate him," recalled Gilligan, "even if he had to tear the place to pieces and that's what terrified Humphrey."[36]

But despite Johnson's intervention, considerable doubt remained whether the supporters of the minority plank would have supported Ginsburg's plank, which Humphrey endorsed. Although its bombing halt clause was less conditional than Johnson's, the minority faction demanded an unconditional bombing halt. And compromise attempts on this issue had failed.

The Platform

On Monday, August 26, the Platform Committee released the Democratic platform to the press. While the delegates generally agreed with the domestic planks, they split over the Johnson Vietnam plank. The doves filed a minority report to take to the convention floor.

The Vietnam plank followed the administration's position. It supported the Paris talks and called for an honorable and lasting settlement. It rejected unilateral withdrawal of American forces, but it would not demand unconditional surrender by the communists. Like the Republican platform, the Democratic platform called for eventual South Vietnamese takeover of their nation's defenses. But while the Republicans advocated a progressive de-Americanization of the war, both military and civilian, the Democrats gave no indication that an expanded Vietnamese role would lead to American troop reductions in the near future. The all-important bombing halt clause read, "Stop all bombing of North Vietnam when this action would not endanger the lives of our troops in the field. This action should take into account the response from Hanoi."

Unlike the Republicans, the Democratic platform avoided the phrase "law and order." It pledged renewed efforts against riots, organized crime, and narcotics but said that fighting crime must not foster injustices: "Lawlessness cannot be ended by curtailing the hard-won liberties of all Americans."

The platform promised to enforce the provisions in the Civil Rights Act. Although it proposed no new civil rights legislation, it pledged "first priority" to legislation long pending in Congress to strengthen the enforcement powers of the Equal Employment Opportunity Commission (EEOC) and endorsed the goal of open housing required under the 1968 civil rights law and renewed the party's commitment to liberal domestic programs and full employment. It promised to replace "the present inequitable, underfinanced, hodge-podge state plans "for welfare aid to the aged, disabled and dependent children and establish federal standards for payments and eligibility. On jobs, it pledged to expand current programs for the hardcore unemployed and endorsed the federal antipoverty programs: the Neighborhood Youth Corps, Head Start, and community action agencies.

The platform called for a strong and balanced national defense along with arms control agreements. It pledged a defense adequate to the task of security and peace. But "defense measures and arms control measures must go hand-in-hand, each serving national security and the larger interests of peace."[37]

To some, Humphrey's acceptance of the Johnson Vietnam plank was a mistake. "It is not exactly the way I personally would have written it," Fred Harris told newsmen.[38] "Humphrey's position," reported the *Miami Herald,* "is a carbon copy of Johnson's policy"; and the *New York Times* added, "Humphrey cannot pretend otherwise."[39] "Now the lines are clearly drawn," declared McCarthy, "and the convention, as a whole, will decide."[40]

Democratic Reforms

Shortly before the convention assembled, McCarthy supporters organized a nonpartisan group to document undemocratic procedures in the delegate selection process. Called the Commission on the Democratic Selection of Presidential Nominees and headed by Governor Hughes of

Iowa, its members discovered numerous undemocratic practices. Over 600 delegates were chosen two years before the convention. Some states did not have written guidelines on delegate selection, and in others, one or more party leaders picked the delegates at unpublicized meetings or caucuses. Those states which operated under the unit rule (Alaska, Arkansas, Georgia, Kansas, Louisiana, Missouri, South Carolina, Tennessee, and Texas), made it impossible for candidates who received less than a majority of the vote in a caucus, convention or primary election to receive any delegates at all.

When the 110 member Rules Committee, chaired by Illinois Governor Shapiro, convened at Chicago's Conrad Hilton Hotel, on August 22 and 23, Hughes submitted the Commission's report. "To an extent not matched since the turn of the twentieth century," it said, "events in 1968 have called into question the integrity of the convention system for nominating presidential candidates."[41] It called for abolishment of the unit rule, delegate selection no earlier than six months before the convention, and a system of proportional representation for minorities. It provided a vitally needed agenda for the improvement of the convention process, said newsman Broder, by attempting to put the one-man, one-vote principle into effect in party affairs.[42]

Just prior to this, Humphrey had sent a letter to the Rules Committee supporting the Hughes report's recommendation to abolish the unit rule for the 1968 convention. Since party sentiment was running against it, Humphrey hoped to place himself on record as favoring democratic procedures. Connally was angry. "He was told one thing," he said, "and then Humphrey did another." "Deeply penitent," Humphrey assured Connally that "the unit rule thing had been a dreadful bureaucratic mix-up," and he would do his best to rectify the mistake.[43]

At a press conference on Friday evening, August 23, Shapiro announced that the Rules Committee had adopted a freedom of conscience resolution suspending application of the unit rule for the 1968 convention. In addition, it created an interim Rules Study Commission to make recommendations on rules changes for the 1972 convention. The McCarthy forces, concluded Mitchell, "won the battle which the Senator himself began long ago in May."[44]

On Saturday afternoon, August 24, Goodwin, at Patrick Lucey's suggestion, called on Connally to discuss the possibility of a McCarthy-Connally alliance. If Connally became McCarthy's running mate, Lucey reasoned, the South might desert Humphrey for McCarthy.[45] According to Herzog, "They played cat-and-mouse on the question of a McCarthy-Connally ticket and Connally did not say no."[46] Later Goodwin, looking "mysteriously optimistic," offered to bet any takers that McCarthy would get the nomination. Although McCarthy must have known about the negotiations, he told his staff "he would rather lose the nomination" than consider Connally as a running mate.[47]

On Monday, August 26, the convention adopted the Rules Committee's unit rule resolution and freed the delegates to vote their consciences. "They have abolished the unit rule with scant concern for the sensitivities of the great state of Texas," editorialized the *Washington Post,* "and have rubbed it in by making the new rules apply at this convention, rather than the next."[48]

The next day the convention approved far-reaching reforms for the 1972 convention. It approved the Rules Committee's minority proposal to abolish the unit rule down to the precinct level and to provide for timely selection of convention delegates beginning in 1972. It established a committee to study state delegates selection processes and to recommend improvements and a committee to insure full participation of all Democrats without regard to race, color, creed or national origin. "The changes in the rules do not sound remarkable," observed the *Washington Post.* "But they will work to open up the Party as never before to minorities and make a closed convention much harder to come by in the future."[49] These reforms, insisted McGovern later, "were the only favorable results of the Chicago convention."[50]

Pre-Convention Clashes

On Thursday, August 22, a few blocks south of Grant Avenue, the police killed Jerome Johnson, a 17-year-old South Dakota Indian. They fired, said police, only after Johnson, identified as a Yippie, fired at them. "We don't want to go overboard in ascribing malevolent intentions to the police," said one demonstrator, "but obviously things are going to be getting very rough here."[51]

The next day, in front of Chicago's Civic Center Plaza, before a crowd of about 250 persons shouting "Pork Power," several Yippies nominated a pig, called Pigasus, for president. "The pig," said one Yippie, "was an ideal candidate because he was born in Montana, is 35 years old, studied law by candlelight for three years and walked five miles through the snow to school plus the fact that he is affiliated with the Roman Catholic and Protestant churches in addition to being a Jew."[52] The police arrested six Yuppies, including Rubin, and locked up Pigasus at the Chicago Humane Society.

On Sunday evening, August 25, in Lincoln Park, the first clash between police and demonstrators occurred. As the 11 o'clock curfew approached, about 200 persons remained in the park. At 11 o'clock, three lines of police, about 60 men, cleared the park and arrested 11 persons for disorderly conduct. "If the curfew ordinance was not enforced," insisted a policeman, "Yippies and others would take it as a sign of weakness; you can't give in to those people."[53]

A Johnson Boomlet

Three days before the convention, a draft Johnson boomlet threatened Humphrey's hold on the South. There was growing sentiment among southerners that Governor Connally should withdraw as a favorite son and nominate Johnson. In that cause, Chairman James Gray of Georgia urged southern favorite sons to remain uncommitted. Governor McKeithen of Louisiana shifted support for Humphrey to favorite son status, and Chairman Robert S. Vance of Alabama advocated a southern move "to rally around the president."[54]

But Johnson publically rejected the rising draft sentiment. Speaking at his alma mater, Southwest Texas State College, on August 24, he declared, "I am not a candidate for anything, except maybe a rocking chair." According to Christian, the rocking chair statement "took the wind out of the draft movement." The following day Connally informed the press that the Texas delegation had no plans to nominate the president. "It is not in accord with his wishes, and we are not here to promote a draft."[55] Reaction differed on whether Johnson ever reconsidered renomination. "Johnson," insisted Murphy later, "had given no hint of reconsideration," and Mary Rather, his personal secretary added, "He had no regrets about withdrawal."[56] "He had used up his capacity to govern," recalled Rostow, and Gilligan said, "Most people did not take it seriously,"[57] but others said he was receptive. "That was why Humphrey was running like a scared rabbit," recalled Gans. "If Hubert should falter," added Sam Johnson, Lyndon's brother, "Lyndon might decide to let the convention nominate him."[58] "Not even after the election," observed Theodore White, "would Humphrey confirm or deny an imminent Johnson sell-out."[59]

Johnson Cancels Convention Visit

Late Tuesday afternoon, August 27, Johnson announced to the press that he would not attend his birthday celebration planned by Daley, at Soldier Field Stadium. He said that the delegates might interpret his appearance in Chicago as an attempt to control the convention, and the Secret

Service was not all that confident about the prospect of being able to protect him. But shortly before his announcement, Boggs cautioned Johnson that if he came to Chicago, his presence "would inflame passions during the Vietnam debate," and Daley told him that "he would likely be booed."[60] According to Busby, "We were just plain outnumbered."[61]

An Edward Kennedy Boomlet

On Friday, August 23, Senator Edward Kennedy sent his brother-in-law, Stephen Smith, to Chicago, to gauge the strength of a draft movement with orders to "avoid at all costs creating the impression of a stark lunge for power."[62] Smith informed Daley that Kennedy was looking for a draft but would not start it, and Daley agreed to wait 48 hours before committing his delegation to a candidate. "Without the South, and without Daley," recalled Goodwin, "Humphrey might be stopped on the first ballot, and then it would be a new convention."[63]

On Sunday evening, August 25, a draft Kennedy movement had surfaced, and by Monday, a full-scale boomlet was in progress. On Sunday, Ohio's former Governor Michael V. DiSalle set up a Kennedy headquarters in his room at the Sherman House. While supporters distributed white stickers with big red letters saying "Draft Ted," high school girls sat on the floor scrawling makeshifts posters. By Monday, Kennedy headquarters moved out of DiSalle's tiny room into larger space on the first floor of the Sherman House and reserved twenty rooms at the Knickerbocker Hotel. By midday, draft Kennedy talk was heard at every bar, restaurant and gathering place in town. Informal polls showed Kennedy's strength rising among the delegates. Governor Shapiro called him a great American, and the California delegation began circulating petitions calling for Kennedy's nomination.

Humphrey skillfully used the Kennedy boomlet to woo wavering southerners. He played on the South's fear of a Kennedy nomination and reassured southerners that he would not pick a running mate unacceptable to them. On Monday and Tuesday, favorite-son governors Buford Ellington of Tennessee, Robert E. McNair of South Carolina, and Connally of Texas, and Senator Smathers of Florida, released their delegates to support Humphrey.

Late Tuesday afternoon, August 27, Smith and McCarthy joined Goodwin in his room at the Conrad Hilton. "I did not initiate the meeting," insisted McCarthy. "Intermediaries suggested to Steve Smith that I wanted to see him in much the same way that they suggested to me that he wished to see me." He told Smith that he could not get the nomination and that he was now willing to ask his delegates to vote for Kennedy. Smith listened but did not commit himself. Before they adjourned, McCarthy said, "I could not have done the same for Senator Robert Kennedy."[64] Smith froze! According to Theodore White, "Smith's emotions still flare with anger as he recalls it."[65]

Throughout Monday and Tuesday, Daley had prodded Smith to get Kennedy to announce. By Tuesday evening, Daley's patience had run out, and he phoned Kennedy to say that he would now throw his support to Humphrey. Without Daley, Kennedy had no choice but to call a halt to the draft movement. He phoned McGovern and Humphrey. "He indicated," recalled McGovern, "that if Daley and others had publicly committed their support, he might have entered the competition."[66] Kennedy told Humphrey:

> "I have been listening, but I am now not a candidate."
> "Is it unequivocal?"
> "Yes."
> "Is the door ajar or unlocked—is the key in it or is it locked," Hubert persisted.
> "The door is locked," Ted told him.[67]

Some argued that Kennedy was not serious about the draft move. "It was an emotionally trying time," recalled Melody Miller; and added Gilligan, "The whole notion of a presidential campaign was absolutely beyond him."[68] Geoghegan agreed, "He was still in total grief."[69] "Kennedy had been in the Senate less than six years," said Sorensen later, "And he saw no reason why he should get in the way of party leaders."[70] According to Sam Brown, "He just never had the fire for it."[71]

Police and Demonstrators Battle

On Monday evening, police enforced Lincoln Park's 11 o'clock curfew. Three hundred policemen, wearing plexiglass face shields and using tear gas, forced 3000 demonstrators into the surrounding streets. Police moved everywhere in pursuit, up streets, walks, and into hallways. "Whether the violence is a matter of policy," editorialized the *Washington Post*, "is not yet altogether clear but very little has yet been done by Mayor Daley to restrain or control it."[72]

On Tuesday evening, after the police again used tear gas to enforce Lincoln Park's 11 o'clock curfew, 2000 demonstrators gathered at Grant Park, where the police allowed them to remain overnight. Folk singers Mary

Travers and Peter Yarrow sang "Blowing in the Wind," "If I Had a Hammer," and "This Land Is My Land." A few delegates drifted into the park and delivered testimonials of their faith in dissent. One speaker, a priest, urged observers in the hotel rooms across the street to "blink your lights if you're with us"; and to the cheers of the crowd, at least fifteen lights in the Conrad Hilton flicked on and off. By now, the exhausted police had asked for assistance from the National Guard. "It was clear the Chicago police had 'had it,'" said a *Washington Post* reporter, and "the kids knew they had made them 'lose their cool.'"[73] At 3 o'clock in the morning, 30 guard vehicles carrying 600 men in full battle dress, with guns, ammunition, and gas, arrived in front of the Conrad Hilton on Michigan Avenue. Their presence increased the tension, but an uneasy truce developed after the Guard assured the demonstrators that they were there only to relieve the police. By dawn, the crowd had dwindled to about 200.

Vietnam Floor Debate

Early Wednesday morning, the doves forced postponement of the Vietnam plank debate. The delegates were tired and irritable, and the doves suspected that the proadministration forces had purposely delayed the debate to deprive them of needed television exposure. According to Gilligan, "they were doing everything they could to submerge the fight."[74] When Boggs asked the clerk to read both the majority and minority planks, the Wisconsin delegation began waving its banner to gain recognition. At first, Boggs and Albert ignored them, but other delegations, notably Missouri, West Virginia, and Ohio, started clapping and shouting in support of Wisconsin's attempts at recognition. Finally, Wisconsin's Chairman Donald Peterson got the floor. He moved to adjourn until 4 o'clock in the afternoon. Albert ruled it an "unrecognizable motion" which generated "a great chorus of boos" that gradually turned into a thunderous chant: "Let's go home, let's go home!" Bailey and Criswell made the television "cut it" signal—fingers slashed across their throats—to Daley. Taking the cue, Daley motioned for adjournment.

Against a backdrop of sporadic chants of "stop the war," the Vietnam plank debate resumed late Wednesday afternoon. Speaking for the majority position, Boggs stressed the importance of supporting a conditional bombing halt. He quoted General Abrams:

> If the bombing in North Vietnam now authorized were to be suspended unilaterally, the enemy in ten days to two weeks could develop a capability in the DMZ area in terms of scale, intensity and duration of combat on the order of five times what he now has.

Sorensen summarized the minority position. He claimed that the plank was not a camouflaged position for surrender or a call for unilateral withdrawal but a change towards peace. He said that the two planks differed in four ways:

> First, we call for an end to the bombing now—they call for an end if and when or maybe.
>
> Second, we call for a mutual withdrawal of all U.S. and North Vietnamese troops now.... The majority plank says maybe, sometime, if all Vietcong hostilities can somehow cease first.
>
> Third, we call for letting the South Vietnamese decide for themselves the shape of their own future. They call for the United States to stay and conform the Vietnamese to our political and economic standards.
>
> Fourth, we call for a reduction of American troops now by reducing our offensive operation. They call for a reduction in troops only when the South Vietnamese Army can take over if that ever comes to pass.[75]

By 1,567 to 1,041, the delegates defeated the minority plank. This produced an outpouring of emotion. Delegates from New York, California, Wisconsin, Colorado, Oregon, and New Hampshire tied black bands around their arms and pinned black crepe on their badges. Hundreds broke into a moaning rendition of "We Shall Overcome." Some knelt in prayer. Cries of "Shalom" and "Amen" were heard. The convention orchestra tried to drown them out with "California Here We Come" and "We've Got a Lot of Living to Do." By 5 o'clock the short demonstration was over. But now, unless the nominee repudiated the Vietnam plank, the division within the party appeared irreconcilable.

Nominations and Balloting

Nomination speeches, beginning at 8:30 Wednesday evening, took almost three hours. Governor Hughes of Iowa called McCarthy the "people's candidate" who would not approach today's problems with yesterday's solutions. Mayor Alioto of San Francisco emphasized Humphrey's liberal record while carefully avoiding the divisive Vietnam issue. Senator Abraham Ribicoff of Connecticut called McGovern the best candidate for America's youth and a man with a solution to Vietnam other than "napalm and gas." And Phillips M. Stern, a District of Columbia delegate, said that Channing Phillips was qualified by experience for the presidency and charged that traditional "experienced leadership has resulted in the barbed wire and helmeted troops."[76]

A little after 11 o'clock, Chairman Albert began the roll-call balloting for president. It lasted less than an hour. Although the two largest delegations, New York and California, cast only 110 of their collective 364 votes for Humphrey, the release of favorite-son senators Stephen Young of Ohio and Birch Bayh of Indiana and Governor Hughes of New Jersey indicated an early Humphrey victory. Illinois gave Humphrey 112 votes; Texas 100 of its votes; and Pennsylvania's 103 votes pushed him past the magic 1,311 votes needed for nomination. The final totals showed Humphrey with 1, 761, McCarthy 601, McGovern 146, and Phillips 67.

Outside his Conrad Hilton suite, Humphrey told cheering supporters, "We are on the victory trail." He appealed for the help of young people in the campaign against Nixon and admitted that the violence in the streets had marred the joy of winning. "Democracy," he said "does not require force or brutality or violence. What it requires are reason, tolerance and forbearance."[77]

The Reaction to Humphrey's Nomination

While McCarthy withheld endorsement, Edward Kennedy and George McGovern pledged their full support to the ticket. Kennedy offered to stump for Humphrey, and McGovern urged his antiwar supporters to back Humphrey but to condition their support on "our faith that now that he is his own man he is going to move in a different direction in Vietnam."[78]

Editorial comment was sympathetic to Humphrey's nomination. "If the Vice President is slightly old fashioned," said Kraft, "he is a good man for fending off the peril of a premature social conflict."[79] "There's still fire in the ashes of the Democratic Party," declared Drummond, and Humphrey is the man who can "Kindle the ashes into flames."[80] "Humphrey confronts a Herculean task," said Evans and Novak, "in attracting Party workers in California and New York—states whose support he desperately needs against Richard M. Nixon."[81] "Only if he is his own man," editorialized the *New York Times,* "making up his own mind, can he hope to lead the nation after November."[82]

Wednesday's Violence

Late Wednesday afternoon, violence broke out in Grant Park. While a speaker was urging draft resistance to an audience estimated in the thousands, a young demonstrator shinnied up a flagpole and lowered the American flag. When the police arrested him, some of the demonstrators started throwing stones and bottles. The police retreated with the arrested youth in hand. According to a *Denver Post* reporter, someone on the stage yelled into the microphone, "Stop throwing things! Stop throwing things."

Shortly thereafter, about fifty policeman waded into the crowd and, flailing with their clubs in all directions, "appeared to have lost all control."[83]

The entire melee, from the first sighting of the boy on the flagpole to the end of the police charge, took place in less than 20 minutes.

At around 8 o'clock Wednesday evening, about 3,000 demonstrators and spectators gathered east of a police line along the two blocks of Grant Park opposite the Conrad Hilton. The crowd included a blend of hippies, straights, newsmen, and cameramen. Some wore helmets, others carried gas masks, and a few were armed with rocks, sticks, and bottles. They faced 300 policemen equipped with helmets, batons, mace aerosol tear gas cans, and revolvers. Behind the police lines, in front of the Conrad Hilton, the fire department set up a high pressure pumper truck. While police loudspeakers ordered the crowd to move to the park area, the protest leaders shouted into loudspeakers, "You don't have to go. Hell no, don't go!" The chant "Pigs, Pigs, Pigs, Pigs" went up.

The police charged into the crowd. It was the most violent clash of the convention week. "All things happen too fast," reported Theodore White: "First, the charge as the police wedge cleaves through the mob; then screams, whistles, confusion, people running off into Grant Park, across the bridges, into hotel lobbies."[84] In the heat of the melee a number of by-standers became trapped in front of the big plate glass window of the Con-rad Hilton's Haymarket Lounge. The window shattered, and screaming men and women tumbled through, some cut badly by jagged glass. A squad of policemen burst into the bar, clubbing indiscriminately, at the same time shouting over and over, "we've got to clear this area."[85]

The Vice Presidential Selection

While the violence continued in the streets, Humphrey and staff assembled in his Conrad Hilton Hotel room to consider a vice presidential choice.

Prior to the convention, Humphrey had considered several staff men for the second spot. Edward Kennedy was Humphrey's first choice, but he declined the offer. Others considered included Mayor Alioto of San Francisco, to help carry California; Cyrus Vance (once deputy Secretary of Defense, but at that moment negotiating with the North Vietnamese in Paris), to add a nonpolitical dimension to the ticket; Senator Fred Harris of Oklahoma, to mollify the South; and Senator Muskie, to appeal to the Catholic and Polish vote. For a time Humphrey even considered Nelson Rockefeller. But despite his hostility toward Nixon and affection for me," recalled Humphrey, "he felt he had to remain a Republican."[86]

By 3 o'clock Thursday morning, August 29, Humphrey had narrowed his choices to Harris and Muskie. At first, Humphrey leaned towards Harris. But it was felt, recalled O'Brien, that Fred was a little too young (37 years old), and "did not provide geographical balance for the ticket."[87] "When it came down to making a choice between Harris and Muskie," Humphrey told Mondale later, "I went for the quiet man. I know I talk too much," and "two Hubert Humphreys might be one too many."[88]

Fifty-four years old, Muskie was noted for his quiet voice and calm, reasoned approach to problems. He had served as state legislator, governor, and senator. In 1954, he became Maine's first Democratic governor in twenty years. He followed a nonpartisan course which proved helpful in steering his programs through the Republican legislature. In 1958, he became senator. Majority Leader Lyndon Johnson regarded Muskie as "a real powerhouse," said a White House aide, "one of the few liberals who's a match for the southern legislative craftsmen."[89] On Vietnam, Muskie was more dovish than Humphrey. "Recently," reported newsman Steven Roberts, "Muskie confirmed that he had written to President Johnson privately last February [1968], and urged a halt to the bombing."[90]

Two names were placed in nomination for vice president. Fred Harris nominated Muskie, and Wisconsin's Vice Chairman Ted Warshafsky nominated Julian Bond. Because he was not yet the required 35 years old, his nomination was only a symbolic gesture. In the middle of the balloting, Daley successfully moved to suspend the rules and declare Muskie the nominee by acclamation.

The press agreed that Muskie was a good vice presidential choice. "His selection," editorialized the *New York Times,* "is not a concession to any particular faction and, if it arouses no marked enthusiasm among his fellow

Democrats, neither does it provoke dismay or outrage."[91] His qualities said the *Washington Post,* "ought to make him, if elected, a loyal and helpful Vice President."[92] "Surely," observed the *Miami Herald,* "he fills the first criterion in Mr. Humphrey's questioning mind: could he be a President? Yes."[93]

Humphrey's Acceptance Speech

Late Thursday evening, Hubert Humphrey took the podium amid outbursts of pro- and anti-Daley shouts from the galleries. "I have never had a more difficult assignment," recalled Humphrey. "It tested every nerve in my body," and it tested his capacity to sway an audience, to "hold a party together that was on the verge of an explosion that would have fractured it for a long, long time."[94] He opened, "Violence breeds counterviolence and

it cannot be condoned, whatever the sources." He quoted St. Francis of
Assisi:

> Listen to this immortal saint: "Where there is hatred, let me know love.
> Where there is injury, pardon. Where there is doubt, faith. Where there is
> despair, hope. Where there is darkness, light."
>
> Those are the words of a saint. And may those of us of less purity listen
> to them well and may Americans tonight resolve that never, never again shall
> we see what we have seen.[95]

Humphrey praised Johnson's domestic accomplishments. (It was the
first time his name had been mentioned since opening night). The delegates
burst into cheers and boos, but Humphrey continued above the sound:

> President Johnson has accomplished more of the unfinished business of
> America than any of his modern predecessors.
>
> And I truly believe that history will surely record the greatness of his con-
> tribution of the people of this land.
>
> And tonight to you, Mr. President, I say thank you, Thank You, Mr.
> President.

Humphrey spoke on three issues. The first was Vietnam.

> Let those who believe that our cause in Vietnam has been right, or those
> who believe that it has been wrong, agree here and now, that neither vindica-
> tion nor repudiation will being peace or be worthy of this country!
>
> I pledge to you and to my fellow Americans that I will do everything
> within my power, within the limits of my capacity and ability to aid the nego-
> tiation and to bring a prompt end to this war!

The second issue was domestic peace. "We do not want a police state,"
declared Humphrey. "Neither mob violence nor police brutality have any
place in America." Third, he asked for unity:

> We must make a great decision. Are we to be one nation, or are we to be a
> nation divided, divided between black and white, between rich and poor,
> between north and south, between young and old? I take my stand—we are
> and we must be one nation, united by liberty and justice for all, one nation,
> under God, indivisible with liberty and justice for all. This is our America....
>
> To my friends Gene McCarthy and George McGovern ... to these two
> good Americans: I ask your help in this difficult campaign that lies ahead. And
> now I appeal, I appeal to those thousands—yes, millions of young Americans
> to join us.... Never were you needed so much, and never could you do so
> much if you want to help now.

Humphrey concluded:

> And I say to America. Put aside recrimination and dissension. Turn away from violence and hatred. Believe—believe in what America can do, and believe in what America can be, and with the help of that vast, unfrightened, dedicated, faithful majority of Americans, I say to this great convention tonight, and to this great nation of ours, I am ready to lead our country.[96]

Humphrey had won the nomination at a terrible price. Forced to reject Ginsburg's compromise Vietnam plank that he preferred, he had accepted Johnson's Vietnam plank and thereby lost whatever chance still existed to persuade the doves to support him. In addition, the violence in the streets emphasized his identification with a party that public sentiment blamed for the recurring riots and disorders.

Although Humphrey's nomination was a victory for the regulars, many feared that close identification with the national ticket would hurt their own local, state, and congressional campaigns. Consequently, he entered the general election without the active support of his own party.

Final Protest Activities

On Thursday evening, Dick Gregory, black comedian and social activist, invited 3,000 demonstrators in Grant Park to accompany him to his home, located south of the Amphitheatre. With Gregory in the lead, the demonstrators, including the Reverend Richard Neuhaus and 26 delegates, walked three abreast heading south out of Grant Park. Several blocks later they encountered a double line of guardsmen, a personnel carrier with a 30mm gun stop, jeeps with protective "bird cages" over the cab and 6x6-foot barbed wire frames mounted on front. A small contingent of police were also present. Guard officials explained that the Secret Service insisted that the marchers could go no farther. Gregory replied that he was only taking some friends home with him. He advised those unwilling to seek arrest to return to Grant Park, but those willing to face arrest should follow him into the "zone of arrest." The Guard arrested 79 persons and used tear gas to disperse the crowd.[97]

Meanwhile, at Grant Park, guardsmen and demonstrators began an uneasy truce. The Guard informed the crowd that they could stay in Grant Park, but could not cross Michigan Avenue. Some demonstrators periodically threw objects at the Guard, which precipitated volleys of gas into the crowd, but guardsmen entered the park only once. The speakers again asked the delegates in the hotel to blink their room lights for support, and some compiled. The crowd settled down, and the night passed uneventfully.

At dawn, on August 30, the police raided McCarthy's headquarters on the 15th floor of the Conrad Hilton. McCarthy's staff used it as a working place and hospitality room for important visitors. A police investigation indicated that hotel crockery, cans of urine, and bags of fecal matter were being thrown from the window of room 1506-A. The hotel security officer evicted everyone from the room. By the elevator lobby, a policeman shoved a McCarthy worker, John Warren, into a card table because he would not move faster. When Warren tried to pick up the table, he was struck on the head with a nightstick which split from the impact. The police also hit George Yumich, another McCarthyite, when he tried to get to the 23rd floor where McCarthy and key members of his team were staying. By this time, a second wave of policemen arrived, cleared other rooms and forced over 40 McCarthyites to accompany them to the lobby.[98]

When informed, McCarthy rushed to the lobby. He found a ring of ten helmeted policemen surrounding his young supporters who were huddled on the floor. Some were bloodied by beatings, and the girls were near hysteria. Very quietly, he told his supporters to rise and go back to the elevator in two's and three's. The police did not follow.

To some, it appeared that the police had overreached. Hotel security men and police insisted that "brutal force was not used against the innocents," but Senator Ralph Yarborough of Texas declared, "McCarthy campaign workers were beaten with clubs in a political atrocity without parallel in American history."[99] "Checking and re-checking later," recalled Theodore White, "I could find no witnesses who had seen or known of anything being thrown from that floor," but one McCarthyite admitted to having seen something dropped from the window.[100] At a Friday morning news conference, McCarthy denounced the police action as "completely out of proportion to anything that has been reported [by the police] to have occurred."[101] But the *Chicago Tribune* remarked, "It may be doubted that this view is shared by the thousands of pedestrians who pass Chicago hotels daily."[102]

By Friday afternoon, August 30, Chicago began to return to normal. The federal troops brought to Chicago for stand-by duty, but never deployed, left for their home bases; the Illinois National Guard headed home; and the police ended their 12-hour shifts and returned to normal duty. On Saturday, a police officer remarked, somewhat incredulously, "It's unbelievably peaceful."[103] By this time, 668 persons had been arrested, and police and medical records estimated hundreds had been injured. Most of those arrested were males under 26 from metropolitan Chicago and with no previous arrest records. Fifty-two were in possession of weapons, primarily rocks and bricks. According to police records, 192 policemen were injured and 49 hospitalized. The Medical Committee for Human Rights, a volunteer medical group, treated 425 civilians at its seven medical facilities.[104]

Reaction to the Week's Violence

Humphrey and Muskie expressed different views on the week's events. Muskie refrained from criticizing the demonstrators and accused the police of using too much force in dispersing them. However, Humphrey said, "I think we ought to quit pretending that Mayor Daley did something that was wrong."[105]

Nixon, Agnew, and Wallace sided with the police. "We cannot have sympathy for provocations that goes beyond peaceful dissent," said Nixon, and Agnew accused the demonstrators with being part of an "unconscious anarchy that young Americans should reject "out of hand."[106] "The Chicago police," Wallace told reporters, "probably showed too much restraint."[107]

The police actions generated mixed reactions from prominent political leaders and groups. "Although there were apparent attempts of anti-war demonstrators to seek a confrontation with the police," said Republican Congressman Gerald Ford of Michigan, "that does not excuse the indiscriminate use of force and the flouting of basic American rights and freedoms."[108] In a joint telegram, the National Council of Churches and the Synagogue Council of America accused the police of "brutality against anti-war demonstrators" and called for an end to such "pagan practices."[109] As an expression of "disgust and revulsion" at police tactics, fifty American painters and sculptors agreed not to exhibit their work in Chicago for the next two years.[110] But Illinois' Republican Senator Dirksen said the Chicago police did an "excellent job."[111] "Those police took a lot of brutality from that mob," insisted Democratic Senator Russell B. Long of Louisiana, "and they did their duty."[112] "If in the excitement," said Roy Wilkins, "the police stepped over the line, it must be said that the provocation came first."[113]

Polls taken immediately after the convention indicated that the public favored the way the Chicago police handled the demonstrators. On August 30, a national survey, conducted by Sindlinger and Company, showed that 71.4 percent of the 1,194 persons questioned agreed with Daley's security measures.[114] Three weeks later the Gallup poll reported that 36 percent of the nation's adults approved of the way the Chicago police dealt with the protesters.[115] "There is," editorialized the *Nation,* "perhaps a majority of the adult population who think that clubbing is too good for hippies—Yippies and dissenters in general."[116] "This may," editorialized the *New York Times,* "reflect a tragic willingness among many Americans to condone high-handed suppression of fundamental freedoms."[117]

The police actions received some editorial support. "The demonstrators were in many cases openly violating the law," said the *Indianapolis News,* "and in general seeking the trouble they got."[118] "We do not sympathize with most of the 'police brutality' talk," editorialized the *New York Daily News.* "Only a Commy or a complete kook, we believe, would say they chose wrongly."[119] According to the *Tulsa Tribune,* "A lot of the bleeding hearts are coming home from Chicago with whole skins because Mayor Daley confined an attempted insurrection."[120]

The editorial sentiment ran against Daley and the Chicago police. "It was true enough," said Wicker, "that the most radical of the demonstrators' leaders wanted a confrontation, but it was Daley and the police who forced it."[121] The police were not neutral, said Joseph Kraft, but "acutely hostile to the student demonstrators and by no means friendly to reporters and cameramen."[122] "On one notorious occasion," said conservative columnist William F. Buckley, "policemen called for the vacating of a street at a speed at which literally, unpracticed sprinters could not comply."[123] "Strong security," observed the *Chicago Tribune,* "does not require the police to beat up newspaper reporters and photographers who are lawfully trying to cover a news event."[124] "The spirit of repression," editorialized the *New York Times,* "has dominated the city, damaged the party and shocked the nation."[125] "The clubbing and kicking of unarmed civilians is intolerable even by a few policemen," editorialized the *Washington Post.*[126] "The Chicago police," reported the *Los Angeles Times,* "appeared to make special targets of reporters and cameramen observing their actions."[127] The *Miami Herald* declared, "Stalag 68 as someone apprehensively called garrison Chicago, a week ago, is a national outrage."[128]

Chapter X

September: Nixon's Month

The Republican Battle Plan

Nixon targeted seven key states. They included New York, California, Illinois, Ohio, Pennsylvania, Texas and Michigan. Of these, he had won only California and Ohio in 1960. But this time he sought to avoid the mistake of 1960, which was to run in all fifty states. Also, he adopted a negative campaign strategy. He criticized the shortcomings of the Johnson Administration but avoided taking positive stands on controversial issues. This was done to conserve Nixon's lead and preserve his coalition of anti-Johnson sentiment.

Nixon hoped to avoid a frontal assault against Wallace. He considered Wallace more of a rival in the South than Humphrey. Nixon's problem was to erode Wallace's southern strength without alienating his own Northern liberal supporters. His main line was that a third party candidate could not win. "Don't waste your vote," he told audiences. "Our theory," Herb Klein told newsmen, "is that the more you mention Wallace, the more stature you give him."[1]

Nixon relied on Thurmond to erode Wallace's southern support, and close observers agreed he was perfect for the job. "In North Florida, South Carolina, and areas in Georgia," recalled Murfin, "Strom was pretty well respected and took votes away from Wallace."[2] "Thurmond had an area of influence," recalled Governor Nunn of Kentucky. "He was able to get publicity and a following."[3] According to Ellsworth, "Thurmond's influence was crucial during the election."[4]

The Kickoff and a Centrist Theme

Nixon attracted large, enthusiastic crowds. At his campaign kickoff, September 4, over 400,000 persons greeted him in Chicago. The following day between 150,000 to 300,000, welcomed him to San Francisco; and on September 7, over 12,000 cheered him at Pittsburgh's airport. Three days later, newspaper accounts reported that he received "the warm embrace of Rockefeller and the tumultuous cheers of a vocal Westchester County (New York) rally."[5] In Philadelphia, on September 20, noontime crowds estimated at 200,000 to 250,000, greeted Nixon at a ticker-tape parade through the downtown business district. "From what we have seen and heard in the South," remarked civil rights leader Vernon Jordan, "the crowds Nixon attracts across the country are lily white, attracting few, if any, Negroes."[6]

Nixon stressed his centrist position. He stood in the middle, he said, between Wallace on the right and Humphrey on the left. Nixon pledged to aim his campaign at the forgotten American: "the non-shouter, the non-demonstrator." "Nixon is running," said Frankel, "in the long and lonely strides of the frontrunner as if he were not just the one, but the only one."[7] "Nixon," observed Lerner, "has pretty effectively scrapped the loser image and replaced it with the comeback image."[8]

The September Polls

Throughout September, the polls favored Nixon. The mid-September Harris poll showed Nixon with 39 percent, Humphrey 31 percent, and Wallace 21. Gallup indicated that Nixon led with 43 percent, Humphrey 31, and Wallace 19; by the end of the month, Nixon still led with 43 percent, but Humphrey had slipped to 28 and Wallace had climbed to 21 percent. A *Newsweek* survey gave Nixon 329 electoral votes from 31 states (59 more than the 270 necessary to win), Wallace 89 in nine states, and Humphrey 54 in seven states. If the election were held on September 24, a CBS News state-by-state survey reported that Nixon would win in a landslide vote and Wallace would come in second. If the poll trends continued, Humphrey's staff agreed that he would be lucky to carry five states in November.[9]

Nixon also led on the two main issues of law and order and Vietnam. On September 8, the Gallup poll indicated that the public considered Nixon the better of the two major candidates to handle the Vietnam War.

When asked which candidate could best maintain law and order, the Harris poll, on September 12, reported that Nixon held a 12-point edge over Humphrey, 38 to 26 percent, with Wallace at 21 percent.

The Agnew Problem

In early September, Agnew generated an uproar by accusing Humphrey of being "soft" on Communism. When newsmen asked whether Agnew thought Humphrey was trying to pin a hardline label on Nixon, Agnew replied, "If you've been soft on inflation, soft on Communism, and soft on law and order over the years, I guess other people look hard."[10] "It is apparent to me," said Lawrence F. O'Brien, "that Agnew has been delegated by Mr. Nixon to travel the low road."[11] Agnew, said *Newsweek,* is playing the heavy "while the standard bearer himself assumes the statesman's mantle."[12] "One wonders," editorialized the *Washington Post,* "whether it is wise for a lieutenant of the new Nixon to sound quite so much like the old Nick."[13]

Most important, Agnew's accusations upset Republican Party leaders. Senator Javits of New York informed Agnew that his "wild statements were acutely embarrassing to him." "Should they continue," said Javits, "he might have to dilute his support."[14] After meeting with top party leaders on the Hill, Senator Dirksen and Congressman Ford told reporters that they knew of no evidence that Humphrey was soft on communism. "We Republicans," explained Ford, "have a wide variety of first-class issues—inflation, crime, lack of leadership. I don't think this one should be pushed at this time."[15]

Although Agnew retracted his statements, he continued to make serious mistakes. He told reporters, "If I left the impression that the Vice President is not a loyal American I want to rectify that."[16] But when a reporter asked him if the low number of blacks in his audiences caused him concern, he replied, "Very frankly, when I am moving in a crowd, I don't look and say, 'Well, there's a Negro, there's an Italian, and there's a Greek, and there's a Polack.'"[17] In Tennessee, a reporter asked him why he did not visit more ghetto areas. "When you've seen one slum," he said blandly, "You've seen them all."[18] While walking down the aisle on a plane trip to Hawaii, he spied Gene Oishi, an old Japanese-American associate from the Annapolis press corps, sleeping. He inquired, "What's wrong with the fat Jap?"[19] "You can view Agnew with alarm," editorialized the *Washington Post,* "or you can point to him with pride, but for now we prefer to look on with horrified fascination. What will he do next?"[20]

But some argued that Agnew's blunders did not hurt Nixon. According to *Time,* "such a note of toughness may attract even more people than it repels."[21] "He was chosen as a sop to the South and border states," recalled O'Brien, "and his blunders didn't lower his appeal in those areas."[22] "Neither Nixon nor anyone on the staff considered Agnew a minus," said McWhorter later.[23] "In the end," added Sears, "people don't really vote over the vice president."[24]

Law and Order and Wallace

Most indicators pointed to law and order as the leading campaign issue. "As the campaign began," said British reporter David English, "it was obvious that the issue of law and order would transcend all others." A mid-September Harris poll indicated that 81 percent of Americans agreed that law and order had "simply broken down." "Law and order turns up as the No. 1 problem in opinion-sounding," reported *U.S. News and World Report.* According to *Time,* "the issue has virtually anesthetized the controversy over Vietnam."[2525]

To some observers, the predominance of the law and order issue signaled a rightward drift among the electorate. The students on the campus may talk about making a revolution," said B. J. Widick in the *Nation,* "but they ignore the real movement in America—a swing to the right."[26] "The conservative revolt," said the *New York Times,* "is a longing for some authority and discipline, a fear that things are getting out of hand."[27] "Precisely because the issue touches such fundamental and even primeval fears," warned the *Wall Street Journal,* "it is ripe for demagogy."[28]

Most observers agreed that the law-and-order issue was Wallace's main appeal. "The twin issues of law and order and race," said Louis Harris, "are both working substantially now for George Wallace." "The law-and-order issue," reported *Time,* "has elevated George Wallace from a sectional maverick to a national force."[29] According to *Newsweek,* "He has called up impulses out of the dark, demonic side of the American spirit," and the *New York Times* observed that "Wallace's strength rises almost correspondingly with the increased militance of the black power radicals in the nation's slums."[30]

In his speeches, Wallace favored the police and promised to curb dissent. When he said, "I commend the Chicago police," he made it clear he commended their rough treatment of journalists as well as peace demonstrators.[31] The way to curtail anarchy, he said, was to "let the police stop it like they know how to stop it," and he told a group of policemen, "I'd like you fellows to run the country for the next couple of years."[32] He would never condone the "treasons" of college professors who advocated a Vietcong victory. He declared, "I would ask the Attorney General to ask the grand jury to prefer charges and indict every person in this country, every professor, that arises and makes a speech saying he wants the Communists, Anarchists, and "free-speech folks."[33]

Hecklers plagued Wallace's campaign, but he considered them necessary to win votes. His staff always carried spare tickets to give to picketers. They entered at their risk, however, since scuffles and fist fights broke out at almost every meeting. When the heckling got out of hand, he soothed his supporters: "That's all right. It's on television." "It's real difficult for me to speak to an orderly crowd," he confessed to a crowd of aerospace workers near Los Angeles. "It really throws me, if you want to know the truth."[34] But he did not emphasize race. If blacks heckled him, he denounced them as anarchists or communists.

But as the campaign progressed, the hecklers adopted tactics that Wallace found difficult to combat. They cut their hair, shaved, and wore Wallace hats and buttons. When he began his usual criticism against communists, they shouted "Kill the Commies! Kill the Commies!" and when he brought up the subject of law and order, they cheered, "Police! Police!" He welcomed the adulation for a few moments and then called for silence, but the hecklers continued to drown him out in his own applause. This got to him. "The anarchists had better have their day now," he warned, "but after November 5, you are through, you are through in this country."[35] He would order the police to throw them out, but the disruptive effect cut into his speaking time.

A number of right-wing organizations backed Wallace. They included the John Birch Society, the Ku Klux Klan, the White Citizens Councils, the American Nazi party, and the Minutemen. The only group whose support he rejected was the Nazi party. The Institute for American Democracy, a nonpartisan organization following the activities of extremist groups, reported that the John Birch Society held key positions in the Wallace campaign, and the leaders of the segregationist White Citizens Councils were active for him in ten states. Many of Wallace's petition gatherers, organizers, and state and county chairmen, reported the Anti-Defamation League of B'nai B'rith, were members of organizations peddling "race hatred, anti-Semitism, or far right extremism." According to the *New York Times,* John Birch Society members held important positions in Wallace campaign headquarters in Idaho, Colorado, Montana, Nevada, and Texas.[36] In at least eight states, editorialized the *Progressive,* "there has been activity on his behalf by a number of the Ku Klux Klansmen and members of other violence-prone hate groups."[37]

Wallace was confident of carrying the 17 southern and border states with their 177 electoral votes. On September 3, Mississippi's regular Democrats endorsed Wallace, and on September 14, Georgia's Governor Maddox endorsed him. According to the *New York Times,* Wallace's strength in Florida, which had voted Republican in three of the last four elections, was especially "noticeable." *Newsweek* estimated Wallace's southern vote at 37 percent, Nixon 30, and Humphrey 26 percent. In a 13-state region, Oklahoma, Kentucky, and 11 former Confederate states, the mid-September Gallup poll indicated that Wallace led with 38 percent, Nixon 31 percent, and Humphrey 25.[38] Wallace's staff added Ohio to the list of states they hoped to win. This would give him 203 electoral votes—67 shy of the 270 needed to win.[39]

Although Wallace's roots were in the South, he had acquired national strength. "The polls," observed Kraft, "show Ohio, Michigan, Texas, and other big industrial states giving the former Alabama Governor as much as 20 percent of their vote." "His crowds," said newsman George Lardner, "include not simply Birchers and blue-collar workers, but real estate brokers, drug salesmen, computer programmers, engineers, and even college students." "It has become a national movement" reported Lerner. "The bulk of Wallace's support," observed *Business Week,* "comes from people who voice despair with domestic unrest and foreign frustration." "His appeal," editorialized the *Wall Street Journal,* "reaches beyond that base [racism] to embrace many voters validly upset by such concerns as crime, disorder, and a general feeling of drift in the nation."

Wallace made large inroads into the Democrats' traditional labor support. Despite labor leadership's support of Humphrey, said George Gallup, the rank and file fail to give the Democratic candidate majority support for the first time since 1936. His mid-September poll estimated Wallace's union strength at 50 percent in the South and 12 percent in the North. According to Louis Harris, the unions represented Wallace's main area of penetration in the North. In a poll of the United Auto Workers' (UAW) Local 599 in Flint, Michigan, Wallace obtained 49 percent, Humphrey 39, and Nixon 12.[40] A Connecticut UAW poll disclosed that 30 percent preferred Wallace over all other candidates.[41] "Listen," admitted a top New Jersey UAW official, "the men in the plants want to zap the Negroes by voting for Wallace." Wallace hurt us, admitted Humphrey later. "In many Northern precincts, Wallace gained support that belonged by habit and tradition to the Democrats."[42]

The UAW and AFL-CIO mounted a huge campaign against Wallace. United Auto Workers President Walter Reuther set up a "Wallace desk" in Detroit and gave the whole operation a matter of top priority. The AFL-CIO's Committee on Political Education (COPE) printed hundreds of thousands of leaflets. They read: "Wallace's Alabama ranks 48th among states in per capita annual income and is $900 below the national average."[43] "Rarely," declared Humphrey staffer Ed Cubberley, "have I seen the full AFL-CIO Executive Board so active in the support of a candidate. "But privately, labor leaders conceded that their campaign to wean white workers away from Wallace was "a long shot."[44]

Despite Wallace's inroads in labor, most observers agreed that he hurt Nixon more than Humphrey. "If it were not for Wallace," said Meany, "Nixon could be expected to carry certain southern states."[45] "Wallace was a spoiler," recalled Nixon. "He would siphon off the protest votes of people who were fed up with the policies of the Great Society."[46] "If Wallace were persuaded to go home and shut up," said Joseph Alsop, "Nixon would have a commanding majority in a race against Hubert Humphrey."[47] "It is just possible," said Buckley, "that Mr. Humphrey will win the election, and altogether likely that he will if a sizeable number of American conservatives vote for Wallace."[48]

The press remained firm in its opposition to Wallace. Only ten newspapers endorsed him, and his own, Alabama's largest, the *Birmingham News* endorsed Nixon.[49] "To be blunt about it," declared Joseph Alsop, "this is also in embryo at least the first successful Fascist movement America has ever seen." "Its mood is one of overwhelming protest and rage," said Lerner, "curiously vigilantist despite its law and order rhetoric."[50] "The trend has all the earmarks of underthinking and overreacting," observed the *Chicago Tribune,* "because those who would turn out the 'liberals' in favor of Mr. Wallace would merely be exchanging the evils of one extreme for the evils of another."[51] "The inherent nature of the Wallace campaign," reported the *Los Angeles Times,* "runs counter to so much of what our Republic should represent."[52] "The Wallace movement is an evil phenomenon," declared the *New York Times.*"[53] "The law," warned the *Washington Post,* "would be what Papa Wallace says it is."[54]

The Democratic Battle Plan

Headed by O'Brien, Humphrey's staff decided to concentrate on the northern urban and industrial areas and virtually concede the South and border states to Nixon and Wallace. They targeted Ohio, California, Illinois,

Michigan, Texas, and New Jersey for special attention. Also, they hoped to reestablish contact with the antiwar liberals and appeal to the younger generation unfamiliar with Humphrey's liberal record.

Humphrey decided to mount a strong partisan assault against Nixon and make Thurmond a major campaign issue. In a staff memo, Cubberley summarized the contest of the strategy: "We must concentrate on the themes of 1) evasive Nixon, and 2) the disaster that his election would be for the American people."[55] Staffer George Reedy added, "Nixon's biggest mistake was to permit Senator Strom Thurmond to be wrapped around his neck. He should not be permitted to do any unwrapping."[56] "Humphrey," said Frankel, "staked everything on the theory that the electorate can be either shamed or frightened into keeping the Democrats in power."[57] By stressing liberal domestic programs and citing his record against the "Republican-reactionary coalition," reported the *New York Times,* Humphrey hopes to portray Nixon and his party as "backward-looking."[58]

Post-Convention Problems

Many problems plagued Humphrey's campaign. Some he minimized, but others would last until the final days of the campaign.

On September 9, Humphrey's Philadelphia kick-off drew only 10,000 persons. "My first major error in judgment," recalled Humphrey, was to compare his opening with Nixon's start in Chicago. "He had been planning that Chicago parade and all the trimmings for six weeks. I had six days."[59] The same day fewer than 3000 persons greeted Humphrey in Denver. At the end of the first week, he told his supporters, "You've got the fight of your life on your hands." "Disinterest in his campaign," reported Frankel, "has so far been a greater problem for the Vice President than outright opposition to his candidacy."[60]

Hecklers continued to follow Humphrey's campaign. They waved Vietcong flags and shouted "Sell Out, Bull Shit, Sieg Heil, and Dump the Hump." "The staff became so wary," recalled Berman, "that they began to pick and choose the spots ... where he could at least get through a speech without a shouting match with the audience."[61] "The filthy hecklers," editorialized the *Wall Street Journal,* "are only interested in drowning out Humphrey."[62] "The press and television," said Theodore White, "would report Humphrey as a victim of the marauders; but the nation is hardly inclined to elect a victim as President."[63]

Lack of money was another problem. The United Democrats for Humphrey had spent $4 million on preconvention campaigning and were now a million dollars in debt. In addition, the Democratic National Committee was $400,000 in debt, and the wealthy patrons of the Democratic Party were not contributing. A continual complaint everywhere in the field was lack of campaign materials. "We just can't afford any of the frills," treasurer Short informed the staff, "no new secretaries or the like."[64] "We had to sit down," recalled Kampelman "and decide that we couldn't spend a nickel on radio and television media until three weeks before the election."[65]

Humphrey's low poll rating hurt his fundraising efforts. The impact of public-opinion polls, stressed Humphrey, was devastating to fundraising. "The contributors, for the most part, never started contributing. And the press just wrote over and over that we couldn't win."[66] "Gallup has done us more harm than any single thing," remarked Short.[67] "We were caught in a vicious circle," explained O'Brien. "The polls showed that Humphrey would lose, therefore people would not give us money, therefore Humphrey would lose."[68]

Adding to his frustration, Humphrey was unable to acquire $700,000 the Democratic Party held on deposit in a New York bank. In 1964, Richard Maguire, then treasurer of the Democratic National Committee, had raised a million and a half for the 1964 campaign by selling tax-deductible advertisements in the convention's official program. In the fall of 1965, Johnson asked Maguire to repeat his technique. He published a book called *Toward an Age of Greatness* with ads sold to corporations at a tax-deductible $15,000 a page. But since the advertising gimmick circumvented federal laws barring corporate political contributions and tax deductions, lawyers said that Maguire's operation may have violated the Federal Corrupt Practices Act.[69] Fearful of legal maneuvers, Johnson had the money placed in trust where it stayed, to Humphrey's dismay, throughout the fall of 1968.

Humphrey also had an image problem. His staff agreed that he came across to voters as indecisive and less experienced than Nixon. But Humphrey's main problem was a badly divided party. The majority of the party's antiwar faction refused to campaign for Humphrey and many regulars shunned him. On his first trip to Texas, Connally was notably absent to greet him on arrival. In California, Humphrey had stumped the first week abandoned by party leadership. In Connecticut, his old friend Abraham Ribicoff kept his distance, and New York's Democratic Reform Clubs seriously debated whether to "disendorse" him. "Democratic leaders," recalled Humphrey, "thought we were beaten, and when it looks as if the head of the ticket can't win, people running for other offices take care of themselves."[70]

McCarthy stubbornly resisted Humphrey's appeal for help. The vice president asked McCarthy to remember their twenty-year association and joint opposition to Nixon. But McCarthy would not endorse Humphrey until he broke with Johnson on the war. "Had Humphrey done that," recalled Gans, "he would have both gotten McCarthy's early support and the support of most of the people who supported McCarthy."[71] "One of the ironies of history," reflected Gilligan "was if Johnson had picked McCarthy in 1964, he would have been out defending the war, and Humphrey would have been a lion in the Senate, demanding an end to the war."[72]

By mid-September, the press agreed that Humphrey's chances of overcoming Nixon were slim. "Humphrey's national organization," reported Evans and Novak, "has yet to make contact either with the Democratic establishment or the burgeoning black vote."[73] "There seemed no possibility left," said newsman Warren Weaver, "that Humphrey could satisfy simultaneously liberal Democrats and independents and those "disturbed by mounting civil violence."[74] "The vice president's prospects are dim," editorialized the *Washington Post* "and Richard M. Nixon has a very good chance of being the next President."[75]

Humphrey and Johnson Clash on the War

At his kickoff appearance in Philadelphia and Denver, on September 9, Humphrey directed his remarks to the doves. In Philadelphia, he declared, "I would think that, negotiations or no negotiations, we could start to remove some of the American forces [from Vietnam] in early 1969, or late 1968," and in Denver, he told precinct workers that he would have had no difficulty accepting the minority plank.[76]

The following evening, in a fist-stumping speech, Johnson defended his Vietnam policy at the fiftieth annual American Legion convention in New Orleans. He rejected Humphrey's prediction of an early troop withdrawal and stressed the need for continual bombing:

> We yearn for the day when the violence subsides and our men can return from Southeast Asia.... No man can predict when that day will come because we are there to bring an honorable stable peace to Southeast Asia, and no less will justify the sacrifices that we and our allies have made....
>
> If the bombing stopped, our casualties would skyrocket, therefore, this Commander-in-Chief has insisted that the bombing will not stop until we are confident that it will not lead to an increase in American casualties.[77]

But in Houston, the same evening, Humphrey insisted that American troops were on their way home. He produced a copy of the morning

Houston Post and pointed to the headline, MARINE REGIMENT HEADS HOME FROM VIETNAM WAR. The headline was misleading, however. Reporters pointed out that the story reported only that the movement was a routine rotation of forces rather than an actual reduction. Humphrey replied that he had information to the contrary. But shortly thereafter, Secretary of State Clark Clifford, repudiated him in public.[78]

Undeterred, Humphrey continued to signal a deviation from Johnson's policies. Once elected, contended Humphrey, "It would be my policy to move toward a systematic reduction in American forces in Vietnam. This could be done in 1969, even if the Paris negotiations were not successful."[79] He implied that the war was a mistake and that the United States "should never again permit itself to 'march' through the quicksands of wars in far away places."[80]

Johnson's Inactivity

Close observers said that Johnson did not actively campaign on Humphrey's behalf. "Johnson was not happy at all with Humphrey's campaign," recalled Christian. "From Johnson's vantage point to be treated like an outsider in the whole thing was not to his liking."[81] According to Rowe, Johnson remained inactive because of Humphrey's vacillation on Vietnam.[82] "But what could Johnson have done?" asked Goodwin later. "The only places he could have campaigned were military installations."[83]

To some, it appeared that Johnson preferred Nixon over Humphrey. He would rather have Nixon than a Democrat who might go against the war.

"If Nixon were elected," reflected Clifford, "Johnson would be the outstanding democrat, sort of the titular leader of the party."[84] But the White House insisted that Johnson was not partial to Nixon. "Anyone who believes that must be on speed," said a long-time Johnson intimate and another White House insider recalled the "many uncomplimentary things he has heard the President say about the GOP candidate."[85] According to staffer Horace Busby, "It was [more] to LBJ's advantage to have a friendly Democrat in the presidency than a Nixon."[86] Johnson demanded of a reporter, "Who got out of the race and opened the way for him? Whose delegates put him over in Chicago?"[87]

Muskie as an Asset

Muskie was an asset to Humphrey. By mid-September, Muskie had become the journalists' favorite, "almost their pet," and the Harris poll re-

ported that the voters preferred Muskie 41 percent to Agnew's 24 percent.
"We felt that Agnew compared rather poorly with Ed Muskie," recalled
O'Brien, "and we did everything we could to force the comparison."[88] By
the end of September, Humphrey was telling audiences, "If you have any
doubts about the top of the ticket, please settle it on the basis of No. 2."[89]
"The long and short of it," said William White, "is that Muskie is over-
shadowing his chief."[90]

Because Muskie was not identified with Johnson and the Vietnam War,
he could better direct his appeal to youth and the antiwar sentiment. He
urged his audiences not to over-react to youthful protesters. "They've met
what they considered defeat," he said. "The worst we can do is throw cold
water on their expectations."[91] And he adopted an ingenious method to
deal with youthful hecklers. He would say, "No, I am not going to out-
shout anybody.... You pick out one of your numbers to come right up here,
right now, and I'll give him ten minutes of uninterrupted attention."[92] In
return, he asked them to give him their undivided attention afterwards.
They usually agreed.

Muskie's speeches were decidedly dovish. He mentioned a bombing
halt, a cease-fire, withdrawal of forces, and establishment of an interim government as areas of risk the United States should be willing to follow in a
peace formula. But he cautioned against defining a specific presidential
decision in advance of events and in advance of the start of a new national
administration next January 20. "Humphrey can't back away from the pro-
Johnson plank which was adopted," editorialized the *Chicago Tribune,* "but
Muskie can."[93]

Muskie urged ethnic and labor groups to reject Wallace and "drumhead
justice." Referring to his own Polish Catholic background, Muskie told the
children of immigrant parents, "You and I should be the first to reject those
who parade under the banner of suppression disguised as law and order.
You and I have gained so much from this great land."[94] He told Wallace
supporters, "Your candidate's whole answer is to build walls between
people, to generate hatred and distrust."[95] He emphasized that the alternative confronting Democrats was "four years or more" of Nixon in the
White House "with all that means in the direction public policy will take."[96]

Humphrey Loosens the Vietnam Knot

In late September, O'Brien, Ginsburg, and Berman persuaded Humphrey that he had to move away from Johnson's Vietnam policy. "We
simply had nothing to lose," insisted O'Brien.[97] But before Humphrey

would agree, he needed to know if Ambassador Averell Harriman, the chief American negotiator in Paris, would repudiate him. George Ball, who had resigned as ambassador to the United Nations, made an unannounced trip to Paris. Harriman assured Ball that an independent move by Humphrey would not hurt the negotiations. This solved Humphrey's dilemma." He could speak out without damaging negotiations."[98] He set aside Monday, September 30, for a television speech on Vietnam.

On Sunday afternoon, September 29, in the dining alcove of his Seattle hotel suite, Humphrey met with staff aides to discuss Monday's speech. Ball had written the speech. "The area for maneuver was narrow," he said later. "Instead of requiring enemy agreement before we stopped the bombing— which had been the Johnson position—we would have Humphrey say that he would 'stop the bombing of North Vietnam as an acceptable risk for peace,' then see what response was clear."[99] "It was weak," insisted O'Brien later, "it begged the question—it was a disaster."[100] "There was no consensus," recalled Humphrey. "I knew what I wanted to say and used the arguments only to bring my own writing to as fine an edge as possible."[101]

On Sunday evening, Humphrey again assembled with his staff to discuss the speech. "They shared with me the sense that this was a moment of truth," related Humphrey, "either the speech would be effective and we would move up, or it would not and our hope for success would be diminished." O'Brien told Humphrey:

> You have to prove you are your own man … You're not going to be elected President unless the people are convinced you stand on your own two feet—and this is the issue you can prove it on!
>
> Damn it, I'm on my own two feet … I'm sick and tired of hearing about how Lyndon Johnson will react or how Gene McCarthy will react. Let's start thinking about what Hubert Humphrey wants. This is my speech and I'll write it myself.[102]

On Wednesday, Humphrey's schedule called for him to tape his speech in the afternoon, call Johnson immediately afterwards to explain its contents, and then have Ball call Johnson to "get him down off the ceiling." Humphrey, however, was not satisfied with the first taping and decided to do it over. Since he did not have time to call Johnson, Ball phoned first:

> I read the language to President Johnson and explained the Vice President's intention. He listened in silence, then replied, "Well, George, nobody's better than you at explaining things to the press and I know you'll be able to persuade them that this doesn't mark any change in the Vice President's position from the line we've all been following."

Though his reaction was not unexpected, I could not leave it at that. "I'm sorry, Mr. President," I said, "But that's not quite the name of the game." I expected an angry riposte but he seemed in a relaxed mood. "Well, George, I know you'll do the best you can."[103]

Humphrey phoned Johnson:

I told him what I intended to say and he said curtly, "I gather you're not asking my advice." I said that was true, but that I felt that there was nothing embarrassing to him in the speech and certainly nothing that would jeopardize peace negotiations. I said we had been in direct contact with Averell Harriman and that George Ball was there with me.[104]

Shortly before the taping, Humphrey staffers told reporters that the speech signaled a greater break than its contents justified. "You have to read between the lines," Berman told reporters. "What he's really saying is he'd pull out the troops and try to end the war January the twenty-first, 1969."[105]

The Salt Lake City Speech

On Monday, September 30, at Salt Lake City, Humphrey gave the most important speech of his campaign. It was his first television appearance since his acceptance speech. Because he sought to speak not for Johnson but for his own candidacy, he had the lectern stripped of his official vice presidential seal and flag. Until then, he had not deviated from the administration's position which coupled a bombing halt with reciprocity from the other side. Now, in a three-point program, he said that he was willing to risk a complete bombing halt in the interests of peace. But he reserved the right to resume bombing if Hanoi showed bad faith. He said:

As President, I would stop the bombing of the North as an acceptable risk for peace because I believe it could lead to success in the negotiations and thereby shorten the war. This would be the best protection for our troops. ... In weighing that risk—and before taking action—I would place key importance on evidence—direct or indirect—by deed or word—of Communist willingness to restore the demilitarized zone between North and South Vietnam,

Now, if the Government of North Vietnam were to show bad faith, I would reserve the right to resume the bombing.

Now secondly, I would take the risk that the South Vietnamese would meet the responsibility they say they are now ready to assume in their own self-defense.

I would move, in other words, toward de-Americanization of the war.

I would sit down with the leaders of South Vietnam to set a specific time-table by which American forces could be systematically reduced while South Vietnamese forces took over more and more of the burden ...

Third, I would propose once more an immediate cease-fire—with United Nations or other international supervision and supervised withdrawal of all foreign forces from South Vietnam....

The ultimate key to an honorable solution must be free elections in South Vietnam—with all people, including members of the National Liberation Front and other dissident groups, able to participate in those elections if they were willing to abide by peaceful processes.[106]

The Reaction to Humphrey's Speech

Nixon feared that Humphrey's speech would increase his support. He called it "detrimental" to American efforts in Vietnam. "Humphrey either has to be for the bombing halt," said Nixon, "or he has to support the negotiations in Paris ... I am not sure which side he is on." "It was regarded as significant," said newsman Warren Meaver, "that Mr. Nixon did not feel called upon to react to Mr. Humphrey's speech with any change in position."[107]

Humphrey's speech made Johnson angry. "It upset Johnson's negotiating procedure," recalled Christian, "and he didn't want the election to be a referendum on him." Johnson told Rowe, "I think Nixon is more for my policies than Humphrey."[108]

To some, Humphrey's proposals appeared to deviate only slightly from Johnson's Vietnam policy. "If Hubert moved out from behind Lyndon," said one long-time Democrat, "it was only about a foot."[109] McCarthy said that Humphrey's speech was "no move at all," and Gans said, "It was nothing but a reiteration of Johnson's policies under peace rhetoric."[110] "It was too little and too late," recalled Goodwin. "He didn't go far enough," said Rauh.[111] According to newsman Murry Marder, "It is the difference, in layman's terms, between a wink and a blink."[112] "It was, editorialized the *Nation,* "obviously a concoction made up under pressure to do something about a lagging campaign."[113] "But," editorialized the *New York Times,* "it is more hopeful than anything the Administration or the Republican candidate has so far offered."[114]

The Humphrey camp insisted that the speech differed considerably from Johnson's position. "President Johnson," said staffers, "wants to know precisely what the communists would do if bombing were stopped. By contrast, all the Vice President wants is 'a wink' from the Communists, and he would, as President, halt the bombing." The speech had a dramatic impact on Humphrey, recalled O'Brien: "it was as if burden had been lifted from his shoulders."[115]

The speech was the turning point in Humphrey's campaign. Throughout September, he was without funds, heckled at every turn, and deserted by his party. The polls indicated that Wallace, a favorite among rank-and-file workers, was closing in. But after Humphrey's Vietnam speech, he began to obtain the needed funds, higher poll ratings, crowds without hecklers, and, most important, a united party.

Chapter XI

October: Humphrey's Month

An Upturn in the Humphrey Campaign

After his Vietnam speech, Humphrey's crowd increased dramatically and the hecklers disappeared. In Knoxville, over 11,000 University of Tennessee students gave him a standing ovation; in Scranton, he filled a noisy field house; and at Utica, the crowd, pressing to greet him, smashed a pane of glass in the front door of the town's auditorium. In Boston, he once struggled to make himself heard over "Dump the Hump," but now college students crowded a Boston courtyard shouting, "We want Humphrey, we need Humphrey." "The Vice President is in excellent spirits," said staffer Orville Freeman; and Joseph Kraft observed, "The Democrats are beginning to come on strong now."[1] "But" said William White, "Can the momentum recently picked up carry Humphrey forward to an upset victory on November 5th?"[2]

Humphrey's Vietnam speech generated needed funds. On October 5, O'Brien informed staffers, "I should report that as of last night we have received some $149,000, as a result of the Vice President's Monday night TV speech."[3] "By October 10th," reported Theodore White, "the first $1,000,000 had been contributed to the Humphrey campaign."[4] The party also began to unite. Many former supporters of Robert Kennedy and McCarthy endorsed Humphrey. They included Rauh, Schlesinger, Dutton, Mankiewicz, Galbraith, Ribicoff, and ten former McCarthyite congressmen, and the ADA. In a visit to Texas in mid-October, Connally and Yarborough, leaders of the rival factions, greeted Humphrey at Carswell Air

Force base, and candidates who would not get near Humphrey earlier "were suddenly clustered about."[5]

But McCarthy continued his nonendorsement stance. On October 8, he told his supporters that the call for party unity is no more acceptable now than it was a year ago.[6] "In time," Humphrey told reporters, "McCarthy will decide that it is better to back [Humphrey] in the pursuit of peace than to contribute, even if indirectly, to the election of Nixon or Wallace."[7]

McCarthy will not cost Humphrey the election, editorialized the *Washington Post,* but "McCarthy's own power and influence will probably suffer."[8]

Johnson began to take a more active role in Humphrey's campaign. In mid-October, he asked Lady Bird and friends "to scour the hills for funds," and in a fifteen minute radio broadcast, Johnson appealed to the nation to elect Humphrey to carry on the administration's progressive programs. In campaign appearances in West Virginia, Kentucky, and Texas, Johnson delivered the familiar Democratic message: "The Republicans are the enemies of the widows, the orphans, the aged, and the poor." "He certainly didn't let Humphrey down," recalled Christian.[9] But others disagreed. "Johnson could have done a hell of a lot more," recalled Rowe.[10] "Johnson didn't help much," added Gilligan.[11] Humphrey later insisted, "but I never went right to him and said, 'You've got to do it.'"[12]

By mid-October, the labor leader's anti-Wallace campaign began showing results. Theodore White observed, "their efforts began to tell on thousands."[13] "I feel we have turned the corner," said Humphrey staffer Al Barkan, and O'Brien added, "I feel that labor involvement is the high water mark of this campaign."[14]

Curtis E. LeMay

Wallace had a difficult time picking a running mate. In early 1968, Marvin Griffin, former governor of Georgia, agreed to accept the position for an eight-month interim basis. This allowed Wallace to fulfill legal requirements for ballot status in several states. Throughout the spring and summer of 1968, Wallace had compiled a list of potential candidates: J. Edgar Hoover, director of the FBI; Louise Day Hicks, a Boston conservative; Paul Harvey, radio commentator; Ezra Taft Benson, former secretary of agriculture from Louisiana; A. B. Chandler, former governor of Kentucky; and Curtis E. LeMay, former air force chief of staff. By September, Wallace had narrowed his choice to Chandler and LeMay. When Chandler would not modify his pro-civil rights' view, Wallace picked LeMay.

A career soldier until his retirement in 1965, LeMay's views were hawkish and conservative. Throughout his 35-year air force career, he participated in the first mass flight of the B-17, the Flying Fortress, to South America in 1937, commanded the 305th Bomber Division that bombed Germany in World War II, took part in the Berlin airlift in 1948, headed the Strategic Air Command in the 1950s and served as air force chief of staff from 1961 to 1965. "My solution to the problem" of North Vietnam, he contended in 1965, "would be to tell them frankly that they've got to draw in their horns and stop their aggression or we're going to bomb them back into the Stone Age." He supported integration, advocated using tactical nuclear weapons in limited wars and reversing the liberal trend on domestic issues.[15]

On October 3, in Pittsburgh, Wallace introduced his running mate to the press. LeMay immediately launched into a discussion concerning the use of nuclear weapons. He said that Americans seemed to have a phobia about nuclear weapons and that most military men considered them just another weapon. The phobia, he said, resulted from propaganda fed the public against the use of nuclear weapons. On Bikini Island, a former nuclear testing ground, he said that the plants were still growing and the animals doing well. "So, I don't believe the world will end if we explode a nuclear weapon."[16]

The press agreed that LeMay was not qualified to hold public office and that Wallace had made a huge mistake in picking him. "Wallace has made his first capital mistake," said William White.[17] "LeMay's selection," reported Evans and Novak, "represents a deviation from Wallace's populistic strategy."[18] According to the *New York Times*, it underscored Wallace's total lack of qualification to have charge of this country's enormous nuclear arsenal."[19]

The Mid-October Polls

In mid-October the polls indicated that Nixon was leading, Humphrey gaining, and Wallace slipping. Since mid-September, Humphrey had gained 4 points in the Harris poll and 8 points in the Gallup poll. Taken on October 18, the Harris poll reported Nixon at 40 percent, Humphrey 35 percent, and Wallace 18. On October 24, the Gallup poll showed Nixon at 44 percent, Humphrey 36 and Wallace 15. "The latest survey," observed George Gallup, "marks the first time since the campaign began that the Wallace vote has shown any signs of slipping."[20] Wallace told his supporters not to worry about the poll findings. "They lie when they poll," he said, "Eastern money runs everything."[21]

Nixon Steps Up the Offensive

As Humphrey began closing the gap, Nixon went on the offensive. He increased his media blitz. He made a series of 15 radio talks, 10 in the last two weeks, covering a wide range of issues from national resources to the problems of senior citizens. "His television performances," observed Reston, "are masterpieces of contrived candor."[22] "All we could do," recalled O'Brien, "was to try to match him the last two or three weeks of the campaign and hope the viewers by then were tired of his spots and curious about ours."[23]

On October 24, in a hard-hitting speech over national radio, Nixon charged the Democrats with creating a security gap. He said that American defenses were close to the "peril point" and "downright alarming." The Soviets, he claimed, had "vigorously advanced their military effort as we put ours in second gear. He said:

> They have raised the quantity and quality of their ballistic missiles. They have greatly increased their submarine-launching ballistic missile capacity. They have developed a landmobile version of an intercontinental missile.... Recently, we learned that they are perfecting ballistic-missile warheads far more powerful than our own. This is a grave menace to the United States.

The response from the administration and Humphrey was immediate. At a Pentagon news conference the following day, Clifford, in a dramatic gesture, reached into his breast pocket for a sheet of intelligence figures on the relative strengths of the two superpowers. "They showed," he insisted, "that the United States still has more than a three-to-one edge in H-bombs." The same day Humphrey stressed the preponderance of American weapons to the Soviets:

> We have over five hundred heavy strategic bombers and over six hundred tankers; the U.S.S.R. has only about one hundred fifty heavy bombers and fifty heavy dual tanker-bomber aircraft....
>
> We have seventy-five nuclear submarines, compared with only eighteen in 1961. The U.S.S.R. had only fifty-seven nuclear submarines, compared with twelve in 1961....
>
> The U.S. has over seven thousand tactical aircraft, the U.S.S.R. has only about fifty-four hundred. Our aircraft have over two hundred sixty-five percent as much payload capacity as the Soviet Force today.
>
> The Soviets are at least two years behind us in simple multiple warheads, and these have already been made obsolete by our technology.[24]

On the security-gap issue, the press favored Humphrey. "Nixon was wrong," said the *Los Angeles Times,* "the Soviet Union has not caught up with us."[25] "The security gap," reported the *New York Times,* "is as imaginary as the missile gap charged by John F. Kennedy, in the 1960 campaign."[26] "It was a disgraceful speech," charged the *New Republic,* "outdoing in its distortions and excessive simplification of complex facts."[27]

A Bombing Halt

On October 9, there was a dramatic change in the Paris negotiations. For five months the Americans and North Vietnamese had, in Dean Rusk's words, "been talking past each other," but now the North Vietnamese appeared more favorable to the three points the American negotiators regarded as crucial: (1) that once the bombing stopped, prompt and serious talks would have to follow, (2) that Hanoi must not violate the demilitarized zone between North and South Vietnam, and (3) that the North Vietnamese and Viet Cong stop large-scale attacks on South Vietnamese population centers.[28] "All intelligence coming to the president," recalled Valenti, "clearly portended a definite break for the better."[29]

Meanwhile, Nixon learned from Professor Henry Kissinger of Harvard, a former secret emissary to the North Vietnamese who continued to have entree into Johnson's inner circles, that "something big was afoot regarding Vietnam." Nixon told Haldeman to have staffer Bryce Harlow phone Dirksen: "Leave the hint that I knew what's going on, and tell Everett to nail Lyndon hard to find out what's happening."[30] On October 16, at the annual Al Smith dinner in New York, Johnson assured Nixon that rumors of an impending breakthrough were false. But on October 22, Nixon received a memorandum from Harlow concerning information received from someone in Johnson's innermost circle. It said that the President was eager for an excuse to order a bombing halt and would accept almost any arrangement. "White Housers still think they can pull the election out for HHH with this ploy; that's what is being attempted."[31]

Nixon made public the fact that a bombing halt was imminent. "I would be walking a fine line between political necessity and personal responsibility," recalled Nixon, but Johnson's actions "were sufficiently political to permit my taking at least some actions."[32] On October 26, Nixon told reporters that the White House was near a bombing halt agreement. "I am also told this spurt of activity is a cynical, last-minute attempt by President Johnson to salvage the candidacy of Mr. Humphrey. This I do not believe."[33]

Three days later, General Creighton W. Abrams, the United States field commander in Vietnam, attended a middle-of-night meeting in the Cabinet Room. Johnson was concerned that a bombing halt might jeopardize American troops. "I have no reservations about doing it," replied General Abrams. He told Johnson that Ambassador Bunker was having trouble obtaining a final agreement with the South Vietnamese. They listed three conditions which had to be met before accepting the American proposal. They sought a firm assurance that Hanoi would deescalate the war, negotiate directly with his government, and agree that the AFL would not attend the conference as a separate delegation. "These conditions were impossible," recalled Johnson. But "we had to go forward with our plans."[34] On October 31, at eight o'clock, Johnson addressed the American people on television. He said that he had ordered all air, naval, and artillery bombardment of North Vietnam to cease early Friday morning. He hoped this decision would lead to a peaceful settlement of the war and stated that negotiations would begin on November 6. He concluded:

> The Government of South Vietnam has grown steadily stronger .... The superb performance of our men . . . has produced truly remarkable results.
>
> Now perhaps some, or all, of these factors played a part in bringing about progress in the talks.
>
> I believe that my responsibilities to the brave men, our men, who bear the burden of battle in South Vietnam tonight and my duty to seek an honorable settlement of the war required me to recognize and required me to act without delay.[35]

Reaction to the Bombing Halt

The candidates reacted cautiously to the bombing halt. Nixon said that he would not "say anything that might destroy the chance to have peace."[36] Humphrey declined to discuss what effect the bombing halt would have on his campaign, but Muskie said that "the bombing halt represents a movement in the right direction."[37] "I couldn't care less about the political effects," said Wallace, and LeMay added, "North Vietnam did not want to see a George Wallace-LeMay administration elected because we would go out and win the war."[38]

The Republicans questioned Johnson's timing, but Democratic reaction was favorable. "The political overtones of the bombing halt appeared rather obvious," said Ronald Reagan, and Republican Senator Bourke B. Kickenlooper of Iowa added, "I think it's tragic that American lives are being played with this way."[39] McCarthy and O'Dwyer welcomed the move, and in a dramatic gesture endorsed Humphrey.[40] "What is important now," observed the *New York Times,* "is that a policy that failed has been put aside."[41]

Most observers agreed that Johnson's peace move had come too late to help Humphrey's campaign. "There was no time for it to sink into the public mind," recalled O'Brien, "no time for Humphrey to follow up on it."[42] The leaders of both political parties, reported the *New York Times* agree that Johnson's move had come too late.[43] Nixon's lead, concluded Evans and Novak, is "too large for last-ditch rescue."[44]

Johnson's speech generated favorable response from abroad. French President Charles de Gaulle, New Zealand's Prime Minister Keith Holyoake, and South Korea's President Park Chung-hee applauded Johnson's bombing halt decision. In West Germany, the Bonn government hoped it would lead to "a just solution for the Vietnamese people."[45] "This is a victory of very important significance," declared Ho Chi Minh; "for our people's great struggle against U.S. aggression, for national salvation."[46]

On November 2, Thieu announced that his government would not attend the Paris talks scheduled for November 6. His move intensified speculation that Johnson's bombing halt was a political ploy as well as undermined its positive effect on Humphrey's campaign. According to Theodore White, "Never was a climax to an election presented to Americans in more blurred form with less time for consideration."[47] But Louis Harris was more emphatic: "It lost Humphrey the election."[48]

The Chennault Connection

The administration suspected the Nixon camp of sabotaging the Paris agreements. The main suspect was Anna Chennault, the beautiful, 45-year-old Chinese-born widow of General Claire L. Chennault who commanded the Flying Tigers in World War II. An American citizen since 1950, Anna Chennault was co-chairman of the Women for Nixon-Agnew National Advisory Committee. Apparently, she advised South Vietnam's ambassador Bui Diem, her close friend, that his country would get a better deal with Nixon and to urge his government not to attend the Paris talks. "Johnson," said Kampelman later, "was fully persuaded that this was all a Nixon conspiracy."[49] "It instilled in him a cold fury," recalled Valenti.[50] "We had tapped the phones in South Vietnam's embassy," related Clifford. "That's how Johnson learned Nixon and his supporters were all involved in it."[51]

Humphrey and Johnson decided not to go public with the Chennault story. But the reason for their silence remained unclear. "What do you prove?" said Rowe, later, "Anna Chennault and the South Vietnamese deny it, and you can't say that Johnson had the South Vietnamese embassy wiretapped, which is what happened."[52] "It wouldn't really accomplish anything," recalled Christian, "and Johnson was having enough trouble with the South Vietnamese as it was."[53] "Both Dean Rusk and Clark Clifford urged the president not to go public with the information," recalled Valenti. "They felt it would fracture the society."[54] But Theodore White later insisted, "Humphrey might have won the presidency if he had gone public with it."[55]

The Final Days

In the final week, Humphrey's Democratic support increased. After McCarthy gave his endorsement on October 29, many of his followers, including Lowenstein, began to support Humphrey. Blue-collar support also picked up. They finally decided to vote "their pocketbooks instead of their prejudices," said *Newsweek*.[56] "Humphrey had reunited the Democratic Party in only nine weeks after the Chicago convention," observed British newsman David English. "It was as impressive a feat as the 1968 Presidential campaign would produce."[57]

Humphrey's final campaign thrust included a two-pronged effort at media saturation and get-out-the-vote drive. O'Brien recalled that they had hoped to spend $6 million on television ads but they only spent half that; Nixon spent twice as much as the Democrats.[58] Humphrey's strategists agreed that the poor and minorities were most likely to vote for him, but they were either not registered or had difficulty getting to the polls. On October 18, O'Brien set the get-out-the-vote drive as the highest campaign priority.[59]

Humphrey's wind-up included numerous parades and rallies, a telethon, and home-to-vote at Waverly, Minnesota. In Chicago, on Friday, November 1, thousands greeted him in the Loop and West Side. The next day he landed in Suffolk County, Long Island. The crowds were "large, noisy, and enthusiastic." On Sunday, November 3, Humphrey flew to Houston. Connally, Senator Yarborough, Robert Strauss, treasurer of the Texas Democratic Party, and Congressman Jim Wright were all on the tarmac waiting. At Houston's Astrodome, Johnson and Humphrey spoke to a wild, cheering packed audience. On Monday, standing on the trunk of a convertible in a lunch-hour motorcade through downtown Los Angeles, Humphrey and Muskie were greeted by nearly 100,000 persons. In the evening they appeared before ABC television cameras to answer questions phoned in by voters across the country. Celebrities Frank Sinatra, Joanne Woodward, Burt Lancaster, and Danny Thomas assisted them. "It was unrehearsed and spontaneous," recalled Humphrey. "No other television we had done was any better or conveyed as well what we were all about."[60]

While Wallace wound up his drive in the South, Nixon stumped through Texas, visited California, where he held a telethon on Monday, November 4, and finally flew to New York, to vote and await the returns. In Texas, he campaigned in San Antonio, Fort Worth, Lubbock, Austin, and El Paso. His message was the same: "If we take Texas, we've won. If the Democrats take Texas, they can't win, and they might cause a constitutional crisis."[61] "We were trying to sit on our lead," recalled Sears. "If you change anything at that point, it looks as though you're rattled."[62] On Monday, Nixon appeared on NBC. Agnew, said observers, was "tucked away in one of the safest Nixon states, far-off Virginia."[63] "Some of my advisers," recalled Nixon, "had thought such a costly and tiring effort was not needed, but I overruled them. I remembered 1960 and felt I should do everything possible that might make the difference in a close election."[64] In the final days, the popular opinion polls were inconclusive. On election eve, November 4, the final Gallup poll gave Nixon 42 percent, Humphrey 40 and Wallace 14; and the Harris poll showed Humphrey leading for the first time with 43 percent to Nixon's 40 percent, and Wallace's 13.[65] The Field Research Corporation's poll reported Nixon leading Humphrey in California, by 50 to 34 percent, and a *New York Daily News* straw poll indicated that Humphrey was leading Nixon in New York.[66] A *New York Times* political opinion spot check indicated Nixon led in 30 states.[67]

The Election Returns

On November 5, 1968, as the election count began, Nixon awaited the results at New York's Waldorf Towers and Humphrey settled in at the Leamington Hotel in Minneapolis. "As the night wore on," recalled Berman, "it became obvious that things were going to be tough, especially in California and Illinois."[68] "The early returns were not encouraging," recalled O'Brien. "They showed us losing New Jersey, a serious blow to our hopes."[69] By midnight, California, Illinois, Missouri, Ohio, and Texas, hung in the balance. Except for Ohio, they were the same states Nixon lost in 1960. By early morning the election appeared to hang on the balance of Illinois, and Nixon feared a repeat performance of losing it and the election. He recalled:

> I became irritated with Daley's stubbornness in not releasing the count in Cook County. I called Bryce Harlow and told him to get Larry O'Brien ... on the phone. 'Bryce, lay it on the line. Don't fool around. Tell O'Brien to tell Hubert to quit playing games. We've won Illinois, so let's get this thing over with.' Harlow reached O'Brien's suite, but either he was not there or would not take the call ....

Just before 8 a.m., Haldeman brought in word that both NBC and ABC had declared me the winner in California and Ohio. But there was still no movement in Illinois, and that was what I needed to confirm victory. One more state.

At 8:30, the door burst open and Dwight Chapin rushed in. 'ABC just declared you the winner!' he shouted. 'They've projected Illinois. You got it. You've won.'[70]

Less than 60 percent of the adult population exercised their franchise. Of the 73,186,819 total votes cast, Nixon polled 31,770,237 (43.4 percent), Humphrey 31,270,533 votes (42.7 percent), Wallace 9,906,141 votes (13.5 percent), and minor party candidate votes totaled 239,908 (0.3 percent). Nixon carried 32 states for 301 electoral votes, Humphrey 13 states and the District of Columbia for 191 electoral votes, and Wallace 5 states for 46 electoral votes. Humphrey had lost the election by one-quarter of 1 percent, or just under 500,000 votes. Nixon's 43.4 percent of the popular vote was the lowest for a president-elect since Woodrow Wilson's 41.9 percent in 1912, and Wallace's 13.5 percent was the largest third-party turnout since Robert LaFollette won 17 percent of the vote in 1924. Although Humphrey's electoral vote was concentrated in the East, he ran almost a dead heat in the national popular vote and did well in California, Illinois, Ohio, and New Jersey. Nixon's gamble on Agnew and Thurmond paid off, and he collected 75 electoral votes in southern and border states.

The Democrats remained in control of Congress, but the ideological make-up shifted slightly to the right. The Republicans gained 5 new Senate seats for a total of 43 to the Democrats' 57. Out of the 435 members of the House, 218 are needed for a majority and the division came to 243 Democrats and 192 Republicans. "Without regard to party label," reported *U.S. News and World Report,* "the 91st Congress is to be more 'conservative' than any in the last decade.[71] But a majority could still be formed from liberal Northern Democrats and moderate Republicans to pass liberal legislation.

In the gubernatorial races, the Republicans elected seven new governors, lost incumbents in two states, for a net gain of five. They jumped from 26 to 31 governorships (the highest since 1920). The Democrats dropped from 24 to 19.

Analysis of the Election

In 1968, the vote represented public dissatisfaction with the Johnson Administration. Between 1964 and 1968, the public mood had changed so dramatically that Johnson could not even defend in the public places of

1968 the domestic and foreign policies he had conducted for four years. And not since 1932 had a major party's vote shrunk so dramatically. The 57 percent total combined votes of Wallace and Nixon, observed Theodore White, represented "an historic turning-of-the-back on all the great promises and domestic experiments of one of the most visionary administrations ever to hold the helm in America."[72]

Nixon's vote was national in character. He won 11 states in the Far West, 9 in the Midwest, 8 in the South and border states, and 4 in the Northeast. Most important, he won Illinois, with the downstate farm vote offsetting the Democratic turnout in Chicago. He carried the crucial Democratic primary states: New Hampshire, Wisconsin, Indiana, Nebraska, Oregon, and California. Although he lost Texas, with its 25 electoral votes, and failed to crack Wallace's stronghold in the five deep South states, he carried a number of upper south and border states: Kentucky, Tennessee, the Carolinas, Florida, Virginia, and Oklahoma. According to the *New York Times,* "He established the Republican Party as a formidable and probably permanent political factor in the South."[73]

Humphrey did well in the industrial North. He carried 6 states in the Northeast, the District of Columbia, 3 in the South and border regions, 2 in the Midwest, and 2 in the Far West. Of the big states, Humphrey carried New York, Pennsylvania, Texas, Michigan, and Massachusetts to Nixon's California, Illinois, Ohio, New Jersey, and Florida. Although he picked up Maine and Washington, which went to Nixon in 1960, Humphrey lost 11 of John Kennedy's states: Arkansas, Delaware, Georgia, Illinois, Louisiana, Missouri, Nevada, New Mexico, New Jersey, North Carolina, and South Carolina. Humphrey carried New York City by more than 797,000 votes and a large 268,000 vote bulge in Philadelphia placed Pennsylvania in his column.

Big-city bosses, intellectuals, and union rank-and-file held for Humphrey. Wallace obtained 18 percent of the union vote, but nearly a third of it came from Republican workers. Also, Humphrey had the edge with women voters: 45 percent to Nixon's 43.[74] "The election," observed *U.S. News and World Report,* "reflected a polarization of Democratic power in 'liberal' and labor union areas of the North, along with the development of new Republican strength in the South."[75]

While Humphrey carried the minority vote, he lost the South. Nationally, he obtained 88 percent of the black vote, and Nixon 12 percent. Relieved of the poll tax, blacks and Mexican-Americans helped Humphrey carry Texas. But the southern Democratic vote plummeted from 50 percent under Lyndon Johnson to Humphrey's 31 percent. This was less than

Nixon's 34.6 and Wallace's 34.3 percent. Humphrey's southern vote came from blacks, labor unions, and "loyal" Democrats.[76] "The old national Democratic Party, observed Theodore White, "has all but disappeared in the South."[77] It raised the question, said Wicker, "of how long it will be before a southern Democratic Party based on the black vote can control the region."[78]

Democrats agreed that party division played a significant role in Humphrey's defeat. Humphrey's staff said that better efforts by Democrat leaders in New Jersey, Illinois, Ohio, and California would have made the difference.[79] The war, recalled McGovern, "shattered Democratic ranks."[80] "If it weren't for Gene McCarthy and Johnson," said Rowe later, "Humphrey would have been president."[81] "It would have been helpful if Johnson would have come out earlier," recalled Kampelman, "but the fact that

McCarthy didn't press his people to help us hurt."[82] "Humphrey's problem," recalled Christian, "was with the other wing of the party. The Johnson people stayed with him solidly."[83] But "Johnson didn't seem to be very upset over Humphrey's defeat," recalled Clifford.[84] "McCarthy's continued non-endorsement after Humphrey's Salt Lake City speech was a mistake," said Sam Brown later.[85] "Nixon," added Stavis, "carried by a very narrow margin several states where the active McCarthy committee refused to help Humphrey very much."[86] "These defections," recalled O'Brien, "were symbolized by Gene McCarthy's performance that fall."[87] "Had McCarthy campaigned early and hard for me and the Democratic Party," recalled Humphrey, "he might have turned it."[88]

Humphrey's strategists split on the importance of the late electoral surge. If the election had been held a week or two later, some argued that Humphrey could have mobilized enough support to swing the electoral vote in his favor, but others contended that voters switching to Humphrey at the last minute would simply have waited longer if the campaign had been extended.[89] "I think Humphrey would have been president if there were another week," said Rowe later. "He was coming very fast."[90] "I don't know," reflected O'Brien. "This one was so tough and so close that it's difficult to make many judgments."[91]

Republican strength in the suburbs, small towns, and farming areas held for Nixon. He obtained 51 percent of the farm vote to Humphrey's 29 and Wallace's 20.[92] The upper-income groups in the suburbs voted Republican.[93] And the Catholic vote, so significant in the 1960 election, had shifted somewhat. In 1960, Nixon obtained 22 percent to John Kennedy's 70; but in 1968, Nixon's percentage had risen to 33 percent to Humphrey's 59.[94]

Most observers agreed that Wallace hurt Nixon. "In terms of electoral votes," said Sears later, "Wallace took forty-five votes from him."[95] Louis Harris agreed, "Richard Nixon would have won a two-way election going away."[96] California, observed *Time*, "fell to Nixon ... in part thanks to a Wallace vote of roughly 7 percent that cut into normally Democratic precincts.[97] Wallace voters, said the *New York Times*, helped Nixon carry Kentucky, Tennessee, and the Carolinas.[98] A large part of the Wallace vote, reported the *Nation*, "would have gone to Nixon if Wallace had not been on the ballot."[99] If it had been a straight two-party contest, reported the *U.S. News and World Report*, Nixon would have won Wallace's southern electoral votes and many of his popular votes collected in the North and West.[100] "Our own guess," editorialized the *National Review*, "is that if he ... had not been in the ring, Nixon would have won by a very large popular and electoral majority."[101]

Although the Vietnam War split the Democratic Party, observers disputed its electoral significance. "Because so little light showed between Nixon and Humphrey on Vietnam," reported *Time*, "it is unlikely that the war played a large part in the presidential vote."[102] "If Hubert would have given the Salt Lake City speech earlier," recalled Gilligan, "the chances were he would have won."[103] But "the war did not control many votes," insisted Sears later.[104] "The net result," reported Theodore White, "was a blurred mandate for Richard M. Nixon rising chiefly from Americans' consideration of their condition at home."[105]

Since the combined votes of Wallace and Nixon came to almost 57 percent, the election signified to many a shift to the right. "The trend was obviously conservative," said *Time*. "White voters seemed to be attracted by Nixon's relatively tough stand on the law-and-order issue."[106] "Taken together," observed *Business Week*, "Nixon's and Wallace's votes added up to a clear rejection of the Johnson-Humphrey Administration and a signal of a swing to the right."[107] "It is a conservative mandate," editorialized the *National Review*. "Not extreme right wing, or even clear-cut unmixed conservative perhaps, but undeniably from the conservative side of the spectrum."[108] "If there were in the country a political consensus still for the old way of the New Deal-Fair Deal coalition," editorialized the *Wall Street Journal*, "Mr. Humphrey would have won."[109]

Chapter XII

Conclusions

In late November, McCarthy entered the race to provide a focal point for antiwar dissent and an educational forum on the Vietnam War. After his large New Hampshire vote on March 12, 1968, he began to consider the possibility of winning the nomination. But his unorthodox campaign style and lack of effort to win over the regulars diminished his strength. Also, unfair delegate selection procedures in state caucuses and conventions favored the regulars. By summer, his staff agreed that he had given up hope of winning the nomination.

Kennedy's staff argued that his decision to enter the race was made before the New Hampshire primary. But unlike McCarthy, he would not enter to champion an issue but only if a real chance existed to win the nomination. McCarthy's large New Hampshire vote persuaded Kennedy that public sentiment was running against Johnson and that a serious bid for the nomination was worthwhile. Some observers called his entry into competition with McCarthy four days after New Hampshire ruthless. This image, first acquired in earlier days, followed him throughout the primaries. Still, if a politician's goal was to win elections, Kennedy's entry made political sense. If anything, he was a better politician than McCarthy.

As the study indicated, Johnson's withdrawal decision was not made in haste. Since the summer of 1967, he had been seriously considering it. In the fall, his aides drew up a withdrawal statement, but he sat on it. He said later that he was waiting for an appropriate time to give it. Others recalled that he appeared somewhat ambivalent. On March 31, 1968, he announced his decision. His reasons, he said, were to promote national and party unity and not have his peace gesture, a partial bombing halt, appear like a campaign ploy. Still, he did not have to withdraw from the race to achieve these goals, and nobody expected him to.

In fact, no president leaves the White House voluntarily, and Johnson was no exception to the rule. Perhaps the Tet offensive, McCarthy's New Hampshire vote, Kennedy's entry, and polls showing him losing Wisconsin and other primaries made his nomination appear uncertain and forced him to withdraw. But his motivation was difficult to pinpoint, and the reason behind his withdrawal remained unclear.

A scenario, however, can be developed suggesting that Johnson may have reconsidered his decision. Throughout the summer, he sought a summit conference with the Soviets. Negotiations broke down after their August 20 invasion of Czechoslovakia. His main intent, apparently, was to get the Soviets to pressure the North Vietnamese for a negotiated settlement. From a successful summit in Europe, he would fly to the convention where the delegates would hail him as a peacemaker. Mayor Daley had reserved Soldier Field Stadium for his sixtieth birthday celebration. Here his supporters could express their love and affection for him, and it would provide him with a needed forum. To a cheering audience, he would announce that events compelled him, though reluctantly, to throw his hat back in the ring. If true, this explained the unprecedented security precautions to keep out demonstrators and hecklers, and his intense concern that the Vietnam plank follow exactly the administration's position.

Nixon was the logical Republican choice. He had worked hard for Goldwater in 1964, congressional candidates in 1966, and spoke at countless Republican fundraisers. In the process, he amassed a strong party following. Primary victories eroded his loser image. In addition party leaders considered Rockefeller too liberal to hold the party together, and Reagan too conservative to win a national following. That left Nixon, the man in the middle, and the convention's choice to challenge the Democrats.

But Thurmond did not, as the press reported, hold the South for Nixon. Reagan's convention announcement came too late. Most of the southern party leaders and their delegates had already pledged to hold to Nixon for a first ballot. Like most Republicans, they considered Reagan unable to win. Also, Nixon promised to support key southern issues. If they helped nominate him, he would be obliged to honor them.

Humphrey announced his candidacy on April 27. He waited until the deadline for entering the primaries was over. This allowed him to quietly

amass delegate support in the states without primaries and to avoid a direct
clash with McCarthy and Kennedy. Because Humphrey considered
Kennedy the stronger opponent, he allowed funds to be channeled into
McCarthy's Oregon campaign and welcomed his subsequent victory. On
June 5, when Kennedy was shot, Humphrey had acquired enough party
support and delegate strength in the non-primary states to assure him the
nomination.

Shortly before the convention, Humphrey considered taking an independent position on the war. He reconsidered, he said later, because Johnson informed him that a break in the Paris negotiations was near. More
likely, he feared that an independent position might cost him the support of
Johnson and the regulars. Nor could he be totally sure that an angry

Johnson might not decide to come back into the race. Nevertheless, he
began to sound more dovish and even suggested that his views and Robert
Kennedy's were similar on most Vietnam issues.

Vietnam was the dominant issue at the Democratic convention. More
specifically, whether the Vietnam plank would contain a conditional or unconditional bombing halt. Humphrey's bombing halt clause was less conditional than Johnson's but the doves demanded an unconditional bombing
halt. Neither side would budge, and thus compromise attempts failed. Then
Johnson intervened and forced Humphrey to adopt the administration process. Further compromise attempts were now hopeless. Humphrey won the
nomination at the price of a divided party.

As the campaign began, Nixon looked unbeatable. He had the full
resources of his party behind him, campaigned to large, enthusiastic crowds;
and the polls showed him leading Humphrey and Wallace by large margins
and indicated that the public considered Nixon the best candidate to handle
Vietnam and maintain law and order. In comparison, Humphrey had to
contend with a divided party, lack of funds, low poll ratings, and hecklers.
Also, Johnson appeared uninterested in the campaign, and Wallace made
serious inroads in labor's Democratic ranks. The press agreed that Humphrey's chances of overcoming Nixon were slim.

Throughout September, Humphrey's staff continued to split on
whether he should break with Johnson on the war. Some argued that he
literally had nothing to lose. Others that Johnson angry could still hurt him.
In late September, Humphrey considered his position desperate and reluctantly agreed with those arguing for a break. On September 30, he stated his
willingness to risk a complete bombing halt. By this time, emotions had
cooled since the turbulent convention, and the regulars and liberals began
to unite behind him.

Still, many liberals only gave Humphrey lukewarm support while others, like McCarthy, continued nonendorsement. They argued that on the war Humphrey was no better than Nixon. This was not the case, however. A large, vocal, antiwar faction existed in the Democratic Party. Its presence forced Humphrey to lean away from Johnson's policy. Nixon had no such faction compelling him to adopt a dovish position. Apparently, the emotions generated at the convention clouded the liberal's judgment.

In mid-October, a break in the Paris negotiations looked promising. Then on October 31, Johnson announced a complete bombing halt. Shortly thereafter, Thieu undermined its impact by announcing that his government would not attend the Paris talks scheduled for November 6. Whether the Chennault connection played an important role in his decision remained unclear. But most observers agreed that Johnson's peace move had come too late to help Humphrey. He lost the popular vote by almost 500,000.

The vote reflected a general dissatisfaction with the Democrats. The public had become intolerant of dissent and protest and blamed them for the riots and disorders. But the election was not a clear-cut turn to the right nor was it a referendum on the war. Neither Humphrey nor Nixon offered a clear indication of the direction of their future policy in Vietnam. The Democrats' failure to recognize that they could not both promote liberalism and social harmony at home and carry on a protracted war abroad without seriously affecting their ability to govern more than anything explained their defeat in the 1968 presidential election.

The Consequences

Although the 1968 election signaled a shift to the right, it was not decisive. The Democrats still dominated both houses of Congress and largely prevented conservative erosion of liberal programs.

Upon entering office, Nixon continued to lack a clear policy on Vietnam. The Paris negotiations, involving the United States, North Vietnam, Saigon, and the Vietcong, had stalled. In April 1970 he ordered the invasion of Cambodia to destroy Vietcong headquarters and supplies. Many Americans considered this a violation of Nixon's pledge not to enlarge the war. Many campuses erupted in protest; and the Senate repealed the Tonkin Gulf Resolution and forbade the president to keep American troops in Cambodia. In February 1971 the communists repulsed a similar raid in Laos by 20,000 South Vietnamese troops operating under American air cover.

By 1971 Nixon's policy began to take shape. Announcing the Nixon Doctrine, he said that the United States would no longer help nations suppress revolutions. He also began a program called Vietnamization: gradual withdrawal of American troops from South Vietnam while enlarging South Vietnam's armed forces in the hope they would win without American troops. But he increased the American air war against North Vietnam, including secret bombings in Cambodia and Laos.

In April 1972 the North Vietnamese launched the largest offensive in four years. They captured the rich rice province of Bing Dinh, but massive American bombing stalled their drive. Another massive American bombing attack took place shortly after Nixon won reelection in 1972. Then in January 1973 the four participants signed a cease-fire agreement. Each side in Vietnam was allowed to hold the territory it then occupied.

In 1975 the communists launched a preliminary offensive. Retreat by South Vietnamese forces turned into a rout, and Saigon fell in seven weeks. This marked the complete defeat for the political-military forces that the United States had backed for fifteen years.

Nixon carried through on his promises to the South. He imposed limits on textile imports from the Far East, opposed busing, and allowed more state control over school desegregation. In 1969, when Chief Justice Earl Warren announced his retirement, Nixon appointed Warren Burger, a conservative with a strong law and order record. The resignation of Justice Abe Fortas the same year allowed an additional appointment, but the Senate rejected Nixon's first two nominees, Clement F. Haynsworth and G. Harold Carswell, both southern conservatives, because of mediocre records. His third nominee, Harry A. Blackmun, another conservative, was confirmed in May, 1970. In September, 1971, when John M. Harlan and Hugo L. Black resigned, Nixon appointed two conservatives, Lewis F. Powell, Jr., and William H. Rehnquist. The Senate confirmed both.

Nixon also carried through on his "hard line" law and order stand. He tripled Federal law-enforcement spending, authorized more wiretapping, and gave the police in the District of Columbia more freedom to tap telephones and enter private dwellings without search warrants.

But Nixon went further than his supporters demanded. In June 1970 he ordered the FBI, CIA, National Security Agency, and Defense Intelligence Agency to formulate a coordinated attack on "internal threats." When FBI Director J. Edgar Hoover refused, Nixon created a Special Investigations Unit (White House Plumbers) under the supervision of Nixon's aide John Ehrlichman to secure evidence against persons considered a threat to the government. In 1972 the so-called "Plumbers" burglarized the office of antiwar activist Daniel Ellsberg's psychiatrist in an attempt to discover incriminating evidence. They also broke into the Democratic headquarters in

Washington's Watergate apartment complex to photograph documents and install wiretaps. Their arrest and the subsequent revelation of Nixon's attempts to cover-up White House involvement led the House Judiciary Committee to recommend impeachment and to his resignation in August, 1974.

Probably the most important consequence of the 1968 Democratic convention was the passage of reform resolutions. They appeared to be of secondary importance at the time, but they led to far-reaching reforms.

In 1969, the Democratic National Committee set up the Commission on Party Structure and Delegate Selection to consider the major problems in delegate selection and to propose solutions. In 1971 the party adopted its recommendations. They included an end to the unit rule at all levels, abolished proxy voting, barred closed or secret delegate meetings designed to exclude rank-and-file Democrats, limited costs and fees to ten dollars, demanded advance posting of times and locations of all caucus meetings, allowed for the opportunity of all delegates to list their presidential preference on the ballot, called for delegate selection during the calendar year of the convention, and stipulated that the appointment method could only apply to 10 percent of the state's delegation. Most important, it called for adequate representation of minorities, young people, and women in reasonable relationship to their presence in the population of the state.

Although more modest than the Democrats, the Republicans also initiated reforms. At the 1968 convention, they authorized the creation of a Committee of Delegates and Organizations to consider the problems and offer solutions to the delegate selection process. The reforms took effect in 1976. They included a call for open meetings in the selection of delegates, banned proxy voting, ex-officio delegates (a practice by which state parties guarantee delegate slots to party and public officials by virtue of their position), and excessive fees. The reforms encouraged, but did not require, that state parties encourage more participation of women, blacks, and the young. The Republicans were compelled to follow many of the Democratic reforms which applied to the primaries. The Democrats controlled most of the state legislatures, and they usually wrote reform legislation to apply to both parties.

In 1972 a brokered convention would probably not have selected an outspoken opponent of the war, but the new rules allowed McGovern, a liberal insurgent, to win the nomination. Party and labor leaders, favoring Humphrey, were angry over their loss of power. Many sat out the election, and for the first time in twenty years, the AFL-CIO, refused to endorse a Democratic nominee. In addition the country's mood was far to the right of

McGovern. The result was the party's greatest electoral defeat in this century.

After McGovern's defeat, the party set up a successor commission to reconsider party rules on delegate selection. Although it reaffirmed the substance of most of the 1972 reform guidelines, it made some gestures towards increasing the role of party leaders in the nominating process. The new guidelines abolished quotas, raised the number of delegates state parties could appoint from 10 to 25 percent, barred winner-take-all primaries at the state level (where the candidate receiving the largest share of the vote wins all the delegates), and established the rule of proportionality: the number of delegates received by a candidate would be proportionate to the percentage of the vote won in the primary. Also, all persons running for delegate slots, in either caucuses or primaries, had to declare their presidential preferences, and a candidate was allowed to approve all of his intended delegates.

In 1978 the party approved further reforms. The most important included elimination of the congressional district level's winner-take-all primary, reduced from 21 to 13 weeks the delegate selection process, expanded state delegations by 10 percent to provide delegate slots exclusively for state party and elected officials, and states that all primary and caucus delegates be bound on the first ballot (22 states already had binding primaries). Under pressure from feminists, the reforms required that one-half of the delegates to the 1980 convention be women.[162]

The reforms literally wedded the party to participatory democracy. Moreover, as a result of the general reform tide, primaries increased from 17 in 1968 to 23 in 1972 to 30 in 1976. By 1980, 35 primaries would choose nearly three-fourths of the delegates.

In retrospect, though it was not clear-cut, the rightward drift continued throughout the 1970s. Liberal strength in Democratic congresses and the 1976 election of a moderate Democrat, Jimmy Carter of Georgia, undermined somewhat the rising conservative trend. But in 1980, public dissatisfaction with Carter's handling of inflation and unsuccessful attempts to obtain the early release of American hostages in Iran brought in ultraconservative Ronald Reagan of California. The Republicans also captured 11 Senate seats which gave them a majority in that house. Thus the shift to the right, beginning in 1968, was now decisive. Reagan seemed to have public and much congressional support to return the nation to the pre-New Deal notion of laissez-faire economics and political conservatism.

Bibliography

I. Primary Sources

Manuscripts

Christian, George. Interview with Joe B. Frantz, June 30, 1970, Oral History Project, Lyndon B. Johnson Library, Austin, Texas.

Clifford, Clark M. Interview with Paige Mulhollan, July 14, 1982, Oral History Project, Lyndon B. Johnson Library, Austin, Texas.

Clifford, Clark M. Papers, Lyndon B. Johnson Library, Austin, Texas.

Goodwin, Richard N. Papers, Library of Georgetown University, Washington, D.C.

Humphrey, Hubert H. Papers, Minnesota Historical Society, Saint Paul, Minnesota.

Johnson, Lyndon B. Papers, Lyndon B. Johnson Library, Austin, Texas.

McCarthy, Eugene J. Papers, Library of Georgetown University, Washington, D.C.

McGovern, George. Interview with Paige Mulhollan, April 30, 1969, Oral History Project, Lyndon B. Johnson Library, Austin, Texas.

McPherson, Harry. Papers, Lyndon B. Johnson Library, Austin, Texas.

Mitchell, Stephen A. Papers, Library of Georgetown University Library, Washington, D.C.

Murphy, Charles S. Interview with Thomas H. Baker, June 29, 1969, Oral History Project, Lyndon B. Johnson Library, Austin, Texas.

Roche, John P., interview with Paige Mulhollan, August 16, 1970, Oral History Project, Lyndon B. Johnson Library, Austin, Texas.

Roche, John P. Papers, Lyndon B. Johnson Library, Austin, Texas.

Rowe, James H. Papers, Lyndon B. Johnson Library, Austin, Texas.

Taylor, Maxwell D. Interview with Dorothy Pierce, February 10, 1969, Oral History Project, Lyndon B. Johnson Library, Austin, Texas.

Temple, Larry. Interview with Joe B. Frantz, June 26, 1970, Oral History Project, Lyndon B. Johnson Library, Austin, Texas.

Temple, Larry. Papers, Lyndon B. Johnson Library, Austin, Texas.

Westmoreland, William C. Interview with Dorothy Pierce McSweeny, Oral History Project, Lyndon B. Johnson Library, Austin, Texas.

Wheeler, Earle G. Interview with Dorothy Pierce McSweeny, Oral History Project, Lyndon B. Johnson Library, Austin, Texas.

Author's Interviews

Brown, Sam. Interview with the author, Sept. 12, 1982.

Busby, Horace. Interview with the author, Aug. 18, 1982.

Christian, George. Interview with the author, August 16, 1982.

Clifford, Clark M. Interview with the author, August 18, 1982.

Dent, Harry S. Interview with the author, August 16, 1982.

Ellsworth, Robert F. Interview with the author, August 21, 1982.

Finch, Robert H. Interview with the author, August 25, 1982.

Gans, Curtis. Interview with the author, August 11, 1982.

Gardner, James C. Interview with the author, August 22, 1982.
Geoghegan, William. Interview with the author, August 13, 1982.
Gilligan, John J. Interview with the author, August 13, 1982.
Ginsburg, David. Interview with the author, August 16, 1982.
Goldthwaite, Alfred. Interview with the author, August 19, 1982.
Goodwin, Richard N. Interview with the author, June 12, 1980.
Hinman, George L. Interview with the author, June 12, 1980.
Hughes, Emmett J. Interview with the author, August 23, 1982.
Kampelman, Max. Interview with the author, August 31, 1982.
Kleindienst, Richard G. Interview with the author, August 25, 1982.
Lukens, Donald. Interview with the author, September 15, 1982.
Mankiewicz, Frank F. Interview with the author, June 23, 1982.
McCarthy, Eugene J. Interview with the author, June 20, 1980.
McWhorter, Charles K. Interview with the author, August 3, 1982.
Miller, Melody. Interview with the author, September 15, 1982.
Murfin, William F. Interview with the author, August 16, 1982.
Nunn, Louie B. Interview with the author, August 23, 1982.
Rather, Mary. Interview with the author, December 22, 1982.
Rauh, Joseph L. Interview with the author, August 3, 1982.
Reed, Clarke. Interview with the author, August 21, 1982.
Rostow, Walt W. Interview with the author, December 22, 1982.
Rowe, James H. Interview with the author, August 5, 1982.
Schlesinger, Arthur M., Jr. Interview with the author, January 28, 1981.
Sears, John W. Interview with the author, September 14, 1982.
Sorensen, Theodore C. Interview with the author, June 16, 1980.
White, Clifton F. Interview with the author, September 7, 1982.
White, Theodore H. Interview with the author, August 3, 1982.

Newspapers

Atlanta Journal, 1968
Capital Times, 1968.
Chicago Tribune, 1968.
Evening Star (Washington, D.C.), 1968
Denver Post, 1968.
Indianapolis News, 1968.
Los Angeles Times, 1968.

Miami Herald, 1968.
New York Times, 1967-1968.
Omaha World-Herald, 1968.
Oregon-Journal, 1968.
San Francisco Chronicle, 1968.
Wall Street Journal, 1968.
Washington Post, 1967-1968.

Periodicals

Atlas, 1968.
Commonweal, 1968.
Fortune, 1968.
The Nation, 1967-1968.
National Review, 1967-1968.
New Republic, 1967-1968.
Newsweek, 1967-1968.
New York Times Magazine, 1967-1968.

Harpers, 1967-1968.
Life, 1968.
Look, 1968.
The Progressive, 1967-1968.
Ramparts, 1968.
Saturday Evening Post, 1968.
U.S. News and World Report, 1967-1968.

Memoirs and Special Studies

Ball, George W. *The Past Has Another Pattern: Memoirs.* New York: W. W. Norton, 1982.

Berman, Edgar. *Hubert: The Triumph and Tragedy of the Humphrey I Knew.* New York: Putnam, 1979.

Christian, George. *The President Steps Down.* New York: Macmillan, 1970.

Dellinger, David. *More Power Than We Know.* New York: Anchor Press, 1975.

———. *Revolutionary Nonviolence.* New York: Bobbs-Merrill, 1970.

Dent, Harry S. *The Prodigal South Returns to Power.* New York: Wiley, 1978.

Galbraith, John K. *A Life in Our Times.* Boston: Houghton Mifflin, 1981.

Halberstam, David. *The Unfinished Odyssey of Robert Kennedy.* New York: Random House, 1968.

Heuvel, William V. and Gwirtzman, Milton. *On His Own: Robert F. Kennedy 1964-1968.* New York: Doubleday, 1970.

Herzog, Arthur, *McCarthy for President.* New York: Viking, 1969.

Hoopes, Townsend. *The Limits of Intervention.* New York: David McKay, 1969.

Hoffman, Abbie. *Soon to be a Major Motion Picture.* New York: G. P. Putnam, 1980.

Humphrey, Hubert H. *The Education of a Public Man.* Edited by Norman Sherman. New York: Doubleday, 1976.

Johnson, Lady Bird. *A White House Diary.* New York: Holt, Rinehart and Winston, 1971.

Johnson, Sam H. *My Brother Lyndon.* Edited by Enrique Hank Lopez. New York: Cowles Book Co., 1970.

Kearns, Doris. *Lyndon Johnson and the American Dream.* New York: Harper & Row, 1976.

Larner, Jeremy. *Nobody Knows.* New York: Macmillan, 1970.

McCarthy, Eugene J. *The Year of the People.* New York: Doubleday, 1969.

McGovern, George. *Grassroots: The Autobiography of George McGovern.* New York: Random House, 1977.

McPherson, Harry. *A Political Education.* Boston: Little, Brown, 1969.

Miller, Merele. *Lyndon: An Oral Biography.* New York: G. P. Putnam, 1980.

Newfield, Jack. *Robert Kennedy: A Memoir.* New York: E. P. Dutton, 1969.

Nixon, Richard M. *The Memoirs of Richard Nixon.* New York: Grosset & Dunlap, 1978.

O'Brien, Lawrence F. *No Final Victories.* New York: Doubleday, 1974.

Plimpton, George, and Stein, Jean., eds. *American Journey: The Times of Robert Kennedy.* New York: Harcourt Brace Jovanovich, 1970.

Rostow, Walt W. *The Diffusion of Power: An Essay in Recent History.* New York: Macmillan, 1972.

Stavis, Ben. *We Were the Campaign.* Boston: Beacon Press, 1969.

Schlesinger, Arthur Jr., *Robert Kennedy and His Times.* Boston: Houghton Mifflin, 1978.

Sorensen, Theodore C. *The Kennedy Legacy,* New York: Macmillan, 1969.

Stout, Richard T. *People.* New York: Harper & Row, 1969.

Taylor, Maxwell D. *Swords and Plowshares.* New York: W. W. Norton, 1972.

Valenti, Jack. *A Very Human Heart.* New York: Pocket Books, 1977.

Walker, Daniel. *Rights in Conflict.* New York: E. P. Dutton, 1968.

Westmoreland, William C. *A Soldier Reports.* Garden City, N.Y.: Doubleday, 1976.
White, Theodore H. *The Making of the President 1968.* New York: Atheneum, 1969.

Articles

Clifford, Clark N. "A Viet Nam Reappraisal: The Personal History of One Man's View and How It Evolved," *Foreign Affairs* 47 (July 1969): 601-622.
Halberstam, David. "The Man Who Ran Against Lyndon Johnson," *Harpers,* December, 1968, pp.47-66.
———. "Travels with Bobby Kennedy," *Harpers,* July, 1968, pp. 51-66.
Goodwin, Richard N. "A Day in June," *Look,* June, 1970, pp. 140-145.
———. "The Night McCarthy Turned to Kennedy," *Look,* October 15, 1968, p. 102.
Hoopes, Townsend. "LBJ's Account of March, 1968," *New Republic,* March 14, 1970, pp. 17-19.
Hughes, Emmett, Jr. "The Tormented Candidacies," *Newsweek,* February 5, 1968, p. 13.
McCarthy, Eugene J. "Why I'm Battling LBJ," *Look,* February 6, 1968, pp. 22-26.
Newfield, Jack. "Kennedy Lays out a 'Gut' Campaign," *Life,* March 29, 1968, pp. 28-29.
———. "Kennedy's Search for a New Target," *Life,* April 12, 1968, p. 35.
Nixon, Richard M. "Nixon Replies," *New Republic,* October 26, 1968, pp. 11-15.
Schlesinger, Arthur, Jr. "Why I Am for Kennedy," *New Republic,* May 4, 1968, pp. 19-23.
White, Theodore H. "The Wearing Last Weeks and a Precious Last Day," *Life,* June 14, 1968. p. 39.

Party Proceedings

The Presidential Nominating Conventions 1968. Washington, D.C.: Congressional Quarterly Service, 1968.
Official Report of the Proceedings of the Twenty-Ninth Republican National Convention, 1968. Baltimore: Dulany-Vernay, 1968.

Government Documents

United States. Congress. Senate. Committee on Armed Services. *Air War Against North Vietnam. Parts 1-5.* Hearings before the Preparedness Investigating Subcommittee, 90th Cong., 1st Sess., August 1967.
———. Department of Defense, *United States-Vietnam Relations, 1945-1967.* 12 vols. Washington, D.C.: United States Government Printing Office, 1971.
———. President. *Public Papers of the Presidents of the United States: Lyndon B. Johnson, 1967.* 2 vols. Washington, D.C.: United States Government Printing Office, 1968.
———. *Public Papers of the Presidents of the United States: Lyndon B. Johnson. 1968-1969.* 2 vols. Washington, D.C.: United States Government Printing Office, 1970.

II. Secondary Sources

Books

Abel, Elie, and Kalb, Marvin. *Roots of Involvement.* New York: W. W. Norton, 1971.

Albright, Joseph. *What Makes Spiro Run*. New York: Dodd, Mead, 1972.

Allen, Gary. *Richard Nixon*. Boston: Western Islands, 1971.

Anson, Robert S. *McGovern*. New York: Holt, Rinehart & Winston, 1972.

Boyarsky, William. *The Rise of Ronald Reagan*. New York: Random House, 1968.

Brown, William, and Brown, Edmund G. *Reagan the Political Chameleon*. New York: Praeger, 1976.

Burns, James M. *Edward Kennedy and the Camelot Legacy*. New York: W. W. Norton, 1976.

Chester, Lewis; Hodgson, Godfrey; and Page, Bruce. *An American Melodrama: The Presidential Campaign of 1968*. New York: Viking, 1969.

Cleveland, Martha. *Charles Percy: Strong New Voice From Illinois*. Harris-Wolfe, 1968.

Cohen, Dan. *Undefeated: The Life of Hubert H. Humphrey*. Minneapolis: Lerner Publications, 1978.

Deakin, James. *Lyndon Johnson's Credibility Gap*. Washington D.C.: Public Affairs Press, 1968.

Dugger, Ronnie. *The Politician: The Drive for Power from the Frontier to Master of the Senate*. New York: W. W. Norton, 1982.

Engelmayer, Sheldon D., and Wagman, Robert J. *Hubert Humphrey: The Man and His Dream*. New York: Methuen, 1978.

English, David. *Divided They Stand*. New Jersey: Prentice-Hall, 1969.

Ernst, Harry W., and Sherrill, Robert. *The Drugstore Liberal*. New York: Grossman, 1968.

Evans, Rowland, and Novak, Robert. *Lyndon B. Johnson: The Exercise of Power*. New York: New American Library, 1966.

Fall, Bernard B. *Hell in a Very Small Place: The Siege of Dien Bien Phu*. Philadelphia: J. B. Lippincott, 1967.

Frady, Marshall. *Wallace*. New York: World, 1968.

Fulbright, William J. *The Crippled Giant: American Foreign Policy and Its Domestic Consequences*. New York: Random House, 1972.

Giap, Nguyen Vo. *The Military Art of People's War*. New York: Monthly Review, 1969.

Goldman, Eric F. *The Tragedy of Lyndon Johnson*. New York: Alfred A. Knopf, 1969.

Goulden, Joseph C. *Truth Is the First Casualty-The Gulf of Tonkin Affair: Illusion and Reality*. Chicago: Rand McNally, 1969.

Graff, Henry F. *The Tuesday Cabinet: Deliberation and Decision on Peace and War under Lyndon B. Johnson*. Englewood Cliffs, N.J.: Prentice-Hall, 1970.

Greenhaw, Wayne. *Watch Out for George Wallace*. Englewood Cliffs, N.J.: Prentice-Hall, 1976.

Guthman, Edwin. *We Band of Brothers*. New York: Harper & Row, 1971.

Hansen, Donald C, and Lippman, Theo, Jr. *Muskie*. New York: W. W. Norton, 1971.

Hartley, Robert E. *Charles H. Percy: A Political Perspective*. Chicago: Rand McNally, 1975.

Haskins, James. *The War and the Protest: Vietnam*. Garden City, N.Y.: Doubleday, 1971.

Hersh, Burton. *The Education of Edward Kennedy*. New York: William Morrow, 1972.

Kimball, Penn. *Bobby Kennedy and the New Politics*. Englewood Cliffs, N.J.: Prentice-Hall, 1968.

Lasky, Victor. *Robert F. Kennedy: the Myth and the Man.* New York: Trident Press, 1968.

Leipold, Edmond L. *Ronald Reagan Governor and Statesman.* Minneapolis: T. S. Denison & Co., 1968.

Lewis, Joseph. *What Makes Reagan Run.* New York: McGraw-Hill, 1968.

Lippman, Theo, Jr., *Spiro Agnew's America.* New York: W. W. Norton, 1972.

Lurie, Leonard. The Running of Richard Nixon. New York: New American Library, 1968.

Mailer, Norman. *Miami and the Siege of Chicago.* New York: New American Library, 1968.

Marsh, Robert. *Agnew and the Siege of Chicago.* New York: Mc Evans & Co., 1971.

Mollenhoff, Clark R. *George Romney, Mormon in Politics.* New York: Meredith Press., 1968.

Murray, David. *Charles Percy of Illinois.* New York: Harper & Row, 1968.

Nevin, David. *Muskie of Maine.* New York: Random House, 1972.

Oberdorfer, Don. *Tet.* Garden City, N.Y.: Doubleday, 1971.

Roberts, Chalmers M. *First Rough Draft.* New York: Praeger, 1973.

Ross, Douglas. *Robert F. Kennedy: Apostle of Change.* New York: Trident Press, 1968.

Salisbury, Harrison E. *Behind the Lines—Hanoi.* New York: Harper & Row, 1967.

Schandler, Herbert Y. *The Unmaking of a President.* Princeton, N.J.: Princeton University Press, 1977.

Trewhitt, Henry L. *McNamara: His Ordeal in the Pentagon.* New York: Harper & Row, 1975.

Windchy, Eugene G. *Tonkin Gulf.* Garden City, N.Y.: Doubleday, 1971.

Witcover, Jules. *85 Days: The Last Campaign of Robert Kennedy.* New York: G. P. Putnam, 1969.

———. *The Resurrection of Richard Nixon.* New York: G. P. Putnam, 1970.

———. *White Knight: The Rise of Spiro Agnew.* New York: Random House, 1972.

Articles

Alexander, Shana. "He Tried to Beat Me With a Dog and an Astronaut." *Life,* June 7, 1968, pp. 36-41.

Astor, Gerald. "Where He Stands On." *Look,* May 14, 1968, pp. 71-78.

Barber, John. "The Making of Hubertism." *Commonweal,* November 1, 1968, pp. 145-149.

Buckley, Tom. "The Battle of Chicago: From the Yippies Side." *New York Times Magazine,* September 15, 1968, p. 28.

Campbell, Angus. "How We Voted—and Why." *Nation,* November 25, 1968, pp. 550-553.

Cannon, James. "Rocky: He Who Runs Least Runs Best," November 18, 1967, pp. 34-35.

Cleghorn, Reese. "Quiet But Angry Rebel." *New York Times Magazine,* October 20, 1968, pp. 38-39.

Curtis, Wilkie. "Who Speaks for Mississippi." *Nation,* August 26, 1968, p. 135.

Duscha, Julius. "Not Great, Not Brilliant, But a Good Show." *New York Times Magazine,* December 10, 1967.

Emerson, Bill. "Mr. Vice President, Are You Going to Win This Election?" *Saturday Evening Post,* October 19, 1968, pp. 29-33.

Evans, Stanton M. "Races to Watch in '68." *National Review,* October 19, 1968, pp. 29-33.

Germond, Jack W. "The Strange Case of Nelson Rockefeller." *Progressive,* June, 1968, pp. 16-20.

Harris, Louis. "Part Way with RFK, the Price He Paid." *Newsweek,* May 20, 1968, p. 35.

Heren, Louis. "Peace and U.S. Politics." *Atlas,* May, 1968, pp. 14-16.

Higdon, Hal. "Indiana: A Test for Bobby Kennedy." *New York Times Magazine,* May 5, 1968, pp. 32-33.

Honan, William H. "A Would-Be Candidate for This Season." *New York Times Magazine,* December 10, 1967.

Ireland, Douglas. "Ready, Willing, and Able." *New Republic,* December 22, 1967, pp. 375-376.

Jordan, Vernon E. "New Game in Dixie." *Nation,* October 21, 1968, pp. 397-399.

Kahn, Roger. "The Revolt Against LBJ." *Saturday Evening Post,* February 10, 1968, p. 7.

Kempton, Murray. "The Decline and Fall of the Democratic Party." Saturday Evening Post, November 2, 1968, pp. 19–21.

Kenworthy, E. W. "Eugene McCarthy Hits the Road." *New Republic,* November 25, 1967, pp. 11–13.

King, Larry L. "The Cool World of Nelson Rockefeller." *Harpers,* February, 1968, pp. 31-40.

Kissinger, Henry A. "The Viet Nam Negotiations." *Foreign Affairs,* 47 (January 1969): 211–234.

Knoll, Erwin. "A Fourth Party?" *Progressive,* November, 1968, pp. 13–15.

Kopkind, Andrew. "The McCarthy Campaign." *Ramparts,* March, 1968, pp. 50–55.

Lardner, George, Jr. "The Backlash Candidate." *Progressive,* November, 1968, pp. 19–22.

McBee, Susanna. "A Bantam—Fact with Talk and the Facts." *Life,* August 2, 1968, pp. 20–23.

McCarry, Charles. "Win with Rockefeller." *Saturday Evening Post,* February 24, 1968, pp. 80–83.

McLuhan, Marshall. "All of the Candidates Are Asleep." *Saturday Evening Post,* August 10, 1968.

McWilliams, Carey. "The Bitter Legacy of LBJ." *Nation,* September 9, 1968, pp. 198–201.

Martin, Harold H. "George Wallace, the Angry Man's Candidate." *Saturday Evening Post,* June 15, 1968, pp. 23–25.

Maynard, Robert. "Negroes Go Local." *Nation,* October 21, 1968, pp. 392–394.

Meryman, Richard. "Hubert Humphrey Talks His Self-Portrait." September 27, 1968, *Life,* pp. 22B–31.

Miles, Michael. "Reagan and the Respectable Right." *New Republic,* April 20, 1968, pp. 25-28.

Miller, Arthur. "The Battle of Chicago: From the Delegates' Side." *New York Times Magazine,* September 15, 1968, pp. 29-31.

Murray, David. "The Rise of Ronald Reagan." *Progressive,* February, 1968, pp. 18-22.

Nevin, David. "Rockefeller: The Old Avidity Is Gone." *Life,* March 29, 1968, pp. 35-35.

Oberdorfer, Don. "Ex-Democrat, Ex-Dixiecrat, Today's Nixiecrat." *New York Times Magazine,* October 6, 1968, pp. 36-37.

O'Mara, Richard. "Discovering Spiro Agnew." *Nation,* September 2, 1968, pp. 175-177.

O'Neil, Paul. "The Party Almost Came Down Around Their Ears." *Life,* September 6, 1968, pp. 22-23.

Pearson, Drew. "The Ghosts That Haunted LBJ." *Look,* July 23, 1968, pp. 25-29.

Quirk, John J. "McCarthy Fights for an Open Convention." *Commonweal,* August 9, 1968, pp. 516-518.

Reddy, John. "Can Humphrey Hold His Party Together?" *Readers Digest,* July, 1968, pp. 105-110.

Reichley, James A. "He's Running Himself Out of the Race." *Fortune,* March, 1968, pp. 113-115.

Roberts, Steven V. "McCarthy Campaign Enters New Phase." *Commonweal,* April 26, 1968, pp. 165-167.

"Edmund Sixtus Muskie Takes the Low-Key Road." *New York Times Magazine,* October 20, 1968, p. 33.

Roddy, Joseph. "The Prime Mover." *Look,* June 25, 1968, pp. 82-88.

Rogers, Warren. "Bobby's Decision." *Look,* April 16, 1968, pp. 73-80.

Ryskind, Morrie. "The Democrats Secret Weapon." *National Review,* August 13, 1968, pp. 801-802.

Schneier, Edward. "The Scar of Wallace." *Nation,* November 4, 1968, pp. 454-457.

Serwer, Arnold. "Gene McCarthy's Winning of Wisconsin." *Progressive,* June, 1968, pp. 24-26.

Sidey, Hugh. "Tortuous Road to Decision—and Lady Bird's Role." *Life,* April 12, 1968, pp. 32-33.

Stevens, Robert. "Disaster in Chicago?" *Commonweal,* August 23, 1968, pp. 550-551.

Wainwright, Loudon. "One More Try for the Heights." *Life,* March 1, 1968, pp. 60-65.

Wechsler, James A. "What Makes McCarthy Run?" *Progressive,* January, 1968, pp. 23-26.

Widick, B. J. "Why They Like Wallace." *Nation,* October 14, 1968, pp. 358-359.

Wilson, Richard. "This Is Humphrey." *Look,* July 9, 1968, pp. 41-46.

Witcover, Jules. "Is There Really a New Nixon?" *Progressive,* March, 1968, pp. 14-26.

Wise, David. "How Bobby Plans to Win It?" *Saturday Evening Post,* June 1, 1968, pp. 23-26.

Zimmermann, Gereon. "Durable Dick Daley." *Look,* September 3, 1968, pp. 16-23

Notes

Introduction

1. U.S. Executive Order 11365, *Report of the National Advisory Commission on Civil Disorders,* prepared for the President by Otto Kerner et al. (Washington, D.C.: U.S. Government Printing Office, 1968), pp. 19-61.
2. Jack Valenti, *A Very Human President* (New York: W. W. Norton, 1975), p. 185.
3. *U.S.-Vietnam Relations* IVC (2) (b), p. 5.
4. Townsend Hoopes, *The Limits of Intervention* (New York: David McKay, 1970), p. 29.
5. Maxwell D. Taylor, *Swords and Plowshares* (New York: W. W. Norton, 1972), p. 337.
6. William C. Westmoreland, *A Soldier Reports* (Garden City, N.Y.: Doubleday, 1976), p. 118.
7. Hubert H. Humphrey, *The Education of a Public Man: My Life and Politics,* ed. Norman Sherman (Garden City, N.Y.: Doubleday, 1976), pp. 322–325.
8. Ibid., p. 320.
9. Westmoreland, *Soldier,* p. 120.
10. *U.S.-Vietnam Relations* IVC (3), p. v.
11. Valenti, *Human,* p. 319.
12. Earle G. Wheeler interview with Dorothy Pierce McSweeny, Aug. 21, 1969, University of Texas Oral History Project, Johnson Library, Austin.
13. Westmoreland, *Soldier,* p. 140.
14. *U.S.-Vietnam Relations* IVC (5), p. 117.
15. Ibid., p. 105.
16. Ibid., p. 8.
17. Ibid., p. 106.
18. George W. Ball, *The Past Has Another Pattern* (New York: W. W. Norton, 1975), p. 397.
19. Lyndon Baines Johnson, *The Vantage Point: Perspectives of the Presidency 1963–1969* (New York: Holt, Rinehart, and Winston, 1971), p. 324.
20. Ball, *Past,* pp. 400–401.
21. Valenti, *Human,* p. 339.
22. Johnson, *Vantage,* p. 148.
23. Valenti, *Human,* pp. 356–358.
24. Westmoreland, *Soldier,* p. 160.
25. *Washington Post,* March 25, 1968.
26. George H. Gallup, *The Gallup Poll: Public Opinion 1935–1971,* 3 vols. (New York: Random House, 1972), 3:2089.
27. Hoopes, *Limits,* p. 83.
28. Westmoreland, *Soldier,* p. 225.
29. *New York Times,* Nov. 20, 1967.
30. Hoopes, *Limits,* p. 90.
31. Doris Kearns, *Lyndon Johnson and the American Dream* (New York: Harper and Row, 1976), p. 320.
32. John P. Roche interview with Paige Mulhollan, July 16, 1970, University of Texas Oral History Project, Johnson Library, Austin.
33. *Washington Post,* Nov. 30, 1967.
34. George Christian interview with Joe B. Frantz, July 1, 1971, University of Texas Oral History Project, Johnson Library, Austin.
35. Roche interview with Mulhollan, July 16, 1970, Johnson Library.

Chapter 1 – The Challengers

1. Curtis Gans interview with the author, Aug. 11, 1982.
2. David Halberstam, "The Man Who Ran Against Lyndon Johnson," *Harpers,* Dec, 1968, p. 49.
3. Gans interview, Aug. 11, 1982.
4. Joseph L. Rauh interview with the author, Aug. 3, 1982.
5. John K. Galbraith, *A Life in Our Times* (New York: Viking Press, 1969), p. 487.
6. Lewis Chester, Godfrey Hodgson, and Bruce Page, *An American Melodrama: The Presidential Campaign of 1968* (New York: Viking Press, 1969), p. 63.

7.   Arthur Herzog, *McCarthy for President* (New York: Viking Press, 1969), p. 24.
8.   David English, *Divided They Stand* (Englewood Cliffs, N.J.: Prentice-Hall, 1969), p. 59.
9.   Richard T. Stout, *People* (New York: Harper and Row, 1970), p. 64.
10. Gans interview, Aug. 11, 1982.
11. Halberstam, "Man," p. 50.
12. Ibid., p. 53.
13. Milton Gwirtzman and William Vanden Heuvel, *On His Own: Robert F. Kennedy 1964–1968* (Garden City, N.Y.: Doubleday, 1970), p. 275.
14. George McGovern, *Grassroots* (New York: Random House, 1977), p. 110.
15. Jack Newfield, *Robert Kennedy: A Memoir* (New York: E. P. Dutton, 1969), p. 184.
16. Ibid., p. 185.
17. Arthur M. Schlesinger, Jr., *Robert Kennedy and His Times* (Boston: Houghton Mifflin, 1978), p. 825.
18. Newfield, *Kennedy,* p. 185.
19. Schlesinger, *Kennedy,* p. 186.
20. Newfield, *Kennedy,* p. 186.
21. Ibid., p. 187.
22. Halberstam, "Man," p. 51.
23. McGovern, *Grassroots,* p. 110.
24. George McGovern interview with Paige Mulhollan, April 30, 1969, University of Texas Oral History Project, Lyndon B. Johnson Library, Austin.
25. Halberstam, "Man," p. 51.
26. McGovern, *Grassroots,* p. 111.
27. Stout, *People,* p. 106.
28. Ibid., p. 108.
29. Eugene J. McCarthy, *The Year of the People* (Garden City, N.Y.: Doubleday, 1969), p. 21.
30. Hubert H. Humphrey, *The Education of a Public Man: My Life and Politics,* ed. Norman Sherman (Garden City, N.Y.: Doubleday, 1976), p. 376.
31. Ibid.
32. Gans interview, Aug. 11, 1982.
33. Chester et al., *American Melodrama,* p. 75.
34. McCarthy, *Year,* p. 58.
35. Gans interview, Aug. 11, 1982.
36. William H. Honan, "A Would-Be Candidate for This Season," *New York Times Magazine,* Dec. 10, 1967, p. 137.
37. Schlesinger, *Kennedy,* pp. 831–832.
38. McCarthy, *Year,* pp. 266–267.
39. *New York Times,* Dec. 1, 1967.
40. Stout, *People,* p. 118.
41. *New York Times,* Dec. 1, 1967.
42. "The McCarthy Bomb," *Newsweek,* Dec. 4, 1967, p. 3.
43. *Washington Post,* Dec. 3, 1967.
44. Ibid., Dec. 1, 1967.
45. *New York Times,* Dec. 1, 1967.
46. *Atlas,* Feb., 1968, p. 13.
47. James H. Rowe interview with the author, August 5, 1982.
48. *New York Times,* Dec. 2, 1967.
49. Ibid., Dec. 1, 1967.
50. Ibid., Jan. 6, 1968, p. 16.
51. George H. Gallup, *The Gallup Poll: Public Opinion 1935–1971,* 3 vols. (New York: Random House, 1972), 3: 2100.
52. *New York Times,* Jan. 22, 1968.
53. McCarthy, *Year,* pp. 58-59.
54. Jeremy Lamer, *Nobody Knows* (New York: Macmillan, 1970), pp. 35–36.
55. Ibid., pp. 286–287.
56. Herzog, *McCarthy,* p. 76.
57. Lamer, *Nobody,* pp. 35–36.
58. McCarthy, *Year,* p. 61.
59. Halberstam, "Man," p. 53.
60. Stout, *People,* p. 138.

61. Herzog, *McCarthy,* p. 80.
62. Ibid., p. 78.
63. Stout, *People,* pp. 131–132.
64. Herzog, *McCarthy,* p. 79.
65. Stout, *People,* p. 138.
66. Lawrence F. O'Brien, *No Final Victories: A Life in Politics—From John F. Kennedy to Watergate* (Garden City, N.Y.: Doubleday, 1974), p. 219.
67. Stout, *People* p. 174.
68. Ibid., p. 175.
69. Gwirtzman, *On His Own,* p. 299.
70. Sam Brown interview with the author, Sept. 12, 1982.
71. Gans interview, Aug. 11, 1982.
72. Abigail McCarthy, *Private Faces/Public Places* (Garden, N.Y.: Doubleday, 1972), p. 319.
73. Ben Stavis, *We Were the Campaign* (Boston: Beacon Press, 1969), p. 14.
74. McCarthy, *Year,* p. 69.
75. Gwirtzman, *On His Own,* p. 301.
76. Stavis, *Campaign,* p. 28.
77. Herzog, *McCarthy,* p. 89.
78. McCarthy, *Year,* p. 73.
79. *New York Times,* Feb. 14, 1968.
80. McCarthy, *Year,* p. 65.
81. Stout, *People,* p. 182.
82. Herzog, *McCarthy,* p. 98.
83. *Progressive,* May, 1968, p. 5.
84. *New Republic,* March 23, 1968.
85. *Washington Post,* March 14, 1968.
86. George Christian interview with the author, Aug. 16, 1982.
87. *New York Times,* March 14, 1968.
88. Gans interview, Aug. 11, 1982.
89. Newfield, *Kennedy,* p. 42.
90. Humphrey, *Education,* p. 374.
91. Newfield, *Kennedy,* pp. 30-31.
92. Gwirtzman, *On His Own,* p. 268.
93. Lyndon Baines Johnson, *The Vantage Point: Perspectives of the Presidency 1963–1969* (New York: Holt, Rinehart and Winston, 1971), p. 99.
94. Theodore C. Sorensen, *The Kennedy Legacy* (New York: Macmillan, 1969), p. 98.
95. O'Brien, *No Final,* p. 219.
96. Newfield, *Kennedy,* p. 199.
97. Jules Witcover, *The Resurrection of Richard Nixon* (New York: G. P. Putnam, 1970), p. 32.
98. Rowe to Johnson, Jan. 16, 1968, Johnson Papers, Johnson Library, Austin.
99. Merle Miller, *Lyndon: An Oral Biography* (New York: G. P. Putnam, 1980), p. 506.
100. Gwirtzman, *On His Own,* p. 294.
101. Earle G. Wheeler interview with Dorothy Pierce, June 7, 1970, Johnson Papers, Johnson Library, Austin.
102. Walt W. Rostow interview with the author, Dec. 22, 1982.
103. Johnson, *Vantage,* p. 284.
104. *New York Times,* Feb. 7, 1970.
105. Christian interview, Aug. 16, 1982.
106. Maxwell D. Taylor interview with Dorothy Pierce, Feb. 10, 1969, Johnson Papers, Johnson Library, Austin.
107. Clark M. Clifford interview with the author, Aug. 18, 1982.
108. *Wall Street Journal,* Feb. 18, 1968.
109. Walter Lippmann, "Defeat," *Newsweek,* March 11, 1968, p. 25.
110. *Washington Post,* March 8, 1968.
111. *New York Times,* March 19, 1968.
112. Ibid., Feb. 17, 1968.
113. Ibid., Feb. 18, 1968.
114. Ibid., Feb. 9, 1968.
115. Ibid., March 14, 1968.

116. Stout, *People,* p. 184.
117. Clifford memorandum of conversation with Senator Robert F. Kennedy and Theodore C. Sorensen, March 14, 1968, Johnson Papers, Johnson Library, Austin.
118. Clifford to Johnson, March 14, 1968, Johnson Papers, Johnson Library, Austin.
119. Clifford interview, Aug. 18, 1982.
120. Abigail McCarthy, *Private,* p. 373.
121. Arthur Schlesinger, Jr., interview with the author, Jan. 28, 1981.
122. Gans interview, Aug. 11, 1982.
123. *New York Times,* March 16, 1968.
124. *Wall Street Journal,* March 25, 1968.
125. *The Evening Star* (Washington, D.C.), March 14, 1968.
126. Gallup, *Gallup Poll,* p. 2112.
127. "The Topsy-Turvy Campaign," *Newsweek,* April 1, 1968.
128. "The Rivals," *Newsweek,* April 8, 1968, p. 35.
129. Christian interview, Aug. 16, 1982.
130. "Under Way with LBJ," *Newsweek,* April 1, 1968, p. 21.
131. "The Rivals," *Newsweek,* April 8, 1968, p. 35.
132. *Time,* March 22, 1968, p. 17.
133. *New York Times,* March 24, 1968.
134. Ibid., March 14, 1968.
135. Schlesinger, *Kennedy,* p. 859.
136. Newfield, *Kennedy,* p. 859.
137. Rauh interview, Aug. 3, 1982.
138. "The Making of Gene McCarthy," *Newsweek,* March 25, 1968.
139. "Mary," *Newsweek,* April 1, 1968, p. 64.
140. Schlesinger, *Kennedy,* p. 858.

Chapter II – The Republican Comeback

1. George H. Gallup, *The Gallup Poll: Public Opinion 1935–1971,* 3 vols. (New York: Random House, 1972), 3:2038.
2. *New York Times,* April 3, 1968.
3. *National Review,* Dec. 12, 1967, pp. 1372-83.
4. *New York Times,* Sep. 7, 1968.
5. Ibid., Aug. 5, 1968.
6. *U.S. News and World Report,* Feb. 19, 1968, p. 52.
7. *New York Times,* Jan. 16, 1968, p. 38.
8. *New York Times,* Aug. 10, 1968.
9. Richard M. Nixon, *Six Crises* (New York: Doubleday, 1962), p. 122.
10. Richard Nixon, *The Memories of Richard Nixon* (New York: Grosset and Dunlap, 1978), p. 76.
11. Ibid., p. 224.
12. Ibid., p. 239.
13. Ibid., p. 245.
14. Theodore White, *The Making of the President 1968* (New York: Atheneum, 1969), p. 43.
15. Harry S. Dent, *The Prodigal South Returns to Power* (New York: Wiley, 1978), p. 76.
16. Nixon, *Memoirs,* p. 279.
17. White, *The Making,* p. 43.
18. *New York Times,* May 28, 1968.
19. *Atlas,* May, 1968, p. 17.
20. Nixon, *Memoirs,* p. 270.
21. *National Review,* Nov. 14, 1967, p. 1266.
22. *Washington Post,* March 8, 1968.
23. *Newsweek,* May 20, 1968, p. 40.
24. *New York Times,* Jan. 14, 1968.
25. Ibid., May 19, 1968.
26. *Newsweek,* Feb. 12, 1968, p. 44.
27. *New York Times,* Feb. 2, 1968.
28. Emmett John Hughes Interview with the author, Aug. 23, 1982.
29. *Time,* March 8, 1968.

30. *Washington Post,* Feb. 29, 1968.
31. Ibid., March 5, 1968.
32. Nixon, *Memoirs,* p. 299.
33. Ibid., p. 357.
34. "Draftmanship," *Newsweek,* March 18, 1968, p. 51.
35. *New York Times,* March 16, 1968.
36. Joseph Albright, *What Makes Spiro Run* (New York: Dodd, Mead, 1972), p. 201.
37. *Washington Post,* March 12, 1968.
38. *New York Times,* March 11, 1968.
39. *U.S. News and World Report,* May 13, 1968.
40. David Murry, "The Rise of Ronald Reagan," *Progressive,* Feb., 1968, p. 19.
41. Julius Duscha, "Not Great, Not Brilliant, But a Good Show," *New York Times Magazine,* Dec. 10, 1967, p. 132.
42. Murry, "The Rise," p. 22.
43. *Atlas,* April, 1968, p. 17.
44. F. Clifton White interview with the author, Aug. 25, 1982.
45. White, *The Making,* p. 35.
46. *Nation's Business,* Jan. 1968, p. 41.
47. *New York Times,* Aug. 6, 1968.
48. *The Presidential Nominating Conventions* (Washington, D.C.: Congressional Quarterly Service, 1968), p. 12.
49. *Washington Post,* March 14, 1968, p. 257.
50. Hughes interview, Aug. 23, 1982.
51. *New York Times,* March 22, 1968.
52. *Wall Street Journal,* March 25, 1968.
53. *New Republic,* March 30, 1968.
54. *Washington Post,* March 23, 1968.
55. Hughes interview, Aug. 23, 1982.
56. *Washington Post,* March 22, 1968.
57. *New York Times,* March 22, 1968.
58. Hughes interview, Aug. 23, 1982.

Chapter III – The Turning Point

1. Lawrence F. O'Brien, *No Final Victories: A Life in Politics—From John F. Kennedy to Watergate* (Garden City, N.Y.: Doubleday, 1974), p. 231.
2. Drew Pearson, "The Ghosts That Haunted LBJ," *Look,* July 23, 1968, p. 27.
3. Hubert H. Humphrey, *The Education of a Public Man: My Life and Politics,* ed. Norman Sherman (Garden City, N.Y.: Doubleday, 1976), p. 361.
4. Edgar Berman, *Hubert: The Triumph and Tragedy of The Humphrey I Knew* (New York: G. P. Putnam, 1979), p. 152.
5. George Christian interview with Thomas H. Baker, August 22, 1978, Johnson Papers, Johnson Library, Austin.
6. Walt W. Rostow interview with the author, Dec. 22, 1982.
7. Lyndon Baines Johnson, *The Vantage Point: Perspectives of the Presidency 1963-1969* (New York: Holt, Rinehart, and Winston, 1971), p. 428.
8. Ibid., p. 492.
9. Ibid., p. 431.
10. Horace Busby interview with the author, Aug. 18, 1982.
11. Christian interview, Aug. 16, 1982.
12. Maxwell D. Taylor, *Swords and Plowshares* (New York: W. W. Norton, 1972), p. 385.
13. Westmoreland, *Soldier,* p. 352.
14. Johnson, *Vantage,* p. 391.
15. Walt W. Rostow, *The Diffusion of Power: An Essay in Recent History* (New York: Macmillan, 1972), p. 520.
16. Johnson, *Vantage,* pp. 392–393.
17. Rostow, *Diffusion,* p. 520.
18. Johnson, *Vantage,* p. 393.

19. Clark M. Clifford, "A Vietnam Reappraisal: The Personal History of One Man's View and How It Evolved," *Foreign Affairs* 47 (July 1969), 609.
20. *New York Times,* Feb. 7, 1970.
21. Taylor, *Swords,* p. 388.
22. Clifford, "Vietnam Reappraisal," p. 611.
23. *U.S.-Vietnam Relations,* IVC (6) (c), p. 59.
24. Johnson, *Vantage,* p. 398.
25. Rostow, *Diffusion,* p. 521.
26. Johnson, *Vantage,* p. 400.
27. William Espinosa and John B. Henry, "The Tragedy of Dean Rusk," *Foreign Policy* 8 (Fall 1972), p. 185.
28. Johnson, *Vantage,* p. 406.
29. Christian interview, Aug. 16, 1982.
30. Johnson, *Vantage,* p. 399.
31. Herbert Y. Schandler, *The Unmaking of a President: Lyndon Johnson and Vietnam* (Princeton, N.J.: Princeton University Press, 1977), p. 180.
32. Clark M. Clifford interview with Paige Mulhollan, July 14, 1982.
33. Clifford, "Vietnam Reappraisal," p. 612.
34. Clifford interview, Aug. 8, 1982.
35. Westmoreland, *Soldier,* p. 358.
36. George Christian, *The President Steps Down: A Personal Memoir of the Transfer of Power* (New York: Macmillan, 1970), p. 115.
37. Clifford interview with Mulhollan, July 14, 1982.
38. Schandler, *Unmaking,* p. 243.
39. Clifford interview with Mulhollan, July 14, 1982.
40. Johnson, *Vantage,* p. 410.
41. Ibid., p. 412.
42. Townsend Hoopes, "LBJ's Account of March, 1968." *New Republic,* March 14, 1970, p. 18.
43. Schandler, *Unmaking,* pp. 250-251.
44. Johnson, *Vantage,* p. 413.
45. Clifford interview with Mulhollan, July 14, 1983.
46. George W. Ball, *The Past Has Another Pattern: Memoirs* (New York: W. W. Norton, 1982), p. 408.
47. Johnson, *Vantage,* p. 416.
48. Taylor, *Swords,* p. 390.
49. Johnson, *Vantage,* pp. 416-417.
50. Ball, *Past,* p. 408.
51. Johnson, *Vantage,* pp. 416-417.
52. Ibid., p. 417.
53. McGeorge Bundy, "Summary of Notes," March 26, 1968, Johnson Papers, Johnson Library, Austin.
54. Taylor, *Swords,* p. 391.
55. Ball, *Past,* p. 408.
56. Schandler, *Unmaking,* p. 264.
57. Johnson, *Vantage,* p. 418.
58. Humphrey, *Education,* pp. 358–359.
59. Busby interview, Aug. 18, 1982.
60. *Public Papers of Lyndon Johnson,* pp. 469-476.
61. *New York Times,* April 4, 1968.
62. Ibid., April 1, 1968.
63. Ibid.
64. O'Brien, *No Final,* pp. 231–232.
65. *New York Times,* April 1, 1968.
66. Richard G. Kleindienst interview with the author, Aug. 25, 1982.
67. *New York Times,* April 1, 1968.
68. John W. Sears interview with the author, Sept. 14, 1982.
69. *New York Times,* April 2, 1968.
70. *Washington Post,* April 3, 1968.
71. *New York Times,* April 2, 1968.
72. *Washington Post,* April 1, 1968.

73. Jack Newfield, "Kennedy's Search for a New Target," *Life*, April 12, 1968, p. 35.
74. Carey McWilliams, "The Bitter Legacy of LBJ," *Nation*, Sept. 9, 1968, p. 199.
75. *Wall Street Journal*, July 9, 1968.
76. *New York Times*, April 2, 1968.
77. Johnson, *Vantage Point*, p. 427.
78. Clifford interview with Mulhollan, July 2, 1969.
79. General Earle G. Wheeler interview with Dorothy McSweeny, June 7, 1970, Johnson papers, Johnson Library, Austin.
80. Jack Valenti, *A Very Human President* (New York: W. W. Norton, 1975), p. 369.
81. *Nation*, July 8, 1968, p. 19.
82. Goodwin interview, Aug. 15, 1982.
83. Christian interview, Aug. 16, 1982.
84. Theodore H. White interview with the author, Aug. 3, 1982.
85. Joseph L. Rauh interview with the author, Aug. 3, 1982.
86. Curtis Gans interview with the author, Aug. 11, 1982.
87. John K. Galbraith, *A Life in Our Times* (Boston: Houghton Mifflin, 1981), p. 494.
88. Frank F. Mankiewicz interview with the author, June 23, 1980.
89. Berman, *Hubert*, p. 158.
90. Christian interview, Aug. 16, 1982.
91. Busby interview, Aug. 18, 1982.

Chapter IV – Aftermath of Johnson's Withdrawal

1. *Wall Street Journal*, April 3, 1968.
2. Charles Murphy, "Notes on Meeting of the President with Senator Robert Kennedy," April 3, 1968, Johnson Papers, Johnson Library, Austin.
3. Hubert H. Humphrey, *The Education of a Public Man: My Life and Politics*, ed. Norman Sherman (Garden City, N.Y.: Doubleday, 1976), p. 361.
4. *New York Times*, June 21, 1968.
5. Richard Wilson, "This Is Humphrey," *Look*, July 9, 1968, p. 44.
6. Richard Meryman, "Hubert Humphrey Talks His Self-Portrait," *Life*, Sept. 27, 1968, p. 24.
7. *New York Times*, August 29, 1968.
8. Humphrey, *Education*, p. 337.
9. Ibid., p. 348.
10. Murphy, "Memorandum of Conversation," April 3, 1968. Johnson Papers.
11. John Osborne, "The Dogged Loyalty That Dogs HHH," *New Republic*, May 4, 1968, p. 12.
12. *Washington Post*, April 4, 1968.
13. Edgar Berman, *Hubert: The Triumph and Tragedy of the Humphrey I Knew* (New York: G. P. Putnam, 1979), p. 66.
14. *U.S. News and World Report*, April 29, 1968, p. 14.
15. *New York Times*, April 28, 1968.
16. *Washington Post*, April 28, 1968.
17. *New York Times*, April 28, 1968.
18. *Washington Post*, April 18, 1968.
19. *New York Times*, April 28, 1968.
20. Ibid.
21. Lewis Chester, Godfrey Hodgson, and Bruce Page, *An American Melodrama: The Presidential Campaign of 1968* (New York: Viking, 1969), p. 267.
22. *Nation's Business*, Jan. 1968, p. 56.
23. *New York Times*, October 30, 1968.
24. *Nation's Business*, Jan. 1968, p. 56.
25. Chester et al., *American*, p. 666.

Chapter V – The Democratic Primaries

1. Richard T. Stout, *People* (New York: Harper & Row, 1970), p. 199.
2. Sam Brown interview with the author, Sept. 12, 1982.
3. Jack Newfield, *Robert Kennedy: A Memoir* (New York: E. P. Dutton, 1969), p. 246.
4. Theodore H. White interview with the author, Aug. 3, 1982.

5. George A. Gallup, *The Gallup Poll: Public Opinion 1935-1971,* 3 vols. (New York: Random House, 1972), 3: 2123.
6. Eugene J. McCarthy, *The Year of the People* (Garden City, N.Y.: Doubleday, 1969), p. 122.
7. Arthur Herzog, *McCarthy for President* (New York: Viking, 1969), p. 158.
8. McCarthy, *Year,* p. 119.
9. Ben Stavis, *We Were the Campaign* (Boston: Beacon Press, 1969), p. 26.
10. McCarthy, *Year,* p. 133.
11. Milton Gwirtzman and William Vanden Heuvel, *On His Own: Robert F. Kennedy 1964-1968* (New York: Random House, 1968), p. 341.
12. Jean Stein and George Plimpton, eds., *American Journey: The Times of Robert Kennedy* (New York: Harcourt Brace Jovanovich, 1970), p. 245.
13. *Indianapolis News,* May 1, 1968.
14. *New York Times,* May 9, 1968.
15. Jules Witcover, *85 Days: The Last Campaign of Robert Kennedy* (New York: G. P. Putnam, 1969), p. 110.
16. *Washington Post,* May 15, 1968.
17. Jeremy Larner, *Nobody Knows: Reflections on the McCarthy Campaign of 1968* (New York: Macmillian, 1970), p. 77.
18. Newfield, *Kennedy,* p. 257
19. Herzog, *McCarthy,* p. 127.
20. Abigail McCarthy, *Private Faces/Public Places* (Garden City, N.Y.: Doubleday, 1972), p. 880.
21. Arthur M. Schlesinger, Jr., *Robert Kennedy and His Times* (Boston: Houghton Mifflin, 1978), p. 880.
22. *New York Times,* May 8, 1968.
23. Joseph Rauh interview with the author, Aug. 3, 1982.
24. McCarthy, *Year,* p. 102.
25. Schlesinger, *Kennedy,* p. 905.
26. *Washington Post,* May 9, 1968.
27. *New York Times,* May 13, 1968.
28. Witcover, *85 Days,* p. 196.
29. Lawrence F. O'Brien, *No Final Victories: A Life in Politics—From John F. Kennedy to Watergate* (Garden City, N.Y.: Doubleday, 1974), p. 239.
30. McCarthy, *Year,* p. 139.
31. Stout, *People,* p. 238.
32. *New York Times,* May 15, 1968.
33. *Oregon-Journal,* May 15, 1968.
34. McCarthy, *Year,* p. 144.
35. *Los Angeles Times,* May 30, 1968.
36. Stein and Plimpton, *American Journey,* p. 268.
37. *Los Angeles Times,* May 30, 1968.
38. *Oregon-Journal,* May 18, 1968.
39. Ibid., May 24, 1968.
40. David Halberstam, *The Unfinished Odyssey of Robert Kennedy* (New York: Random House, 1968), p. 182.
41. Stavis, *Campaign,* p. 67.
42. *Oregon-Journal,* May 14, 1968.
43. Ibid., May 25, 1968.
44. Schlesinger, *Robert Kennedy,* p. 906.
45. McCarthy, *Year,* p. 124.
46. Stout, *People,* p. 258.
47. Larner, *Nobody,* p. 97.
48. *Los Angeles Times,* May 23, 1968.
49. Herzog, *McCarthy,* p. 166.
50. Larner, *Nobody,* pp. 100-101.
51. *New York Times,* May 27, 1968.
52. Ibid., May 27, 1968.
53. Larner, *Nobody,* p. 72.
54. *New York Times,* May 29, 1968.
55. McCarthy, *Year,* p. 150.
56. Newfield, *Kennedy,* p. 270.

57. Theodore H. White, "The Wearing Last Weeks and a Precious Last Day," *Life*, June 14, 1968, p. 39.
58. Theodore H. White, *The Making of the President 1968* (New York: Atheneum, 1969), p. 177.
59. *Los Angeles Times,* May 29, 1968.
60. *New York Times,* May 30, 1968.
61. *Washington Post,* May 30, 1968.
62. *Omaha World-Herald,* May 30, 1968.
63. *Los Angeles Times,* May 30, 1968.
64. *San Francisco Chronicle,* May 16, 1968.
65. *New York Times,* June 2, 1968.
66. Ibid.
67. Herzog, *McCarthy,* p. 177.
68. *San Francisco Chronicle,* May 31, 1968.
69. Stout, *People,* p. 268.
70. Ibid., p. 272.
71. *Washington Post,* June 2, 1968.
72. McCarthy interview, June 30, 1980.
73. *Washington Post,* June 3, 1968.
74. Ibid., June 3, 1968.
75. *San Francisco Chronicle,* June 3, 1968.
76. *New York Times,* June 3, 1968.
77. Stein and Plimpton, *American Journey,* p. 314.
78. Schlesinger, *Robert Kennedy,* p. 912.
79. Brown interview, Sept. 11, 1982.
80. Stout, *People,* p. 265.
81. Newfield, *Kennedy,* p. 290.
82. Richard N. Goodwin, "A Day in June," *McCalls,* June 1970, p. 140.
83. Schlesinger, *Robert Kennedy,* p. 913.
84. Stein and Plimpton, *American Journey,* pp. 336-338.
85. Newfield, *Kennedy,* p. 300.
86. Witcover, *85 Days,* p. 277.
87. Goodwin, "Day in June," p. 140.
88. O'Brien, *No Final,* p. 243.
89. Stout, *People,* p. 280.
90. Stavis, *Campaign,* p. 126.
91. Hubert H. Humphrey, *The Education of a Public Man: My Life and Politics,* ed., Norman Sherman (Garden City, N.Y.: Doubleday, 1976), p. 373.
92. *New York Times,* June 6, 1968.
93. *San Francisco Chronicle,* June 6, 1968.
94. *Atlas,* July, 1968, p. 12.

Chapter VI – The Republicans Before Their Convention

1. Emmett John Hughes interview with the author, Aug. 22, 1982.
2. *New York Times,* May 1, 1968.
3. *Washington Post,* May 1, 1968.
4. *Wall Street Journal,* May 2, 1968.
5. *Atlas,* April, 1968, p. 17.
6. *Indianapolis News,* May 1, 1968.
7. *Washington Post,* May 1, 1968.
8. *New York Times,* March 22, 1968.
9. Ibid., May 1, 1968.
10. *U.S. News and World Report,* Aug. 19, 1968, p. 31.
11. *Newsweek,* May 13, 1968, p. 31.
12. *New York Times,* May 1, 1968.
13. *Washington Post,* May 1, 1968.
14. *New York Times,* May 1, 1968.
15. *Washington Post,* May 1, 1968.
16. Richard M. Nixon, *The Memoirs of Richard Nixon* (New York: Grosset & Dunlap, 1978), p. 302.

17. *Oregon-Journal,* May 1, 1968.
18. *New York Times,* May 2, 1968.
19. *Washington Post,* March 13, 1968.
20. *New York Times,* May 14, 1968.
21. Nixon, *Memoirs,* p. 303.
22. *New York Times,* May 15, 1968.
23. *Oregon-Journal,* May 18, 1968.
24. *Washington Post,* May 26, 1968.
25. William Murfin interview with the author, Aug. 16, 1982.
26. Clarke Reed interview with the author, Aug. 21, 1982.
27. Harry S. Dent interview with the author, Aug. 16, 1982.
28. Reed interview, Aug. 21, 1982.
29. Harry S. Dent, *The Prodigal South Returns to Power* (New York: Wiley, 1978), p. 78.
30. Alfred Goldthwaite interview with the author, August 19, 1982.
31. Dent interview, Aug. 16, 1982.
32. John W. Sears interview with the author, Sept. 14, 1982.
33. Alfred Goldwaithe interview, Aug. 19, 1982.
34. *Washington Post,* May 23, 1968.
35. Clifton White interview with the author, Sept. 7, 1982.
36. Theodore White interview with the author, Sept. 7, 1982.
37. *Los Angeles Times,* May 21, 1968.
38. Sears interview with the author, Sept. 14, 1982.
39. *Washington Post,* May 25, 1968.
40. Ibid., May 19, 1968.
41. *San Francisco Chronicle,* May 27, 1968.
42. Ibid., May 30, 1968.
43. *New York Times,* May 29, 1968.
44. Dent interview, Aug. 16, 1982.
45. Dent, *Prodigal,* p. 82.
46. *New York Times,* June 2, 1968.
47. Theodore White, *The Making of the President* (New York: Atheneum, 1969), p. 138.
48. Nixon, *Memoirs,* p. 305.
49. Ibid., pp. 306-307.
50. Ibid., p. 307.
51. *New York Times,* July 19, 1968.
52. Hughes interview, Aug. 23, 1982.
53. *New York Times,* July 16, 1968.
54. White, *Making,* p. 234.
55. *New York Times,* June 25, 1968.
56. Hughes interview, Aug. 23, 1982.
57. *New York Times,* July 23, 1968.
58. Ibid., June 16, 1968.
59. Clifton White interview with the author, Sept. 7, 1982.
60. Louie B. Nunn interview with the author, Aug. 23, 1982.
61. *New York Times,* July 9, 1968.
62. *Washington Post,* Aug. 1, 1968.
63. Ibid., Aug. 2, 1968.
64. *New York Times,* Aug. 4, 1968.

Chapter VII – The Republican Convention

1. *Newsweek,* Aug. 19, 1968.
2. Robert H. Finch interview with the author, Aug. 25, 1982.
3. *New York Times,* July 31, 1968.
4. *The Presidential Nominating Conventions 1968* (Washington, D.C.: Congressional Quarterly Service, 1968), p. 15.
5. *Washington Post,* July 31, 1968.
6. Louie B. Nunn interview with the author. Aug. 23, 1982.
7. Emmett John Hughes interview with the author, Aug. 23, 1982.

8. *Washington Post,* Aug. 7, 1968.
9. *Los Angeles Times,* Aug. 7, 1968.
10. *Indianapolis News,* Aug. 8, 1968.
11. Alfred W. Goldthwaite interview with the author, Aug. 19, 1982.
12. Clifton White interview with the author, Sept. 7, 1982.
13. *Washington Post,* Aug. 6, 1968.
14. *New York Times,* Aug. 6, 1968.
15. Finch interview, Aug. 25, 1982.
16. *Washington Post,* Aug. 6, 1968.
17. Lewis Chester, Godfrey Hodgson, and Bruce Page, *An American Melodrama: The Presidential Campaign of 1968* (New York: Viking, 1969), p. 458.
18. John W. Gardner interview with the author, Aug. 23, 1982.
19. Harry S. Dent, *The Prodigal South Returns to Power* (New York: Wiley, 1978), p. 95.
20. Harry S. Dent interview with the author, Aug. 16, 1982.
21. *New York Times,* Aug. 11, 1968.
22. Dent, *Prodigal,* p. 98.
23. *Miami Herald,* Aug. 11, 1968.
24. *Official Report of the Proceedings of the Twenty-Ninth Republican National Convention* (Baltimore: Dulany-Vernay, 1968), pp. 240-266.
25. Dent interview, Aug. 16, 1982.
26. *Newsweek,* Aug. 19, 1968, p. 25.
27. Goldthwaite interview, Aug. 19, 1982.
28. John W. Sears interview with the author, Sept. 14, 1982.
29. Finch interview, Aug. 25, 1982.
30. Theodore White interview with the author. Sept. 7, 1982.
31. Donald Lukens interview with the author, Sept. 15, 1982.
32. *New York Times,* Aug. 7, 1968.
33. *Newsweek,* Aug. 19, 1968.
34. Chester et al., *American Melodrama* p. 471.
35. Dent interview, Aug. 16, 1982.
36. Ibid.
37. Clifton White interview with the author, Sept. 7, 1982.
38. Clarke Reed interview with the author, Aug. 21, 1982.
39. Dent, *Prodigal,* p. 100.
40. White interview, Sept. 7, 1982.
41. William F. Murfin interview with the author, Aug. 16, 1982.
42. Lukens interview, Sept. 15, 1982.
43. Dent, *Prodigal South,* p. 99.
44. Lukens interview, Sept. 15, 1982.
45. Murfin interview, Aug. 16, 1982.
46. Lukens interview, Sept. 15, 1982.
47. White interview, Sept. 7, 1982.
48. Hughes interview, Aug. 23, 1982.
49. Murfin interview, Aug. 16, 1982.
50. *Twenty-Ninth Republican National Convention,* pp. 372-373.
51. *New York Times,* Aug. 9, 1968.
52. *Los Angeles Times,* Aug. 9, 1968.
53. *Chicago Tribune,* Aug. 6, 1968.
54. *Miami Herald,* Aug. 11, 1968.
55. *Indianapolis News,* Aug. 9, 1968.
56. *Miami Herald,* Aug. 10, 1968.
57. *Washington Post,* Aug. 9, 1968.
58. *Miami Herald,* Aug. 10, 1968.
59. *New York Times,* Aug. 8, 1968.
60. Ibid., Aug. 9, 1968.
61. James C. Gardner interview with the author, Aug. 22, 1982.
62. Sears interview, Sept. 14, 1982.
63. Richard M. Nixon, *The Memoirs of Richard Nixon* (New York: Grosset & Dunlap, 1978), p. 312.
64. *New York Times,* Aug. 9, 1968.

65.   Nixon, *Memoirs,* p. 312.
66.   *New York Times,* Aug. 11, 1968.
67.   Murfln interview, Aug. 16, 1982.
68.   Nunn interview, Aug. 23, 1982.
69.   Dent, *Prodigal,* p. 103.
70.   Finch interview, Aug. 25, 1982.
71.   Nixon, *Memoirs,* pp. 312–313.
72.   Reed interview, Aug. 16, 1982.
73.   Murfin interview, Aug. 16, 1982.
74.   Dent interview, Aug. 16, 1982.
75.   *New York Times,* Aug. 9, 1968.
76.   Ibid., Aug. 8, 1968.
77.   Hughes interview, Aug. 23, 1982.
78.   *New York Times,* Aug. 10, 1968.
79.   *Nominating Conventions,* 1968, p. 44.
80.   *New York Times,* Aug. 9, 1968.
81.   *Washington Post,* Aug. 9, 1968.
82.   *Wall Street Journal,* Aug. 16, 1968.
83.   *Miami Herald,* Aug. 11, 1968.
84.   *Chicago Tribune,* Aug. 11, 1968.
85.   *Washington Post,* Aug. 9, 1968.
86.   *Miami Herald,* Aug. 16, 1968.
87.   *New York Times,* Aug. 9, 1968.
88.   Nixon, *Memoirs,* p. 314.
89.   *Newsweek,* Sept. 2, 1968.
90.   Nixon, *Memoirs,* p. 314.
91.   *Twenty-Ninth Republican National Convention,* pp. 440–452.

Chapter VIII – The Democrats Before Their Convention

1.   George H. Gallup, *The Gallup Poll: Public Opinion 1935-1971,* 3 vols. (New York: Random House, 1972), 3:2127.
2.   Melody Miller interview with the author, Sept. 15, 1982.
3.   Lawrence F. O'Brien, *No Final Victories: A Life in Politics—From John F. Kennedy to Watergate* (Garden City, N.Y.: Doubleday, 1974), pp. 244-245.
4.   Theodore C. Sorensen, *The Kennedy Legacy* (New York: Macmillan, 1969), p. 281.
5.   Arthur Herzog, *McCarthy for President* (New York: Viking, 1969), p. 214.
6.   Robert Stevens, "Disaster in Chicago?" *Commonweal,* Aug. 23, 1968, p. 550.
7.   Herzog, *McCarthy,* p. 196.
8.   Ben Stavis, *We Were the Campaign* (Boston: Beacon Press, 1969), pp. 146–147.
9.   *New York Times,* June 20, 1968.
10.   *Wall Street Journal,* June 27, 1968.
11.   Jeremy Lamer, *Nobody Knows: Reflections on the McCarthy Campaign of 1968* (New York: Macmillan, 1969), p. 131.
12.   Herzog, *McCarthy,* p. 221.
13.   *New York Times,* June 28, 1968.
14.   *New Republic,* Aug. 23, 1968, p. 550.
15.   David Halberstam, "The Man Who Ran Against Lyndon Johnson," *Harper's,* Dec. 1968, p. 58.
16.   Stavis, *Campaign,* p. 136.
17.   Lamer, *Nobody,* p. 143.
18.   Stavis, *Campaign,* p. 156.
19.   Sam Brown interview with the author, Sept. 12, 1982.
20.   Stavis, *Campaign,* p. 170.
21.   Brown interview, Sept. 12, 1982.
22.   Halberstam, "Against Lyndon Johnson," p. 55.
23.   Brown interview, Sept. 12, 1982.
24.   *New York Times,* July 23, 1968.
25.   Hubert H. Humphrey, *The Education of a Public Man: My Life and Politics,* ed. Norman Sherman (Garden City, N.Y.: Doubleday, 1976), p. 375.

26. Arthur Schlesinger, Jr., interview with the author, Jan. 28, 1981.
27. *New York Times,* July 7, 1968.
28. John J. Gilligan interview with the author, Aug. 13, 1982.
29. Humphrey, *Education,* p. 355.
30. *Washington Post,* July 17, 1968, Humphrey Papers.
31. O'Brien, *No Final,* p. 299.
32. Max Kampelman interview with the author, Aug. 31, 1968.
33. *New York Times,* July 20, 1968.
34. Joseph L. Rauh interview with the author, Aug. 3, 1982.
35. George McGovern, *Grassroots: The Autobiography of George McGovern* (New York: Random House, 1977), p. 118.
36. Richard N. Goodwin interview with the author, Aug. 15, 1982.
37. Sam Anson, *McGovern: A Biography* (New York: Holt, Rinehart and Winston, 1972), p. 196.
38. *New Republic,* Aug. 24, 1968, p. 4.
39. *New York Times,* Aug. 11, 1968.
40. *New Republic,* Aug. 24, 1968.
41. *New York Times,* Aug. 15, 1968.
42. *Progressive,* Sept. 1968, p. 5.
43. *New York Times,* Aug. 23, 1968.
44. Theodore C. Sorensen, *The Kennedy Legacy* (New York: Macmillan, 1969), pp. 298–299.
45. *New York Times,* Aug. 18, 1968.

Chapter IX – The Democratic Convention

1. George McGovern, *Grassroots: The Autobiography of George McGovern* (New York: Random House, 1977), p. 130.
2. *New York Times,* Aug. 26, 1968.
3. David Dellinger, *More Power Than We Knew* (New York: Anchor Press, 1975), p. 92.
4. *New York Times,* Aug. 18, 1968.
5. Abbie Hoffman, *Soon to Be a Major Motion Picture* (New York: G. P. Putnam, 1980), p. 144.
6. Lewis Chester, Godfrey Hodgson, Bruce Page, *An American Melodrama: The Presidential Campaign of 1968* (New York: Viking, 1969), p. 579.
7. Jeff Pressman to Bob Axelrod, Aug. 15, 1968, McCarthy Papers.
8. David Halberstam, "The Man Who Ran Against Lyndon Johnson," *Harper's,* Dec, 1968.
9. *New York Times,* Aug. 29, 1968.
10. Ibid., Aug. 28, 1968.
11. Lawrence F. O'Brien, *No Final Victories: A Life in Politics—From John F. Kennedy to Watergate* (Garden City, N.Y.: Doubleday, 1974), p. 256.
12. Richard N. Goodwin, "Convention Notes," Aug. 23, 1968, McCarthy Papers.
13. *New York Times,* Aug. 23, 1968.
14. William Geoghegan interview with the author, Aug. 13, 1982.
15. *New York Times,* Aug. 19, 1968.
16. Ibid., Aug. 20, 1968.
17. John J. Gilligan interview with the author, Aug. 13, 1982.
18. Chester et al., *American,* p. 532.
19. George Christian interview with the author, Aug. 16, 1982.
20. Theodore H. White, *The Making of the President 1968* (New York: Atheneum, 1969), pp. 277–278.
21. *New York Times,* Aug. 23, 1968.
22. *Los Angeles Times,* Aug. 25, 1968.
23. Theodore C. Sorensen, *The Kennedy Legacy* (New York: Macmillan, 1969), p. 285.
24. *New York Times,* Aug. 24, 1968.
25. Geoghegan interview, August 13, 1982.
26. David Ginsburg interview with the author, Aug. 25, 1982.
27. *New York Times,* Aug. 27, 1968.
28. Hubert H. Humphrey, *The Education of a Public Man: My Life and Politics,* ed. Norman Sherman (Garden City, N.Y.: Doubleday, 1976), pp. 389-390.
29. Chester, et al., *American,* p. 536.
30. Ginsburg interview, Aug. 25, 1982.
31. *New York Times,* Aug. 27, 1968.

32. Humphrey, *Education,* p. 389.
33. Ibid., p. 390.
34. James H. Rowe interview with the author, Aug. 5, 1982.
35. Richard N. Goodwin interview with the author, Aug. 15, 1982.
36. Gilligan interview, Aug. 13, 1982.
37. *New York Times,* Aug. 27, 1968.
38. Ibid., Aug. 30, 1968.
39. *Miami Herald,* Aug. 20, 1968.
40. *New York Times,* Aug. 27, 1968.
41. *The Presidential Nominating Conventions 1968* (Washington, D.C.: Congressional Quarterly Service, 1968), p. 115.
42. *New York Times,* Aug. 20, 1968.
43. Chester et al., *American,* p. 557.
44. *Nominating Conventions,* 1968, p. 115.
45. *Washington Post,* Sept. 1, 1968.
46. Arthur Herzog, *McCarthy for President* (New York: Viking, 1969), p. 259.
47. Goodwin, "Convention Notes," McCarthy Papers.
48. *Washington Post,* Aug. 28, 1968.
49. Ibid., Aug. 25, 1968.
50. McGovern, *Grassroots,* p. 134.
51. Daniel Valker, *Rights in Conflict* (New York: E. P. Dutton, 1968), p. 133.
52. *New York Times,* Aug. 24, 1968.
53. Walker, *Rights,* p. 138.
54. *New York Times,* Aug. 25, 1968.
55. Ibid., Aug. 26, 1968.
56. Mary Rather interview with the author, July 17, 1982.
57. Gilligan interview, Aug. 13, 1982.
58. Sam Houston Johnson, *My Brother Lyndon,* ed. Enrique Hank Lopez (New York: Cowles Book Co., 1970), pp. 261–262.
59. White, *Making ... 1968,* pp. 279–280.
60. *Capital Times,* Sept. 2, 1968.
61. Horace Busby interview with the author, Aug. 18, 1982.
62. *New York Times,* Aug. 28, 1968.
63. Goodwin, "Convention Notes," Aug. 25, 1968.
64. Eugene J. McCarthy, *The Year of the People* (Garden City, N.Y.: Doubleday, 1969), p. 211.
65. White, *Making of the President 1968,* p. 284.
66. McGovern, *Grassroots,* pp. 124–125.
67. *New York Times,* Sept. 1, 1968.
68. Melody Miller interview with the author, Sept. 15, 1982.
69. Geoghegan interview, Aug. 13, 1982.
70. Theodore C. Sorensen interview with the author, June 16, 1980.
71. Sam Brown interview with the author, Sept. 12, 1982.
72. *Washington Post,* Aug. 28, 1968.
73. Walker, *Rights,* p. 211.
74. Gilligan interview, Aug. 13, 1982.
75. *New York Times,* Aug. 29, 1968.
76. *Nominating Conventions 1968,* p. 155.
77. *New York Times,* Aug. 29, 1968.
78. *Washington Post,* Aug. 29, 1968.
79. Ibid., Aug. 30, 1968.
80. Ibid., Aug. 31, 1968.
81. Ibid., Aug. 30, 1968.
82. *New York Times,* Aug. 29, 1968.
83. Walker, *Rights,* p. 221.
84. White, *Making ... 1968,* pp. 297-299.
85. Walker, *Rights,* p. 221.
86. Humphrey, *Education,* pp. 490-491.
87. O'Brien, *No Final,* p. 253.
88. White, *Making ... 1968,* p. 304.

89. *New York Times,* Aug. 30, 1968.
90. Steven V. Roberts, "Edmund Sixtus Muskie Takes the Low-key Road," *New York Times Magazine,* Oct. 20, 1968, p. 33.
91. *New York Times,* Aug. 30, 1968.
92. *Washington Post,* Aug. 30, 1968.
93. *Miami Herald,* Aug. 31, 1968.
94. Humphrey, *Education,* p. 394.
95. *New York Times,* Aug. 30, 1968.
96. Ibid., Aug. 30, 1968.
97. Walker, *Rights,* pp. 344-345.
98. McCarthy, *Year,* p. 219.
99. *Chicago Tribune,* Sept. 5, 1968.
100. White, *Making ... 1968,* p. 309.
101. *New York Times,* Aug. 31, 1968.
102. *Chicago Tribune,* Sept. 5, 1968.
103. *New York Times,* Sept. 1, 1968.
104. Walker, *Rights,* p. 354.
105. *New York Times,* Aug. 30, 1968.
106. Ibid., Sept. 5, 1968.
107. Ibid., Aug. 30, 1968.
108. Ibid., Sept. 1, 1968.
109. Ibid., Aug. 31, 1968.
110. Ibid., Sept. 5, 1968.
111. Ibid., Aug. 30, 1968.
112. *Nominating Conventions 1968,* p. 177.
113. *Los Angeles Times,* Sept. 9, 1968.
114. *New York Times,* Aug. 31, 1968.
115. Ibid., Sept. 18, 1968.
116. *Nation,* Sept. 16, 1968.
117. *New York Times,* Sept. 1, 1968.
118. *Indianapolis News,* Aug. 30, 1968.
119. *Chicago Tribune,* Aug. 30, 1968.
120. Ibid., Aug. 28, 1968.
121. *New York Times,* Sept. 1, 1968.
122. *Los Angeles Times,* Sept. 4, 1968.
123. Ibid., Sept. 6, 1968.
124. *Chicago Tribune,* Aug. 28, 1968.
125. *New York Times,* Aug. 30, 1968.
126. *Washington Post,* Aug. 31, 1968.
127. *Los Angeles Times,* Aug. 30, 1968.
128. *Miami Herald,* Aug. 29, 1968.

Chapter X: Nixon's Month

1. *Los Angeles Times,* Sept. 19, 1968.
2. William F. Murfin interview with the author, Aug. 16, 1982.
3. Louie B. Nunn interview with the author, Aug. 23, 1982.
4. Robert F. Ellsworth interview with the author, Aug. 21, 1982.
5. *New York Times,* Sept. 11, 1968.
6. Vernon E. Jordan, Jr., "New Game in Dixie," *Nation,* Oct. 21, 1968, p. 394.
7. *New York Times,* Sept. 30, 1968.
8. *Los Angeles Times,* Sept. 30, 1968.
9. Hubert H. Humphrey, "Campaign Policy Committee Minutes," Sept. 27, 1968, Humphrey Papers, Minnesota Historical Society, Saint Paul.
10. *New York Times,* Sept. 11, 1968.
11. Ibid., Sept. 12, 1968.
12. *Newsweek,* Oct. 7, 1968, p. 39.
13. *Washington Post,* Sept. 12, 1968.
14. Ibid., Sept. 19, 1968.

15. *New York Times,* Sept. 13, 1968.
16. *Washington Post,* Sept. 14, 1968.
17. Ibid., Sept. 25, 1968.
18. Jules Witcover, *White Knight* (New York: Random House, 1972), p. 247.
19. Jules Witcover, *The Resurrection of Richard Nixon* (New York: G. P. Putnam, 1970), p. 387.
20. *Washington Post,* Sept. 25, 1968.
21. *Time,* Sept. 20, 1968, p. 20.
22. Lawrence F. O'Brien, *No Final Victories: A Life in Politics—From John F. Kennedy to Watergate* (Garden City, N.Y.: Doubleday, 1974), p. 267.
23. Charles K. McWhorter interview with the author, Aug. 3, 1982.
24. John W. Sears interview with the author, Sept. 14, 1982.
25. *Time,* Oct. 4, 1968, p. 21.
26. B. J. Widick, "Why They Like Wallace," *Nation,* Oct. 14, 1968, p. 359.
27. *New York Times,* Aug. 26, 1968.
28. *Wall Street Journal,* Sept. 10, 1968.
29. *Time,* Oct. 4, 1968, p. 21.
30. *New York Times,* Aug. 5, 1968.
31. Ibid., Sept. 3, 1968.
32. Ibid., Sept. 23, 1968.
33. George Lardner, Jr., "The Backlash Candidate," *Progressive,* Nov., 1968, p. 21.
34. *Washington Post,* Sept. 14, 1968.
35. *New York Times,* Oct. 14, 1968.
36. Ibid., Sept. 29, 1968.
37. *Progressive,* Nov., 1968, p. 6.
38. George H. Gallup, *The Gallup Poll: Public Opinion 1935–1971,* 3 vols. (New York: Random House, 1972), 3:2159.
39. *New York Times,* Sept. 17, 1968.
40. Ibid., Oct. 6, 1968.
41. *Miami Herald,* Aug. 23, 1968.
42. *Newsweek,* Sept. 30, 1968.
43. Lewis Chester, Godfrey Hodgson, and Bruce Page, *American Melodrama: The Presidential Campaign of 1968* (New York: Viking, 1969), p. 708.
44. *Washington Post,* Oct. 2, 1968.
45. *New York Times,* Sept. 17, 1968.
46. Richard M. Nixon, *The Memoirs of Richard Nixon* (New York: Grosset & Dunlap, 1978), p. 320.
47. *Washington Post,* Aug. 7, 1968.
48. William F. Buckley, "The Doubts About Agnew," *National Review,* Nov. 5, 1968, p. 1097.
49. *Chicago Tribune,* Oct. 10, 1968.
50. *Washington Post,* Oct. 4, 1968.
51. *Chicago Tribune,* Oct. 25, 1968.
52. *Los Angeles Times,* Oct. 4, 1968.
53. *New York Times,* Sept. 22, 1968.
54. *Washington Post,* Sept. 24, 1968.
55. Ed Cubberley to Hubert Humphrey, Sept. 27, 1968, Humphrey papers, Minnesota Historical Society, Saint Paul.
56. George E. Reedy to Humphrey, Sept. 9, 1968, Lyndon B. Johnson Papers, Johnson Library, Austin.
57. *New York Times,* Sept. 23, 1968.
58. Ibid., Sept. 9, 1968.
59. *Time,* Oct. 25, 1968.
60. *New York Times,* Sept. 24, 1968.
61. Edgar Berman, *Hubert: The Triumph and Tragedy of the Humphrey I Knew* (New York: G. P. Putnam, 1979), p. 201.
62. *Wall Street Journal,* Oct. 30, 1968.
63. Theodore H. White, *The Making of the President 1968* (New York: Atheneum, 1969), pp. 335–337.
64. Cubberley to Humphrey, Sept. 23, 1968, Humphrey Papers.
65. Max Kampelman interview with the author, Aug. 31, 1982.
66. Humphrey, *Education,* p. 492.
67. *New York Times,* Oct. 18, 1968.

68. O'Brien, *No Final,* p. 260.
69. *Washington Post,* Oct. 4, 1968.
70. Humphrey, *Education,* pp. 397-399.
71. Curtis Gans interview with the author, Aug. 11, 1982.
72. John J. Gilligan interview with the author, Aug. 13, 1982.
73. *Washington Post,* Sept. 10, 1968.
74. *New York Times,* Aug. 30, 1968.
75. *Washington Post,* Aug. 30, 1968.
76. Ibid., Sept. 10, 1968.
77. Ibid., Sept. 11, 1968.
78. Berman, *Hubert,* p. 199.
79. *New York Times,* Sept. 26, 1968.
80. *Chicago Tribune,* Sept. 27, 1968.
81. George Christian interview with the author, Aug. 16, 1982.
82. Joseph L. Rauh interview with the author, Aug. 3, 1982.
83. Richard N. Goodwin interview with the author, Aug. 15, 1982.
84. Clark Clifford interview with the author, Aug. 18, 1982.
85. *Wall Street Journal,* Oct. 23, 1968.
86. Horace Busby interview with the author, Aug. 18, 1982.
87. George Christian, *The President Steps Down: A Personal Memoir of the Transfer of Power* (New York: Macmillan, 1970), p. 148.
88. O'Brien, *No Final,* pp. 263-264.
89. Nixon, *Memoirs,* p. 320.
90. *Washington Post,* Oct. 14, 1968.
91. *Time,* Oct. 4, 1968, p. 19.
92. *Washington Post,* Oct. 14, 1968.
93. *Chicago Tribune,* Sept. 12, 1968.
94. *New York Times,* Sept. 18, 1968.
95. Ibid., Oct. 6, 1968.
96. Ibid., Sept. 17, 1968.
97. O'Brien, *No Final,* p. 259.
98. Humphrey, *Education,* p. 401.
99. George W. Ball, *The Past Has Another Pattern* (New York: W. W. Norton, 1982), p. 446.
100. O'Brien, *No Final,* p. 259.
101. Humphrey, *Education,* p. 401.
102. Ibid., p. 402.
103. Ball, *Memoirs,* pp. 446-447.
104. Humphrey, *Education,* p. 403.
105. Berman, *Hubert,* p. 220.
106. *New York Times,* Oct. 1, 1968.
107. Ibid., Oct. 2, 1968.
108. James H. Rowe interview with the author, Aug. 5, 1982.
109. *New York Times,* Oct. 2, 1968.
110. Gans interview, Aug. 11, 1982.
111. Rauh interview, Aug. 3, 1982.
112. *Washington Post,* Oct. 3, 1968.
113. *Nation,* Oct. 14, 1968, p. 12.
114. *New York Times,* Oct. 2, 1968.
115. O'Brien, *No Final,* p. 261.

Chapter XI – October: Humphrey's Month

1. Ed Cubberley to Larry O'Brien, Oct. 3, 1968, Humphrey Papers, Minnesota Historical Society, Saint Paul.
2. *Washington Post,* Oct. 21, 1968.
3. Cubberley to Humphrey, Oct. 5, 1968, Humphrey Papers.
4. Theodore H. White, *The Making of the President 1968* (New York: Atheneum, 1969), p. 356.
5. Hubert H. Humphrey, *The Education of a Public Man: My Life and Politics,* ed. Norman Sherman (Garden City, N.Y.: Doubleday, 1976), p. 403.

6.   *Washington Post,* Oct. 9, 1968.
7.   Ibid., Oct. 10, 1968.
8.   Ibid., Oct. 11, 1968.
9.   George C. Christian interview with the author, Aug. 16, 1982.
10. James H. Rowe interview with the author, Aug. 5, 1982.
11. John J. Gilligan interview with the author, Aug. 13, 1982.
12. Merle Miller, Lyndon: *An Oral Biography* (New York: G. P. Putnam, 1980), p. 524.
13. White, *Making of the President 1968,* p. 366.
14. Cubberley to Humphrey, Sept. 25, 1968, Humphrey Papers.
15. *New York Times,* Oct. 31, 1968.
16. *Washington Post,* Oct. 4, 1968.
17. Ibid.
18. *Washington Post,* Oct. 7, 1968.
19. *New York Times,* Oct. 4, 1968.
20. *Washington Post,* Oct. 27, 1968.
21. *New York Times,* Oct. 27, 1968.
22. Ibid., Oct. 30, 1968.
23. Lawrence F. O'Brien, *No Final Victories: A Life in Politics—From John F. Kennedy to Watergate* (Garden City, N.Y.: Doubleday, 1974), pp. 261-262.
24. *Washington Post,* Oct. 26, 1968.
25. *Los Angeles Times,* Oct. 29, 1968.
26. *New York Times,* Nov. 2, 1968.
27. *New Republic,* Nov. 9, 1968, p. 5.
28. *New York Times,* Oct. 26, 1968.
29. Jack Valenti, *A Very Human President* (New York: W. W. Norton, 1975), p. 373.
30. Richard M. Nixon, *The Memoirs of Richard Nixon* (New York: Grosset & Dunlap, 1978), p. 323.
31. Ibid., p. 323.
32. Ibid., p. 327.
33. *Washington Post,* Oct. 26, 1968.
34. Lyndon Baines Johnson, *The Vantage Point: Perspectives of the Presidency 1963–1969* (New York: Holt, Rinehart, and Winston, 1971), p. 524.
35. *New York Times,* Nov. 1, 1968.
36. Nixon, *Memoirs,* p. 328.
37. *Washington Post,* Nov. 1, 1968.
38. *New York Times,* Nov. 1, 1968.
39. *Washington Post,* Nov. 1, 1968.
40. Ibid., Nov. 2, 1968.
41. *New York Times,* Nov. 1, 1968.
42. O'Brien, *No Final,* p. 268.
43. *New York Times,* Nov. 3, 1968.
44. *Washington Post,* Nov. 4, 1968.
45. Ibid., Nov. 2, 1968.
46. Ibid., Nov. 3, 1968.
47. White, *Making ... 1968,* pp. 379–380.
48. Max Kampelman interview with the author, Aug. 31, 1982.
49. Ibid.
50. Christian interview, Aug. 31, 1982.
51. Clark M. Clifford interview with the author, Aug. 18, 1982.
52. Rowe interview, Aug. 5, 1982.
53. Christian interview, Aug. 16, 1982.
54. Valenti, *Human,* p. 374.
55. Theodore H. White interview with the author, Aug. 3, 1982.
56. *Newsweek,* Nov. 11, 1968, p. 32.
57. David English, *Divided They Stand* (Englewood Cliffs, N.J.: Prentice-Hall, 1969), p. 391.
58. O'Brien, *No Final,* p. 257.
59. John Hoving to Terry Sanford, Oct. 18, 1968, Humphrey Papers.
60. Humphrey, *Education,* p. 406.
61. Lewis Chester, Godfrey Godson, and Bruce Page, *An American Melodrama: The Presidential Campaign of 1968* (New York: Viking 1969), p. 751.

62. John W. Sears interview with the author, Aug. 14, 1982.
63. Jules Witcover, *The Resurrection of Richard Nixon* (New York: G. P. Putnam, 1970), p. 445.
64. Nixon, *Memoirs,* p. 329.
65. George H. Gallup, *The Gallup Poll: Public Opinion 1935-1971* (New York: Random House, 1972), p. 2168.
66. *New York Times,* Oct. 29, 1968.
67. *Time,* Nov. 1, 1968, p. 15.
68. Edgar Berman, *Hubert: The Triumph and Tragedy of the Humphrey I Knew* (New York: G. P. Putnam, 1979), p. 227.
69. O'Brien, *No Final,* p. 265.
70. Nixon, *Memoirs,* pp. 332-334.
71. *U.S. News and World Report,* Nov. 18, 1968, p. 42.
72. White, *Making ... 1968,* pp. 396-398.
73. *New York Times,* Nov. 7, 1968.
74. Richard M. Seammon and Ben J. Wattenberg, *The Real Majority* (New York: Coward-McCann, 1970), p. 333.
75. *U.S. News and World Report,* Nov. 18, 1968, p. 15.
76. Ibid., p. 44.
77. White, *Making ... 1968,* p. 401.
78. *New York Times,* Nov. 7, 1968.
79. Ibid., Nov. 8, 1968.
80. George McGovern, *Grassroots: The Autobiography of George McGovern* (New York: Random House, 1977), p. 109.
81. Rowe interview, Aug. 5, 1982.
82. Kampelman interview, Aug. 31, 1982.
83. Christian interview, Aug. 16, 1982.
84. Clifford interview, Aug. 18, 1982.
85. Sam Brown interview with the author, Sept. 12, 1982.
86. Ben Stavis, *We Were the Campaign* (Boston: Beacon Press, 1969), p. 201.
87. O'Brien, *No Final,* p. 262.
88. Humphrey, *Education,* p. 377.
89. *New York Times,* Nov. 8, 1968.
90. Rowe interview, Aug. 5, 1982.
91. *New York Times,* Nov. 8, 1968.
92. Seammon and Wattenberg, *Real,* p. 333.
93. *U.S. News and World Report,* Nov. 18, 1968, p. 43.
94. Seammon and Wattenberg, *Real,* p. 333.
95. Sears interview, Sept. 14, 1982.
96. Seammon and Wattenberg, *Real,* p. 182.
97. *Time,* Nov. 15, 1968, p. 23.
98. *New York Times,* Nov. 10, 1968.
99. Angus Campbell, "How We Voted—And Why," *Nation,* Nov. 25, 1968, p. 551.
100. *U.S. News and World Report,* Nov. 18, 1968, p. 41.
101. *National Review,* Nov. 19, 1968, p. 1152.
102. *Time,* Nov. 15, 1968, p. 19.
103. Gilligan interview, Aug. 13, 1982.
104. Sears interview, Sept. 14, 1982.
105. White, *Making ... 1968,* p. 398.
106. *Time,* Nov. 15, 1968, p. 19.
107. *Business Week,* Nov. 9, 1968, p. 27.
108. *National Review,* Nov. 19, 1968, p. 1150.
109. *Wall Street Journal,* Nov. 7, 1968.

Index